Read This First

The information in this book is as up to date and accurate as we can make it. But it's important to realize that the law changes frequently, as do fees, forms, and other important legal details. If you handle your own legal matters, it's up to you to be sure that all information you use—including the information in this book—is accurate. Here are some suggestions to help you do this:

First, check the edition number on the book's spine to make sure you've got the most recent edition of this book. To learn whether a later edition is available, go to Nolo's online Law Store at www.nolo.com or call Nolo's Customer Service Department at 800-728-3555.

Next, because the law can change overnight, users of even a current edition need to be sure it's fully up to date. At www.nolo.com, we post notices of major legal and practical changes that affect a book's current edition only. To check for updates, go to the Law Store portion of Nolo's website and find the page devoted to the book (use the "A to Z Product List" and click on the book's title). If you see an "Updates" link on the left side of the page, click on it. If you don't see a link, there are no posted changes—but check back regularly.

Finally, while Nolo believes that accurate and current legal information in its books can help you solve many of your legal problems on a cost-effective basis, this book is not intended to be a substitute for personalized advice from a knowledgeable lawyer. If you want the help of a trained professional, consult an attorney licensed to practice in your state.

6th edition

The Independent Paralegal's Handbook

How to Provide Legal Services Without Becoming a Lawyer

by Ralph Warner, Catherine Elias-Jermany,
and Stephen Elias

NOLO

Sixth Edition:	February 2004
Editor:	Emily Doskow
Book Design:	Terri Hearsh
Illustrations:	Mari Stein
Proofreading:	Mu'Afrida Bell
Printing:	Delta Printing Solutions, Inc.

Warner, Ralph E.
    The independent paralegal's handbook: how to provide legal services without becoming a lawyer / by Ralph Warner, Catherine Elias Jermany, and Stephen Elias.-- 6th ed.
      p. cm.
    ISBN 0-87337-343-X
    1. Legal assistants--United States--Handbooks, manuals, etc. I. Elias Jermany,
Catherine. Elias, Stephen. III. Title.

KF320.L4W37 2003
340'. 023'73--dc21   2004056239

Quantity sales: For information on bulk purchases or corporate premium sales, please contact the Special Sales department. For academic sales or textbook adoptions, ask for Academic Sales, 800-955-4775, Nolo, 950 Parker Street, Berkeley, CA, 94710.

Acknowledgments

Many wonderful people have contributed to this book over the years. A part of all of them can be found throughout. We specifically wish to thank Karen Chambers, Rosemary Furman, Toni Ihara, Lois Isenberg, Jolene Jacobs, Bob Mission, Robin Smith, Glynda Dixon, Bob Anderson, Virginia Simons, Sharon Goetting, Jon and Mel Lebewitz, Ian Gardner, Sylvia Cherry, Rose Palmer, Debbie Chalfie, Bill Fry, Glen Nishimura, Tony Mancuso, Kay Ostberg, Michael Phillips, Salli Rasberry, Susan Cornell, Stephanie Harolde, and Stan Jacobsen.

We are grateful to attorney Richard Lubetsky for sharing his vast storehouse of information about bankruptcy petition preparers and the trials and tribulations they face at the hands of the bankruptcy trustees.

We also wish to express our complete delight with our editor Emily Doskow, new to Nolo but old in the excellence for which Nolo is widely known.

About the Authors

Ralph Warner is a cofounder of Nolo and one of the pioneers of the self-help law movement. Educated as a lawyer, Warner quit the practice in the early 1970s. Along with Charles Sherman he founded Nolo in 1971 and the WAVE Project, one of the first self-help divorce typing services, the next year. He is the author of a number of self-help law books, and the co-author of *29 Reasons Not to Go to Law School.*

Catherine Elias-Jermany, an innovator for over thirty-five years in the fields of legal training and career and business development, served as the director of Paralegal Training and Career Development for the National Legal Services Corporation between 1974 and 1980. She then turned her expertise to designing and implementing a series of legal and business education programs for Nolo, the National Association for Independent Paralegals, and the National Paralegal Institute. Catherine currently is the executive director of the National Self Help Law Project, president of Lake County Community Radio, program producer for KPFZ FM, and the mother and grandmother of four.

Stephen R. Elias received a law degree from Hastings College of Law in 1969 and practiced law in California, New York, and Vermont until 1980 when he hooked up with Nolo. In 2000, Steve retired from Nolo, and with his wife Catherine, launched the National Self-Help Law Project, an organization that is dedicated to creating and improving the infrastructure necessary for self-help law to thrive. Steve also operates a storefront bankruptcy law practice in Lakeport, California, and is deeply involved with a local community radio station.

Table of Contents

Introduction

4 • Legal Areas Open to Independent Paralegals

5 • Naming Your Business

6 • Establishing an Office

11 • Computers, the Internet, and the Independent Paralegal

12 • Customer Recourse

13 • Working for Volunteer, Community, or Social Change Organizations

14 • Political Organizing for Change

Appendix A • Arizona Code of Conduct for LOPs

Appendix B • Interviews

Index

Introduction

In 1971, a new company known as Nolo Press published its first self-help law book, *How to File Your Own Divorce in California,* by Charles Edward Sherman. Two years later, Sherman and Nolo cofounder Ralph Warner (also a co-author of this book) launched an independent chain of clerical divorce service centers to assist people using the book. In essence, these centers operated as public legal secretaries, taking their directions from their customers who were acting as their own attorneys. Most of the centers are still in business more than 25 years later.

Almost from the beginning, these centers came under the scrutiny of the State Bar of California. As is true in all states, California has a statute prohibiting the unauthorized practice of law (UPL). As we point out in Chapter 2, this type of statute is almost always ill-defined, that is, the statute doesn't define the practice of law but rather leaves it to the courts to decide on a case by case basis, after the fact, whether a particular activity is or is not the practice of law.

The Original Independent Paralegal Model

Not surprisingly, given the fact that the judges who make these decisions are all lawyers, court decisions that take up the issue of UPL tend to label as UPL any activity that might compete with the legal profession. However, as it turned out, the divorce centers managed to avoid being hauled into court by explaining to the investigating officials that they:

- made it clear to their customers that they were not lawyers and were not providing legal advice or other services that only lawyers could offer

- required their customers to make their own decisions on the basis of what they learned in Nolo's divorce book, and did not themselves deliver legal advice, and

- only provided secretarial services that were, in all respects, the same as scrivener services that have long been held not to involve the practice of law even if a legal document is involved.

In other words, the centers convinced the District Attorney that their services could not remotely be considered the practice of law.

Independent Paralegalism Spreads to Other States

Since the advent of the California divorce centers, many other nonlawyer divorce services have opened in California and other states. And as the idea took hold, services were offered for people handling their own legal matters in such areas as bankruptcy, personal injury settlements, guardianships, name changes, and restraining orders against domestic abuse. Over the years, the folks offering these services began to refer to themselves as independent paralegals (IPs). Other names that are commonly used to describe IPs are legal technicians, form preparation services, legal typing services, and most recently in California, legal document assistants. In this book we stick with the IP label to avoid confusion.

The Original Independent Paralegal Model Gets Stretched

As the concept of self-help law and independent paralegal services became more accepted in California and several other states, including Oregon, Florida, and Arizona, the original model under which the California divorce services operated became increasingly stretched. For instance, instead of requiring their customers to use published written materials, some services would prepare their own brochures. Instead of restricting their role to essentially clerical services, the staff of some services would find it more convenient to advise their customers as to their basic choices. And instead of letting their customers select the appropriate forms, some services would select the forms for them.

All of this made sense from the IP's standpoint, since it was often the case that the IP knew more about divorce at the level it was being practiced than most divorce attorneys. After all, in a regular law office, the nitty gritty work of completing and filing the forms is almost always done by nonlawyer staff, not by the lawyers themselves. Nevertheless, the looser the IPs got with the original model, the easier it was for the organized bar to pounce. And pounce they did. Especially in the 1980s, a number of IPs in various states were hounded by lawyer organizations and prosecutors into closing up their services. And, in those states where UPL is a crime, a few IPs actually did some jail time. A more systematic history of UPL enforcement in this country is set out in Chapter 2.

The point we are making here is that departures from the original model leave IPs vulnerable to attacks by the organized bar. Close compliance with the original independent paralegal model, on the other hand, historically has worked to keep the lawyers at bay. If this book has one central purpose, it is to teach you how to stay within the original model to avoid trouble with organized lawyerdom.

The California Legislative Breakthrough

Ironically, exactly 25 years after the creation of the California divorce centers, and several thousand new California IPs later, the California legislature finally decided to recognize and regulate this new profession.

As of Jan. 1, 2000, all California independent paralegals must be registered with the State's Department of Consumer Affairs. While this registration affords the IPs an official status that has previously been denied them, the law also restricts the IPs to the original model, that is, no personal legal advice. Also, to qualify for registration, the IPs must post a bond and prove some combination of a minimum level of education and experience. We describe this law in more detail in Chapter 14, Section A. A copy of the law is also included in Chapter 14.

You Can Never Be Certain When Lawyers Are in Control.

Because lawyers have so much power, we can't guarantee that your service won't experience some harassment, even if you strictly follow the original independent paralegal model. Nolo itself learned how whimsical UPL enforcement can get when it was investigated in 1998 by a Texas Supreme Court committee for engaging in UPL by selling its software and books in Texas. In its near 30-year history, Nolo had never before faced this type of accusation and was forced to expend a sizeable chunk of money on a top-rate Texas law firm to make the problem go away. The lesson we learned from our Texas escapade is that you're never completely safe as long as lawyers are in control of the courts and the legislature.

More recently, on September 17, 2003 an unauthorized practice of law subcommittee in Dallas, Texas, filed a lawsuit against the *We the People* independent paralegal franchise. Although *We the People* uses a different delivery model than the one we espouse in this book, their franchise has operated in many different states without serious incident. The Texas lawsuit undoubtedly came as a rude shock.

What Is the Demand for Independent Paralegal Services?

Despite the obstacles created by the legal profession in most states, the independent paralegal movement is growing rapidly all across America. The average American, faced with almost daily news stories about the glut of lawyers (close to one million at last count), at the same time that he finds even routine legal services prohibitively expensive, is increasingly supportive of high-quality, low-cost paralegal alternatives. For example, in states such as Arizona and California more than 60% of divorces and 30% of bankruptcies are now done without lawyers.

The growth in independent paralegal services is being fueled by the dramatic increase in the availability of plain English legal materials made possible by the World Wide Web. Just a few years back, it was necessary to call a lawyer or visit a law library to get legal questions answered or to obtain forms and instructions required for a particular legal task, unless of course Nolo happened to have a book on the subject. Now, the answers, forms, and instructions are often only a mouse click away. As people find it easier to learn about the law, they also win more confidence in their ability to handle their own legal affairs, especially if they have some knowledgeable clerical help such as that offered by IPs.

Courts also are starting to provide quality information to people handling their own cases. In some cases the courts are operating self-help websites that let you download official legal forms. For an example, visit the California Judicial Council's Self-Help Center at www.courtinfo.ca.gov. In other cases, courts are establishing brick and mortar self-help law centers in the court buildings themselves, in which plain English forms and instructions, and help from special clerks, are available for a wide variety of legal tasks. This court-sponsored assistance will only increase the number of people who seek the services of an IP to help them complete their paperwork.

How Will This Book Help Me Operate an Independent Paralegal Service?

In this book we offer a number of suggestions that should ease the way for the nonlawyer willing to deliver competent services in the hostile shadow of the American legal profession. By way of example, this book covers:

- What types of legal paperwork an independent paralegal can safely and profitably prepare;

- How to get the necessary training to work as an independent paralegal;
- How to name your business;
- How to market your services in a cost-effective way;
- How to make sure customers know you are not a lawyer;
- How to work with lawyers when appropriate;
- How to minimize the chance of harassment by the bar;
- What to do if you are threatened by the bar or a district attorney;
- How much to charge for your services;
- How to think about working with computers and the Internet.

In addition, this book contains interviews with a number of people who pioneered the independent paralegal field and successfully delivered services to the public for many years. In many ways, these interviews, which you will find in the Appendix, are the most important part of the book and we urge you to take the time to read them carefully.

Many of the suggestions in this book are aimed at helping you to deal with problems you are sure to face as part of starting any new business. These range from choosing a name and finding a good location, to getting a business license and buying necessary equipment. Sometimes it is necessary to borrow money to begin. Certainly, once your doors are open, it is important to quickly generate a positive cash flow. None of this is easy, especially when you remind yourself that embarking on a career as an independent paralegal involves not only putting yourself through normal "new business trauma," but simultaneously coping with the likely hostility of the legal profession.

This raises the question of why anyone would want to become an independent paralegal. Or, to ask the question more directly, "Why do you even consider working in a field where persecution, or at least official harassment, is a distinct possibility, and criminal conviction, including even a jail sentence, is not completely out of the question in many states?"

Why Should You Become an Independent Paralegal?

One obvious answer to this question is that running an independent paralegal business is potentially profitable. Lawyers' fees are so outrageous that independent paralegals can significantly undercut them (often by as much as 70%) and still make an excellent living.

But the prospect of making good money doesn't begin to explain why so many pioneer paralegals have been willing to assume the risk inherent in challenging organized lawyerdom. In talking to dozens of independent paralegals, some of whom have been in business for 30 years, we sense that, for most, the determination to persevere is drawn from the same sort of stubborn conviction that motivated Massachusetts colonists to toss chests of tea into the Boston Harbor in 1773. Like their colonial forefathers, angered by King George III's nasty monopoly on tea, these men and women stand up to organized lawyerdom's even nastier monopoly over the delivery of legal services, because they deeply believe it is wrong to deny access to our legal system to those who can't afford lawyers.

While obviously we don't minimize the problems inherent in embarking on a career as an independent paralegal, we believe that with a lot of determination and a little luck, you can establish a profitable business and provide a valuable service helping nonlawyers with their own legal paperwork. This should become easier in the future, as public support for deregulation of the legal profession is almost sure to grow.

For example, the federal Fair Trade Commission (FTC) and the U.S. Attorney General's office recently issued a joint response to a proposal by the American Bar Association to toughen up the nation's UPL laws, in which the federal agencies warned against anticompetitive behavior by lawyers (www.usdoj.gov/atr/public/comments/200604.htm). The FTC/AG response concluded:

"By including overly broad presumptions of conduct considered to be the practice of law, the [ABA's] proposed Model Definition likely will reduce competition from nonlawyers. Consumers, in turn, will likely pay higher prices and face a smaller range of service options. The Task Force makes no showing of harm to consumers from lay service providers that would justify these reductions in competition.

"As the New Jersey Supreme Court has concluded: 'Not every such intrusion by lay persons into legal matters disserves the public: this Court does not wear public interest blinders when passing on unauthorized practice of law questions. We have often found, despite the clear involvement of the practice of law, that nonlawyers may participate in these activities, basing our decisions on the public interest.'

"Likewise, the Task force, in recommending a proposed Model Definition of the practice of law, should allow lay competition that is in the public interest, and craft an appropriate definition of the practice of law that is based upon a careful view of the harms and benefits of lay participation in any service that the Definition would cover."

A Few Words About Terminology

Because lawyers in private practice, legislatures, bar associations, prosecutor's offices, and judge's robes have all been trained to defend their monopoly to deliver legal services, we often refer to them here with the shorthand terms "organized lawyerdom" or "the bar" except when it's important to distinguish among them.

Also, as noted, for convenience we refer to nonlawyers who help other nonlawyers deal with the legal system as "independent paralegals" (IPs) even though some people in the field describe themselves in other ways—as a "legal technician," "form preparer," "legal typing service," "legal information specialist," "divorce counselor," "public paralegal," or "legal document assistant" (in California).

In fact, in California, IPs are prohibited from referring to themselves as paralegals. (Cal. Bus. & Prof. Code, §§ 6450-6456.) The stated purpose of this bill was to protect consumers against confusion. The traditional California paralegal organizations that pushed the bill argued that when customers hear that someone is a paralegal, they assume supervision by an attorney. That this conclusion is almost the exact opposite of what people really think didn't bother the California legislature one bit.

When describing the people who use independent paralegals, we use the word "customer," rather than "client." We do this both because we believe it is wise for paralegals to distinguish themselves from lawyers as much as possible and because we personally don't like the word client, which has Latin roots in the terms "to hear" and "to obey." "Customer," on the other hand, conjures up the image of an empowered person, someone who expects good and conscientious service and who won't patronize a business again if she isn't satisfied.

And then there is the pesky personal pronoun. Our solution to the problem of how to handle gender is to use "he" and "she" more or less alternately throughout the book. While this solution isn't perfect, it makes more sense to us than only using "he" or adopting other cumbersome schemes such as writing "he and she," "he/she" or "s(he)" every time an abstract person must be identified.

New to the Sixth Edition

In addition to general updating, the Sixth Edition:

- contains the most recent changes to the California law (SB 1418) that governs practice by Legal Document Assistants
- provides a detailed description of the Arizona rules governing Legal Document Preparers (as the IPs are now called in that state);
- contains updated marketing, advertising, and business development materials
- provides new information about the World Wide Web and how independent paralegals can make use of it and its legal resources when operating and marketing their business
- includes a profile of the California Association of Legal Document Assistants, and
- sets out and discusses recent comments by the Federal Trade Commission and the American Bar Association about better access to the legal system for unrepresented persons.

ICONS TO HELP YOU ALONG

Throughout the book, we use several icons to advise you of some special alert.

 The "fast track" arrow alerts you that you can skip some material that isn't relevant to your situation.

 A "caution" icon warns you of potential problems.

 This icon refers you to helpful books or other resources for further information.

 The "tip" icon gives you hints on dealing with special situations.

 The "attorney" icon lets you know when we believe you need the advice of an attorney. ■

Chapter 1

The Historical Background

A person who decides on a career as an independent paralegal almost by definition must engage in a struggle with organized lawyerdom, a powerful adversary. Before you do this, you should learn some history—that is, understand the historical forces that have led to the current confrontation between independent paralegals and organized lawyerdom. Second, while you should respect these lessons, you should not allow them to control your strategy or tactics. Does this sound paradoxical? It isn't. Because we live in an age of unprecedented change, the lessons of history, while important, should be only one element in your strategy to keep your business from being suppressed by organized lawyerdom.

Reading history and not being ruled by it is never easy. Unfortunately, the natural human response is to draw such inflexible lessons from past events that history is repeated. Thus, it is a cliché that the best-trained generals tend to refight the last war, learned economists make predictions based on yesterday's recession, and baseball managers repeatedly rely too much on aging players who hit last year's home runs.

Until the 1990s, independent paralegals had one dubious advantage over generals and coaches, who try to extrapolate past successes into future victories: there were precious few successes to extrapolate. Indeed, even today, an independent paralegal who slavishly applies history's lessons is likely to conclude that a career as an independent paralegal is hopeless. Why? The lawyers have been firmly in charge since the dawn of the twentieth century and have moved to crush any type of service that looks remotely like competition.

Fortunately, some very important successes have occurred in Florida, California, and Arizona. We hope that these will create a springboard from which a revitalized independent paralegal movement can be launched in the next decade. For example, California is now the first state to have a regulatory scheme that legitimizes independent paralegals who operate their businesses in a way that is very close to what we recommend in this book. (See Chapter 14, Section A, for more on the California independent paralegal regulations.)

Florida has taken a different approach. There, independent paralegals are allowed to prepare hundreds of forms that have been approved by the Florida Supreme Court. Arizona has taken a third approach. In

July 2003, new court rules became effective under which Arizona IPs are renamed Legal Document Preparers. Once certified under specific eligibility criteria, the newly minted LDPs are authorized to provide a wide range of legal and factual information to their clients—but not any kind of specific advice, opinion, or recommendation to a consumer about possible legal rights, remedies, defenses, options, or strategies. We discuss the Arizona program in more detail in Chapter 14, Section A.

A. An American Tradition: "Every Man His Own Lawyer"

Let's look back four-and-one-half centuries. What can we say about the practice of law in colonial America? Very little, because in the early days of the American experience neither a lawyer elite nor a lawyer-dominated dispute resolution system existed in most colonies. Especially in Puritan New England, the Quaker communities in Pennsylvania, and the Dutch settlements in New York, there was a strong religious and egalitarian spirit, hostile to the very notion of lawyers. Colonists solved their disputes within the community, which in those early days was heavily influenced by the church. Church elders were expected to guide disputing members of their congregations to a "just" result. The ultimate punishment for deviant behavior was exile from both church and community. For example, Anne Hutchinson, a woman who challenged several orthodox views in the Massachusetts Bay Colony, was tried by the church for heresy and exiled to the wilderness; she eventually ended up in Rhode Island.

When a particular dispute proved intractable, formal mediation techniques, similar to those newly popular today, were often used to help the disputants arrive at their own compromise. In 1635, a Boston town meeting ordered that no congregation member could litigate before trying arbitration, and Reverend John Cotton, the leading Puritan minister of the time, stated that to sue a fellow church member was a "defect in brotherly love." In 1641, the "Body of Liberties" adopted by the Massachusetts Bay Colony prohibited all freemen from being represented by a paid attorney:

Every man that findeth himselfe unfit to plead his own cause in any court shall have libertie to employ any man against whom the court doth not except, to help him, Provided he give him noe fee or reward for his pains.

In the second half of the seventeenth century, England increasingly asserted its political authority over the colonies, with the result that the common law tradition—complete with courts, trial by jury, and inevitably, lawyers—began to take hold. Once established, it didn't take these first American lawyers long to try to suppress competition. Indeed, in Virginia, as early as 1642, legislation prohibited pleading a case without license from the court. Apparently, however, the egalitarian, every-man-his-own-spokesman tradition was strong even in relatively affluent Virginia; lawyers who charged for their services were banned from Virginia courts in 1645. They were allowed back in 1647, licensed in 1656, again prohibited from receiving compensation in 1657, and finally again allowed to practice with pay, if licensed, in 1680. Similar legislative ambivalence toward lawyers was evident in other colonies.[1]

One hundred years later, by the middle 1700s, lawyers were in evidence in all colonial commercial centers. Their prominence reflected the fact that although respect for religion still ran strong in America, ecclesiastical control of nearly all aspects of colonial life had receded before new waves of colonists more interested in secular than heavenly success.

In America in the 1750s, there were no law schools as we know them today. Young lawyers served an apprenticeship with an established practitioner. When they had learned enough legal ropes, they were questioned by a local judge (who had very likely received much the same sort of catch-as-catch-can training) and admitted to practice. When it came to legal knowledge, the gap between an attorney and the average educated citizen was less than great in the cities and almost nonexistent in rural America. Even James Madison and Thomas Jefferson, authors of many of the important documents leading up to American independence, thought of themselves as farmers who happened to study some law.

Many notable patriots of the Revolutionary War, including John Adams, Alexander Hamilton, Aaron Burr, and Patrick Henry, had legal training. Indeed, depending on how you define the term, about 40% of those who signed the Declaration of Independence were lawyers. Despite the prominence of these lawyer-patriots, the American Revolution marked the beginning of a long period of declining prestige for the legal profession. Much of the reason for this is traceable to the fact that the majority of the established bar sided with King George III rather than George Washington, and when the war was lost, left the colonies for England or Canada. As Thomas Jefferson remarked in a letter to James Madison, "Our lawyers are all Tories."

It should also be noted that a number of patriots with legal training, such as Jefferson and Madison, were radical ideologists, interested in legal theory as it contributed to the creation of a new social order, but not enamored with the traditional practice of law. Many patriot-lawyers saw the English legal system, with its formal rules of pleading and courts of equity, as fundamentally undemocratic, and opposed its wholesale adoption after independence. In this context, the creation of a written constitution guaranteeing citizens certain fundamental rights can be seen as a reaction against the English common law system, which consisted of a collection of laws and court decisions that could be changed, willy-nilly, by Parliament and the King.

Despite the fact that there were plenty of lawyers in late eighteenth century America, there is strong evidence that most citizens did not rely on them as a primary source of legal knowledge. Eldon Revare James, in *A List of Legal Treatises Printed in the British Colonies and the American States Before 1801,* found that:

> *In the hundred years between the publication in 1687 of William Penn's gleanings from Lord Coke and the issuance of the American editions of Buller's* Nisi Prius *and Gilbert's* Evidence *in 1788, not a single book that could be called a treatise intended for the use of professional lawyers was published in the British Colonies and American States. All of the books within this period which by any strength of definition might be regarded as legal treatises were for the use of laymen.*

One of the most popular of these law books directed at the non-lawyer was entitled *Every Man His Own Lawyer*, which was in its ninth edition by 1784. Published in London, but widely distributed in the colonies, this was a comprehensive guide to both civil and criminal law, divided into six sections covering the following diverse topics:

I.   Of Actions and Remedies, Writs, Process, Arrest and Bail.
II. Of Courts, Attorneys and Solicitors therein, Juries, Witnesses, Trials, Executions, etc.
III. Of Estates and Property in Lands and Goods, and how acquired; Ancestors, Heirs, Executors and Administrators.
IV. Of the Laws relating to Marriage, Bastardy, Infants, Idiots, Lunaticks.
V.   Of the Liberty of the Subject, *Magna Charta,* and *Habeas Corpus* Act and other statutes.
VI. Of the King and his Prerogative, the Queen and Prince, Peers, Judge, Sheriffs, Coroners, Justices of Peace, Constables, etc.

Use of this book was sufficiently widespread that it appears in a historical vignette featuring the second President of the United States, John Adams. It seems that before the Revolution, Adams, then a Boston lawyer and farmer, campaigned against "pettifoggers" (a derogatory term for independent paralegals and even some marginal lawyers) and led lawyer efforts to suppress the practice of law by "untrained" persons. Adams, like so many members of the profession today, worried about the loss of fees when he remarked that "looking about me in the country

I found the practice of law grasped into the hands of deputy sheriffs, pettifoggers and even constables who filled all the writs upon bonds, promissory notes and accounts, received the fees established for lawyers and stirred up many unnecessary suits."

Apparently to prove the extent of the problem presented by the proliferation of nonlawyer practitioners, Adams relates this story about a pettifogger and tavern keeper named Kibby: "In Kibby's barroom, in a little shelf within the bar, I spied two books. I asked what they were. He said, 'Every Man His Own Lawyer and Gilbert on Evidence.' Upon this, I asked some questions of the people there and they told me that Kibby was a sort of lawyer among them; that he pleaded some of their cases before justices, arbitrators, etc."[2]

As the new nation took shape, lawyers, with a number of conspicuous exceptions, tended to be poorly trained if they were trained at all. Indeed, except in Eastern commercial centers such as Boston, where at times an apprentice lawyer was required to work in a law office for as long as seven years before gaining admission to the bar, an American lawyer was little more than a man who could read and write and who owned a fireproof box. Still, in the last years of the eighteenth century and first decade of the nineteenth, urban lawyers were able to hold onto many of the prerogatives of their profession, thanks to laws in a number of states that established professional licensure requirements. This hard-won prominence was not to last, however. Along with a number of other "establishment" groups, from bankers to Freemasons, the legal profession did not fare well as America moved west. According to Daniel Lewolt, writing in *Americans for Legal Reform*, Vol. 5, No. 1 (Fall 1984):

> *The final blows were administered to legal professionals during the Andrew Jackson years. Frontiersmen, whose muddy boots had been allowed to trample White House rugs during Jackson's inaugural celebration, believed that justice should be popular and egalitarian and that experience was the best teacher. After 1830, even the requirement of reading [law] with a lawyer as a condition of practicing law was eliminated, and virtually anyone could practice law.*

Lewolt's view is supported by Leonard Tabachnik, who finds in *Professions for the People* (Schenkman Publishing, 1976) that:

The belief that professionalism advances science and protects the public from quackery was completely rejected by state legislators during the Age of Jackson: ...By 1840, only 11 of 30 states maintained regulations for admission to the Bar.

With the legal profession in retreat during these years, how did people settle disputes? The average citizen settled many on his own, without formal legal help, relying on one of several lay legal guides, such as Thomas Wooler's Every Man His Own Attorney, published in 1845.[3] In an interesting parallel to modern self-help law books, Wooler wrote in his introduction:

When attorneys are employed, they must be paid; and their charges are not always regulated whether by their abilities or their services to a client, but by their own desire to make as much as they can. This evil can only be remedied by making their clients well informed on common subjects, and able to see what course they are taking in matters of more intricacy.

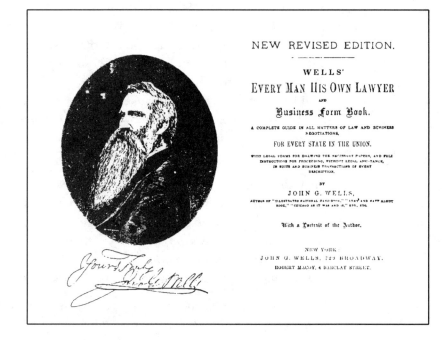

In addition, John Wells's *Every Man His Own Lawyer* (a different book than the one of the same title behind Kibby's bar that so annoyed John Adams and the members of the other, more powerful, bar), was sold as "a complete guide in all matters of law and business negotiations for every State in the Union, containing legal forms and full instructions for proceeding, without legal assistance, in suits and business transactions of every description." Apparently the popularity of this book was widespread. The author writes in the introduction to the 1879 edition:

> *The original edition of this work was prepared and presented to the public many years ago and was received with great favor, attaining a larger scale [hundreds of thousands according to Wells] it is believed, than any work published within its time.*

One might imagine that during the middle years of the nineteenth century, when almost any American could practice law and there was widespread interest in and support for self-help alternatives to lawyers, the intellectual quality of work done by the legal profession was low and individual lawyers were members of an endangered species. Just the opposite was true. As noted by Barlow Christensen in his article, "The Unauthorized Practice of Law: Do Good Fences Really Make Good Neighbors—Or Even Good Sense?" in the *American Bar Foundation Research Journal* (1980, No. 2):

> *The history of the profession during this period is paradoxical. On the one hand, this time is generally acknowledged to have been the great formative era in American law, during which were produced the great institutional cases that formed the foundation for the legal system as it exists today. It was also an era of great lawyers—Luther Martin, William Pinkney, William Wirt, Jeremiah Mason, Daniel Webster, Rufus Choate. In addition, it was an era of great judges, including James Kent, John Marshall and Joseph Storey. On the other hand, however, it was, as well, an era of decentralization and deprofessionalization of the profession, a return to the virtually unregulated profession of the colonial period.*

It's also worthy of note that Abraham Lincoln, a lawyer who had almost no formal education and never went to law school, appeared in court to represent clients as a paralegal before he was admitted to the bar.[4]

B. The Lawyers Take Over

By now, you are probably asking, "So what happened?" How did lawyers develop their stranglehold over almost every aspect of making, administering, and carrying out our laws? The full answer to this question is complex, a subject worthy of a book of its own. Here we can only suggest some of the historical forces that combined to produce the political climate conducive to lawyers' virtual monopoly over our legal system. These include:

- **Non-English speaking immigrants.** In the late nineteenth and early twentieth centuries, huge numbers of non-English speakers immigrated to the United States. These new Americans had a stiff language barrier to overcome. In addition, they had not been brought up in the comparatively democratic, always argumentative, every person on his feet having his say, tradition of the English Protestant church and, to a lesser extent, English common law. In short, this influx of humanity created a huge group that was, at least initially, at a considerable disadvantage when dealing with the American legal system. In an age when unsuspecting new immigrants really were sold shares in the Brooklyn Bridge, many people were taken advantage of by all sorts of quick-buck artists, including the legal variety. As a result, confidence that the average citizen could competently handle her own legal affairs began to erode, and calls for better professional standards began to be heard.

- **Rapid urbanization.** The decline of communities where people knew each other undoubtedly had a negative effect on legal self-reliance. The New England town meeting style of local government, so much a part of rural small-town America in the eighteenth and nineteenth centuries, didn't work in the urban America of the early twentieth century. Similarly, the power of many nineteenth century spiritual and immigrant communities dedicated to solving disputes without the intervention of lawyers began to wane.[5] After the Civil War, New York, Chicago, and a dozen more big, anonymous cities that had been growing for decades came to dominate the states in which they were located, and, through their newly huge banks, insurance companies, and stock exchanges, the commercial and political life of the nation. In the large cities, family and church ties had little power to bind people and help them settle their disputes outside of court. Increasingly, disputes now had to be dealt with in the public arena of the civil and criminal courts—the traditional spider-webs of the professional bar—complete with their arcane language, obfuscatory procedures and long delays.

- **New technology and business concentration.** Unprecedented development of new technologies in almost every industry, particularly energy, transport, and telecommunications, changed the relationship of Americans to their employers, spurred the growth of big labor unions to protect workers' rights, and required more and better-trained lawyers to invent and administer (and all too often manipulate) the business and legal infrastructure. For example, within the relatively few years between the end of the Civil War and the beginning of the First World War, modest factories, clustered mostly in areas with access to water and power, gave way to institutions such as Standard Oil, the Ford Motor Company, General Electric, railroads that spanned half a continent, and yes, even the Coca-Cola Company. In this brave new corporate world, disputes that would have been settled face to face in simpler times were now routinely turned over to big-city law firms.

- **The closing of the frontier.** In the last decade of the nineteenth century, America ran out of free farm and range land. No longer could the average person realistically hope to pack up the wagon, gather the kids, hitch up old Dobbin, and head west to homestead a free 160 acres. This is important because the American tradition of always moving west had helped prevent establishment groups, including lawyers, from dominating American political and legal institutions. For hundreds of years, no sooner did one city gain economic clout and its professionals start building themselves mansions on the hill, than the nation's center of economic gravity lurched west, leaving established elites behind. When America ran out of open land, lawyers and other establishment figures, including bankers, insurance agents, physicians, and brokers, had a chance to catch up with western migration for the first time in almost 300 years. Before long, they were able to control the political and economic life of the new states, just as they already did in the old, and the winds of legal change that had usually blown from the west were substantially stilled.

- **Consumer reform.** The early consumer movement, which fought for reasonable standards of product safety, honest and accountable business practices, and a ban on price-fixing and other monopolistic practices, paradoxically played an important role in the increase in organized lawyerdom's power. The reformers (often called "muckrakers"), inspired by authors like Upton Sinclair (*The Jungle*) and Lincoln Steffens (*The Shame of the Cities*), broke with the common law tradition of caveat emptor ("let the buyer beware") to argue that in an industrial society dominated by large-scale capitalism, the government must intervene in the commercial life of the nation to see that the ordinary citizen has a reasonable opportunity to avoid cynical exploitation by big business. This consumer crusade resulted in much of the progressive legislation adopted during the presidencies of Theodore Roosevelt and Woodrow Wilson, and laid the foundation for later reforms that have resulted in all sorts of good things, from purer food to safer workplaces. But it often produced negative results as it related to traditional professional groups such as lawyers and doctors. These "professionals" used the consumer reform movement to sell the nation on the rationale of "professional responsibility" and to justify organizing themselves into publicly sanctioned monopolies. For example, when it came to training new lawyers, the legal profession now emphasized formal schooling over the traditional apprenticeship method, and pushed required written examinations as an alternative to being admitted to practice on the recommendation of a practitioner or judge.

All of these changes quickly worked to the pecuniary benefit of American lawyers. Already by the turn of the century, lawyers had gained substantially in wealth, power, and community standing. Among the presidents elected between 1890 and 1932, Cleveland, Harrison, McKinley, Taft, Coolidge, Harding,[6] and Franklin Roosevelt were members of the bar, and Supreme Court justices Oliver Wendell Holmes and Louis Brandeis were among the most respected men in America. Even Teddy Roosevelt spent a year at Columbia law school before concluding that the practice of law was too boring.

The Great Goddess Gobbledygook and Her Devotees

It was particularly remarkable how quickly lawyers were able to use the new educational and certification requirements to eliminate non-lawyer competition. As late as 1890, fewer than half of the states and territories had meaningful educational requirements for lawyers. But by 1915, only 13 states and one of the remaining territories allowed admission to law practice without attending law school. By 1940, all but a few states effectively required professional study to be a lawyer.[7] Perhaps because it was so easy for organized lawyerdom to sell the American public on the image of an educated professional bar dedicated to high standards of integrity and service, lawyers had little incentive to actually back up this image with substantive consumer protection. For example, once new lawyers passed a general knowledge examination that had little to do with the day-to-day work of a practicing lawyer, there were absolutely no requirements for continuing skills testing or education. And legal consumers who were cheated or overcharged by the professional incompetence of individual lawyers were then, as now, provided with little meaningful recourse.

It wasn't until the Depression of the 1930s that lawyers really had to defend their newly minted monopoly. Bad economic times hit the legal profession particularly hard, striking as they did at the roots of its new power base as the protector of corporate America. Suddenly, from skyscraper to street corner, there were too many lawyers chasing too few clients—at least those who could pay their bills. The result might have been a legal profession that made a concerted effort to try to make good cheap legal help available to millions of newly poor Americans. In fact, despite lip service to helping widows and orphans, organized lawyerdom did just the opposite, banding together as never before to fix prices by use of a number of anticompetitive devices. These included, most prominently, bar association-mandated minimum fees, "treaties" with other professions, including bankers, accountants, and real estate brokers, designed to respect each other's service monopolies, and a concerted campaign to eliminate all nonlawyer competition.

Just as the Depression caused a lot of people to consider handling their own legal work or seeking help from more reasonably priced nonlawyer practitioners, the bar adopted a surprisingly militant campaign to rid the nation of the last vestiges of the self-help law movement that had survived from the nineteenth century.[8] If you doubt the accuracy of this assertion, consider that the first American Bar Association committee ever to deal specifically with unauthorized practice was formed in 1930, and by 1938, over 400 state and local bar associations had formed similar committees.

The great increase in interest in unauthorized practice by bar associations led naturally to an increase in the number of nonlawyers who were prosecuted. As noted by Deborah Rhode in her fascinating 1981 study of unauthorized practice published in the *Stanford Law Review*,[9] a 1937 survey of reported unauthorized practice cases devoted 94 pages to all pre-1930 decisions and 619 pages to unauthorized practice suits decided between 1930 and 1937. Much of the reason for this increase in enforcement was the passage of new unauthorized practice statutes with tougher penalties. Most of this new legislation was orchestrated by the newly organized local and state bar unauthorized practice committees, all of which claimed their activities were designed not to feather the nest of the legal profession but to protect the public from unqualified and incompetent law practitioners. Interestingly, Deborah Rhode's in-depth study finds almost no evidence that the public ever asked for, or needs, this "protection."

When good economic times returned after the Second World War, the legal profession suddenly found that there weren't enough lawyers to go around. This isn't surprising when you realize that relatively few lawyers were trained during the Depression. This shortage of lawyers, coinciding as it did with the unprecedented expansion and prosperity of the American middle class, resulted in an economic golden age for lawyers. Or, put simply, in the 1950s it was a snap to make big bucks in the law business. And just in case any nonlawyers were tempted to try to participate in this bonanza, the tough unauthorized practice statutes passed in the 1930s were still on the books to keep out interlopers.

In fairness, it should be noted that during the Eisenhower years, the average American's newfound admiration for "professionalization" also contributed to the maintenance of organized lawyerdom's monopoly. In the prosperous 1950s, it seemed as if everyone wanted their kids to be lawyers, doctors, or orthodontists (as popular as law school was, learning to straighten middle-class children's teeth was surely the growth profession of the decade). Against this background, it wasn't hard for the legal profession to convince most people that "a person who represents himself has a fool for a client."

C. The Modern Movement Away From Lawyers

Paradoxically, just as the legal profession reached the zenith of its power in the early 1960s, the first hints of its current vulnerability were becoming apparent. In its effort to clamp down on potential competitors, organized lawyerdom acted as if it, and it alone, was equipped to serve the legal needs of the broad American public. Although many lawyers believed it (and despite two generation's accumulation of evidence to the contrary, a few still do), this was far from true. Lawyers had gained status and wealth serving corporate America, the growing bureaucracy of federal and state governments, and, to a lesser extent, individuals in upper-income brackets. Except for a few profitable but very limited legal areas, such as personal injury litigation, divorce, wills, and probate, the legal profession barely dealt with the average American of 1965.

That the majority of middle-class Americans were underserved by the legal profession (and that blue-collar and ethnic Americans were hardly served at all) became embarrassingly obvious in the late 1960s. This widespread recognition was triggered in part by the Johnson administration's sponsorship of federally funded legal services for the poor (legal aid), the first-ever coordinated delivery of legal help nation-wide. Everyone who worked in a legal services office in those years (and increasingly reporters who covered the war on poverty) was struck by an incredible fact—despite the bargain basement ambiance of the largely ghetto-based offices, each had to employ a number of people who did nothing but turn away middle-class Americans not poor enough to qualify for legal aid, but not affluent enough to retain a lawyer under the traditional fee-for-services model. In short, when middle-class Americans began to line up on the streets of Watts, Bedford-Stuyvesant, and the South Side of Chicago (places they had gone previously only after rolling up the windows and locking the doors of their Pontiacs) to wait in line to talk to a lawyer, the fiction that American lawyers served the average American was revealed to be just that.

But it wasn't only the discovery that lawyers had priced their services out of the financial reach of most Americans that resulted in the profession's great fall in the public regard. Widespread latent dissatisfaction with the legal profession also surfaced during the investigation of the Watergate break-in in 1973. Many, if not most, of the people accused of illegal conduct—including Dean, Erlichmann, Colson, Chapin, Segretti, Mitchell, and Nixon himself, were lawyers. Instead of admitting they were wrong, these men first told a series of whopping lies and then, even after they were forced to admit their culpability, tried to wriggle off the hook on one or another legal technicality. In short, almost every

American with a TV set learned that being a lawyer had little to do with the bar association's image of a profession dedicated to the pursuit of truth and justice. Woody Guthrie, it seemed, had been right all along when he sang about a profession which did its robbing not with a six-gun but a fountain pen.

After Watergate, most Americans understood that a majority of lawyers were out to make a pile of money fast, and if ignoring the rules they were supposed to respect helped them achieve their goal quicker, so be it. And when it came right down to it, why should this be shocking? Wasn't this trend of "life in the fast lane," "damn the rights of others," "winning is everything" approach equally fashionable among stockbrokers, doctors, football coaches, morticians, bankers, car salespeople, and others? Yes, but since these other groups hadn't tried so hard to put their occupation on a pedestal, they were less vulnerable to attack.

Not only did the public, as a whole, lose respect for the legal profession, some individuals with legal questions and problems began to look for ways to solve them without lawyers. One consequence was that America began to rediscover its strong historical tradition of legal self-help. By the middle 1970s, Norman Dacey's *How to Avoid Probate* and Ed Sherman's *How to Do Your Own Divorce in California* were best-sellers. In California, Nolo had been established, and had published over 20 successful self-help law books. Now, the Nolo catalog has over 150 titles. And of particular interest to readers of this book, nonlawyer (independent paralegal) typing services began to offer legal form preparation services directly to the public.

By the early 1980s, about 100 independent paralegals existed in Florida, California, and several other Western states. In addition to divorce, those pioneers began preparing legal forms for other problems, including bankruptcy, stepparent adoption, and change of name. Later in the 1980s, as more form-preparation services were added, many IPs began to prosper. So much so that by the mid-1990s, California alone had as many as 2,000 IPs, and in a number of other states, including Florida, Arizona, and Oregon, IP practice was common. Unfortunately, this has not meant that organized lawyerdom has given up trying to suppress its competitors.

As the IP movement has gained momentum, legislation affecting this new business was introduced in a number of states. Some bills were designed to make it clear that the delivery of basic legal form preparation services by nonlawyers is legal. In other states, bills were proposed to study what, if any, state regulation of this new industry was needed. In 1998 the first major legislative breakthrough came in California with passage of SB 1418. See Chapter 14 for a brief history of recent events in California. In July 2003, new court rules in Arizona took it a step further and established a certification structure under which IPs (now called Legal Document Preparers) can provide general legal and factual information to their clients as long as they don't give specific advice as to available options. And since the early 1980s, rules issued by the Florida Supreme Court have permitted IPs to prepare forms issued by the Florida Supreme Court. See Chapter 14 for more information about both of these states' rules.

endnotes

[1] We are indebted to Charles Warren, *A History of the American Bar* (Boston, Little Brown), and Roscoe Pound, *The Lawyer From Antiquity to Modern Times* (West Publishing Co., 1953), for much of this historical background.

[2] See Roscoe Pound, *The Lawyer From Antiquity to Modern Times* (West Publishing, 1953).

[3] We are indebted to a fascinating article by Mort Reber, entitled "A Return to Self-Reliance," which appeared in the *People's Law Review* (Nolo, 1980), for much of this information.

[4] See *Lincoln,* by David Donald (Simon and Shuster, 1995), page 71.

[5] In the nineteenth century, all sorts of groups, including Shakers, Seventh Day Baptists, Swedenborgians, the Socialist followers of Owen and Fourier, Orthodox Jews, and literally hundreds of others, established communities that handled disputes without lawyers. Rather typically, John Noyes, the founder of the Oneida community, considered litigation "as the private equivalent of war," and it was said that the members of the Amana community in Iowa "live[d] in

such perpetual peace that no lawyer is found in their midst." For more on the story of how a number of American communities tried to do without lawyers entirely, see Jerold Auerbach, *Justice Without Law: Resolving Disputes Without Lawyers,* Oxford University Press (1983).

[6] Warren Harding was as unsuccessful as a lawyer as he was as president, quitting the profession early on to go into the newspaper business.

[7] Willard Hurst, *The Growth of American Law: The Law Makers* (Little Brown & Co., 1950).

[8] The American Bar Association also led a 50-state effort to close down unaccredited, mostly night law schools which, in the previous several decades, had produced the majority of American lawyers. The idea was frankly to limit the supply of new lawyers in an effort to push up legal fees. For the fascinating story of the suppression of America's unaccredited law schools, see Richard Abel's *American Lawyers* (Oxford University Press, 1989).

[9] Rhode, "Policing the Professional Monopoly: A Constitutional and Empirical Analysis of Unauthorized Practice Prohibitions," *Stan. L. Rev.,* Vol.34:1 (1981).

■

The Law

This chapter is concerned with the laws, court rules and powers claimed by bar associations that, taken together, define the unauthorized practice of law. Mastering this information is crucial to your success as an independent paralegal because the unauthorized practice laws are organized lawyerdom's principal way to attack nonlawyers who challenge its monopoly power to deliver legal services. As we go through this chapter, it's important to keep in mind the general truth that it's one thing to know what any law says and quite another to understand what the words mean in the real world. Especially in the context of regulations governing the unauthorized practice of law, which are incredibly vague, it is necessary to understand the nuances of both community and law enforcement attitudes in your city and state.

In Chapter 3, we discuss in detail what an independent paralegal can do to avoid charges of unauthorized practice of law. Basically, as an IP, you should do three things: tell the world you are not a lawyer, make sure your customers have the written or electronic information they need to make their own decisions, and limit yourself to legal form preparation.

A. Introduction to the Concept of Unauthorized Practice of Law (UPL)

What exactly is the practice of law and how can you avoid doing it? Unfortunately, the term "practice of law" is nowhere clearly and unambiguously defined. In many states the courts prescribe who can deliver legal services on a case-by-case basis under their inherent power to regulate law practice. Unfortunately, the reasoning in these cases tends to be circular: Only lawyers can practice law, and therefore, doing what lawyers do is practicing law. Statutes that make unauthorized practice a crime in the majority of states are no more helpful, defining the practice of law as "what lawyers do" or "activities that require a trained legal mind," terms that are impossible to interpret by any meaningful objective standard.

But all hope is not lost. Although you probably can't get much help from definitions of the practice of law, you may be able to get some guidance from finding out what is not considered to be the practice of law. Probably the best place to look is at the court decisions of your own state, the rules that regulate your state's bar, and any pronouncements on the subject issued by your state's supreme court.[1] For example, in the aftermath of the Rosemary Furman affair (see Interview in the Appendix), the Florida Supreme Court provided some guidance in the Rules Regulating the Florida Bar. With some small changes, these now read:[2]

> *...[I]t shall not constitute the unlicensed practice of law for a non-lawyer to engage in limited oral communications to assist a person in the completion of blanks on a legal form approved by the Supreme Court of Florida. Oral communications by nonlawyers are restricted to those communications reasonably necessary to elicit factual information to complete the blanks on the form and inform the person how to file the form.*

Since then, the Florida Supreme Court has approved hundreds of pages of legal forms involving divorce, landlord-tenant, and other routine legal issues, thus allowing Florida independent paralegals to help consumers prepare these forms, free of worry that they will be charged with UPL.

Let's take a look at some case decisions that will give you a sense of the approaches different state courts have taken in deciding what constitutes UPL.

California. In *The People v. Landlords Professional Services*,[3] a California case involving an eviction service that helped people prepare and file unlawful detainer actions, the court applied a statute that allowed law enforcement officers to shut down businesses that ran afoul of the California UPL law, and held that the service was engaged in the unauthorized practice of law because:

1. The advertisement suggested that the eviction service did more than simply provide clerical assistance. The ad implied that the service actually accomplished evictions.

2. "Call and talk to us" on the ad and "counselor" on the business card were general invitations for discussion and suggested that the service sells expertise.

3. The service provided specific information and advice directed to the client's personal problems and concerns.

The court found that the service provided by the IP business would not amount to the "practice of law" as long as the service was "merely clerical," because:

- It is not UPL to make forms available for clients' use.
- It is not UPL to fill in forms and file and serve them at the specific direction of the client.
- It is not UPL to give a client a detailed manual containing specific advice.
- It is not UPL as long as the service doesn't personally advise the client with regard to her particular case.

Washington. An opinion written by the Washington Supreme Court illustrates just how unpredictable application of UPL regulations to any specific situation can be.[4] Here the court invoked its own inherent power to regulate the practice of law to find that the preparation of certain real estate forms necessary to buy and sell houses, which had, in the past, always been prepared by lawyers, could now be completed by nonlawyers. In allowing nonlawyer involvement in real estate transactions, the court relied on the public's interest in freedom of choice, convenience, and the lower costs provided by nonlawyers. In doing so, the court specifically ruled that:

> *There are sound and practical reasons why some activities that fall within the broad definition of the "practice of law" should not be unauthorized simply because they are done by laypersons.*

This thinking was mirrored in a recent Kentucky Supreme Court opinion in which the court held that nonlawyers can handle real estate closings without running afoul of the states' UPL laws. (*Countrywide Home Loans, Inc. v. Kentucky Bar Association*, No. 2000-SC-0206-KB (Ky. 08/21/2003).)

Oregon. In 1995, Robin Smith, a longtime IP and owner of People's Paralegal in Beaverton, Oregon, was suddenly enjoined from doing many of the things that had been a basic part of her legal form preparation business for over eight years. (See interview in the Appendix.) Although the judge's decision in *Oregon State Bar v. Smith,* No. C940-597CV (Washington Co. Circuit Court, 1995), was considered outrageously pro-lawyer by many, it has been upheld by the Oregon Court of Appeal. (*Oregon State Bar v. Smith,* 149 Ore App 171, 942 p.2d 793 (1997).) Among other things, Smith was enjoined from:

- Any personal contact with customers in the nature of consultation, explanation, recommendation, or advice regarding legal matters.
- Meeting with customers to discuss their individual facts and circumstances, their need or desire for legal forms, services, or assistance.
- Advising customers regarding their legal eligibility for, or the advisability of, legal remedies to address the customer's particular legal matter.
- Advising customers regarding procedural functions of the court system as it relates to customers' particular legal matters.
- Assisting in selecting particular forms, documents, or pleadings for customers to address their legal matters.

In the accompanying discussion, Judge McElligott wrote:

In the circumstance in which a person proceeds pro se, the person alone brings knowledge of the law to bear. If the person has none, none can be gained from someone who is not a member of the Bar. The person who proceeds pro se must "practice all the law," though they can buy and utilize forms. These forms can be legally sold. Defendants undertake to do so. However, while Defendants can legally offer and sell forms, the pro se must determine which forms are appropriate. Defendants violate the law by making this determination.

Just as anyone can sell forms, anyone can legally type forms. But the typist cannot supply the words and phrases and sentences to be typed. Only a lawyer as the pro se can. Defendants violate the law by doing so.

B. Criminal Penalties for Unauthorized Practice

More than two-thirds of states in the U.S. have criminal statutes that make unauthorized practice a misdemeanor. Typically, fines are limited to between $1,000 and $5,000, and jail time to one year or less in a county correctional facility. For example, in California, the UPL statute reads like this:

> *Any person advertising or holding himself or herself out as practicing or entitled to practice law or otherwise practicing law who is not an active member of the State Bar, or otherwise authorized pursuant to statute or court rule to practice law in this state at the time of doing so, is guilty of a misdemeanor punishable by up to one year in a county jail or by a fine of up to one thousand dollars ($1,000), or by both that fine and imprisonment.*[5]

In states where UPL is a crime, public prosecutors play a key role in UPL enforcement. A deputy District or State's Attorney decides if a particular independent paralegal is committing unauthorized practice and should either be prosecuted or pursued in a civil action. (See Section D, below, for more on enforcement of UPL laws.)

FINDING YOUR STATE'S UPL LAWS

Your state's UPL laws come from three possible sources: statutes passed by your state legislature, decisions made by your state's courts in specific cases dealing with UPL issues, and court rules issued by your state's supreme court. All of these sources of UPL law can be found on the Internet or in your local law library. Here we provide a brief overview of how you can find these resources yourself. However, we strongly recommend that you get a copy of *Legal Research: How to Find and Understand the Law*, by Elias and Levinkind (Nolo), to help you navigate the shoals of legal research, online and in the law library.

The Internet

We recommend that you start with the Legal Research Center on the Nolo website. On the Nolo.com Homepage, you will see a link to other research. This link will lead you to a page that lists all 50 states. Click the link for your state and you will be taken to a page that lists a number of different types of state resources, including a link to your state's statutes (usually in the form of a code), regulations, and recent cases. As a general rule, you can enter key words, such as "unauthorized practice of law," or you can browse the different sections of the code until you come to the UPL statutes themselves. Through a little trial and error you can find the set of statutes that govern UPL in your state.

Court decisions are a little harder to find, but it is vitally important that you become familiar with how your state courts define UPL and how they have treated particular activities in previous cases, such as drafting a living trust or helping a customer choose the correct divorce forms. While cases decided by your state courts over the past several years are available over the Internet for free, chances are you'll want to find older cases. To do this you'll have to subscribe to a service that lets you search for archived cases. Our favorite is Versuslaw at www.versuslaw.com. Non-attorneys can subscribe for $11.95 a month. Once you find your way to the Versuslaw case search section, simply enter the words "unauthorized practice of law" in the search engine box and start skimming the cases that your search pulls up. You should pay particular interest to any case that deals with the type of law (divorce, bankruptcy, estate planning, etc.) that you plan to feature in your business.

Rules issued by your state's supreme court regarding the unauthorized practice of law can usually be found on the court's website. The best way to find a court website is to start with Findlaw at www.findlaw.com. Click the link for "U.S. state resources," then the link for your state, then the link for your state's courts, then the link for your state's supreme court. The rules should be there.

Law Library

Go to a large public library or, better yet, a law library (often found at county courthouses or publicly funded law schools). Find the book containing your state's laws (often referred to as statute books or code books). If possible, use the "annotated" version of your legal code, which contains not only the laws themselves but also useful information about relevant court cases, articles, and other secondary sources that discuss each law. Locate the volume entitled General Index and look up the Unauthorized Practice of Law, which will refer you to the appropriate code and section.

Once you have found and read the law in the hardbound volume, check the same statute number in the inserted "pocket part" (just inside the back cover). This will contain any changes passed by your state's legislature from the time the hardbound book was published up to about six months to one year ago. If your legislature has met since then, ask a law librarian to show you how to check to see if there have been even more current changes.

Next, look up and read any court cases decided in your state very carefully. To find UPL cases in your state, there are a number of ways to proceed. The first place to check is the case notes, which you will find with your state's UPL statute in the annotated code. (See "How to Look Up Your UPL Statutes," earlier in this chapter.) Once you locate at least one relevant case and read it, you will almost surely be referred to other UPL cases. Also, with the case citation you have, use Shepard's Case Citations to get citations to all other cases that mention that case.

Another way to check for UPL cases is to check a case digest for your state. (All populous states have them.) A digest is a collection of case summaries that are organized by subject matter and indexed. To use a digest for your state, check the subject-matter index under "unauthorized practice of law."

A third way to identify cases in your state is to read all the cases mentioned in the text and footnotes of this chapter. Typically, these will refer to (cite) UPL cases from other states, one of which may be yours.

Also, law review articles on UPL cite a number of cases. The important articles are:

- Rhode, "Policing the Professional Monopoly: A Constitutional and Empirical Analysis of Unauthorized Practice Prohibitions," *Stanford Law Rev.*, Vol. 34:1 (1981).
- Michelman, "Guiding the Invisible Hand: The Consumer Protection Function of Unauthorized Practice Regulation," *Pepperdine L. Rev.*, Vol. 12, No. 1 (1984).
- Wolfram, "Lawyer Turf and Lawyer Regulation—The Role of the Inherent-Powers Doctrine," *University of Arkansas at Little Rock Law Journal*, Volume 12, No. 1 (1989-90).
- Rhode, "The Delivery of Legal Services by Nonlawyers," *Georgetown Journal of Legal Ethics*, Vol. 4:209 (1990).

Finally, check the Index of Legal Periodicals under the heading "Unauthorized Practice." This publication lists all law review and law journal articles in the unauthorized practice area. You may well find a current one that discusses the case law of your state.

Legal Research Note: Nolo's *Legal Research: How to Find and Understand the Law* (Elias and Levinkind) thoroughly explains how to accomplish all the tasks mentioned here.

C. Civil Enforcement of Criminal UPS Statutes

In some states it is possible for independent paralegals to be sued under civil statutes that prohibit unfair business practices. These statutes often define unfair business practices to include violations of criminal law. Unfair business practice suits can be brought by law enforcement attorneys (attorneys general, district attorneys, etc.) or by private parties, including attorneys. In California, for example, a private attorney brought a civil enforcement action under California Business and Professions Code Section 17200 against a large number of independent paralegals in the Los Angeles area. The suit sought to put the IPs out of business and sought disgorgement of fees the IPs had collected for the previous three years (the period allowed by Section 17200). The lawsuit was finally settled when the California legislature passed a law permitting independent paralegal activity along the lines we suggest in this book. See Chapter 14, Section A.

The primary relief offered by this type of unfair business practices statute is injunctive relief, meaning an order from the court that IPs must do some act (like close down their business) or refrain from doing some act (like advising clients). Injunctive relief may, as a practical matter, drive paralegals out of business if the injunction is broad enough. Frequently, the statutes also provide for restitution to anyone harmed by the unfair business practice, disgorgement of fees taken in by the business during a several year period preceding the lawsuit, and attorney fees. Because they are considered civil cases, unfair business practice cases are easier to prove than are criminal UPL charges. Also, because unfair business practice causes of action are statutory in origin (made by the Legislature) rather than based on the common law (made by a judge), jury trials usually are not allowed.

To determine whether your state has an unfair business practice law, locate your state's statutes and search for "unlawful business practice," "unfair competition," or "unfair business practice."

D. Judicial Penalties for Unauthorized Practice — the Inherent Powers Doctrine

Courts in most states assert the power to define and regulate the practice of law. In legal parlance, this is often referred to as the "inherent powers doctrine."[6] For example, in the preamble to its new rules governing legal document preparers in Arizona, the court states: "The supreme court has inherent regulatory power over all persons providing legal services to the public, regardless of whether they are lawyers or nonlawyers. The court recognizes, however, that the need to protect the public from possible harm caused by nonlawyers providing legal services must be balanced against the public's need for access to legal services." Judges claim this power originally comes from their inherent authority to regulate what happens in their own courts, and by extension the practice of law generally. This inherent powers doctrine is then elevated to constitutional dimensions by the "separation of powers" clause, which grants each branch of government (executive, legislative, and judicial) the right to regulate its own affairs. For example, if a state legislature passes a law or regulation that affects lawyers or the practice of law, the state supreme court can find it unconstitutional because it invades the exclusive province of the judiciary. In practice, they often don't, as long as the law strictly limits what nonlawyers can do. However, courts are far more likely to overrule legislation when they believe it goes too far in allowing nonlawyers to perform legal tasks. In the following sections, we will review some court decisions that will give you an idea of how the inherent powers doctrine is applied and how it might be relevant to you as an IP.

1. Court Regulation of Independent Paralegals Who Appear Before State Administrative Hearings

Some administrative agencies are created by state statute and basically exist to facilitate a legislative purpose, such as administering health, labor, or retirement programs. Many of these agencies provide court-like procedures to hear and resolve disputes. For example, a person who is denied unemployment insurance benefits normally has the right to an administrative hearing and, if he loses, to at least one appeal. In many states (if not most) nonlawyers may represent people in these and many similar administrative agency proceedings.

Because many state courts assert inherent powers to regulate the entire legal system, nonlawyers who represent people before state (and sometimes even federal) agencies may be charged with unauthorized practice. Occasionally, this can be true even though the state legislature or the agency itself allows nonlawyers to appear before it. And if this isn't confusing enough, consider that, in some states, judges choose not to use their inherent power to block legislation that allows nonlawyers to represent people before agencies, while others just say no. With this in mind, let's look at a few cases.

In a decision by the Florida Supreme Court, the court found that the preparation of documents and presentation of noncontested juvenile dependency cases by lay counselors was unauthorized practice.[7] The court said if advice involved important rights and required knowledge of law greater than that of the average citizen, it constituted unauthorized practice.

In Rhode Island, the Supreme Court considered two statutes that allowed nonlawyers to represent people in informal hearings within the Department of Workers' Compensation.[8] The purpose of these nonlawyer "employee assistants" was to give help and advice to employees under the Workers' Compensation Act. The court concluded that although the activities subject to the statutes could be considered the practice of law, they were okay because any definition of the practice of law must be responsive to the public interest. The court explicitly states that the legislature may aid the court's inherent power to define the practice of law and determine who may practice, but the legislature must abide by the court's standard. The court points out that it has not interfered with a number of legislative acts that, in effect, carved out exceptions to the practice of law because they constituted a response to a public need.

In other words, while theoretically the Rhode Island legislature's power to regulate state administrative proceedings is second to the courts, in practice, the court will not upset the legislature's decision if it agrees with the public policy being advanced. This approach, which leaves the final decision up to the courts, is the prevailing approach in the United States,[9] according to legal commentator Gregory T. Stevens.[10]

Because of the differences between what a state law or agency regulation says and what actually happens, it is not always easy to know whether an independent paralegal can appear before a particular agency on behalf of a claimant or not. Probably the best approach is to simply call any agency you are interested in and ask.

2. Federal Administrative Agency Hearings

The federal system gives exclusive regulatory control of federal agencies to Congress. The Administrative Procedure Act (5 U.S.C. 555(b)) authorizes federal agencies to allow nonlawyers to practice before them without regard to whether the activities would be unauthorized practice in the state where the agency proceeding occurs. One example of where this occurs is in the Social Security system, where nonlawyers are permitted to represent people appealing from the denial of a disability claim. This does not mean that all federal agencies allow nonlawyers to do this, only that each agency has the power to allow nonlawyer representation if it so chooses. The IRS, the U.S. Citizenship and Immigration Service (USCIS), and the Patent and Trademark Office are other agencies that allow considerable nonlawyer practice. According to one U.S. Supreme Court decision, states cannot restrict the right of any person to perform a function that falls within the scope of federal authority.[11] However, to guarantee the right of nonlawyers to appear, the agency in question must explicitly allow nonlawyer representation. If it fails to do so, states can assert this right to prohibit what they see as UPL, even in a federal agency proceeding.

For example, in Florida, the state bar's committee on the unauthorized practice of law wanted the court to find that certain nonlawyer involvement in preparing pension plans was unauthorized practice. In this instance, federal statutes and regulations authorized nonlawyers to practice before federal agencies. The Florida Supreme Court ruled that because the federal agency granted such authority, the states could not use their own definition of UPL to limit it, and thus, the court did not find unauthorized practice in this instance.[12]

3. Federal Bankruptcy Court Law

Federal Law 11 U.S.C. § 110(g)(1), adopted in 1994, recognizes the occupation of Bankruptcy Petition Preparer (BPP). It also establishes technical rules as to how a BPP can operate his business. For example, a BPP must put his name, address, and Social Security number on every bankruptcy petition he prepares, and can't use the word "legal" or any similar term in advertising.[13]

So far so good. But unfortunately, there are some less attractive aspects of this law. They include:

- **Fee caps.** The act allows bankruptcy courts to establish a "fair price" for preparing bankruptcy forms. In most locations, BPPs are allowed to charge between $125 and $200. A few courts are more restrictive and some are more liberal. Many BPPs have been forced out of the business.

- **Bounties.** The act allows bankruptcy trustees and creditors to collect a $1,000 bounty from a BPP who violates the technical rules discussed above, or commits a fraudulent, unfair, or deceptive act, or whose negligence or violation of bankruptcy rules causes a case to be dismissed. In some areas of the country, lawyers have used this bounty law to go after IPs. In addition to the bounty, a BPP who is found to have violated these rules must pay a customer $2,000, or twice any losses, whichever is greater.

Despite the ridiculous severity of 11 U.S.C. § 110 (g)(1), in many parts of the country, bankruptcy form preparers as a group have benefited from its passage. After all, by tightly regulating this occupation, this law also recognizes its legitimacy.

KNOW THE BPP LAW

To say the least, no one should consider preparing a bankruptcy petition unless they fully understand every nuance of 11 U.S.C. § 110(g)(1). Richard Lubetzky, a Los Angeles lawyer who has undoubtedly represented more IPs charged with the unauthorized practice of law than any other attorney, emphasizes that in addition to complying with the technical rules of 11 U.S.C. § 110(g)(1), BPPs still must be extremely concerned about the unauthorized practice of law (UPL), since that Act specifically states that it doesn't change existing law in that area. He counsels IPs to particularly watch out for trustees who ask people filing bankruptcy how they decided which exemptions to pick. If your customer replies, I read about exemptions in a book such as *How to File for Chapter 7 Bankruptcy*, by Elias, Renauer, and Leonard (Nolo), there is no problem. But if the customer says the bankruptcy petition preparer told her which ones to choose, that's considered the practice of law and makes the independent paralegal vulnerable to UPL charges.

Lubetzky also provides a succinct analysis of the bankruptcy petition preparer law.

Some of the most common problems encountered by bankruptcy petition preparers involve the unauthorized practice of law, understanding the limitations on what petition preparers can do, using the term 'legal' in advertising, handling the bankruptcy court filing fee, making the proper disclosure where the petition preparer is a corporation, and determining the fee to be charged.

Some bankruptcy petition preparers believe that Section 110 authorizes them to perform activities regarding bankruptcy that would otherwise be prohibited by their state's UPL. This is not true. In fact, Section 110(k) specifically provides that Section 110 may not be used to legitimize the practice of law by a petition preparer, where state law prohibits the practice of law. Courts use the UPL laws of the state where the bankruptcy court is located to assess whether a particular BPP activity constitutes UPL.

To avoid UPL charges, BPPs should be especially careful about how the exemptions are chosen. If a customer is asked at the creditor's meeting about how the exemptions were selected and the customer answers that the BPP selected them, the BPP will most likely be accused of UPL. If, however, the customer answers that the exemptions were selected from a published source, such as Nolo's How to File for Chapter 7 Bankruptcy, *there should be no problem.*

Generally, bankruptcy courts have differed on what BPPs may do beyond merely typing bankruptcy documents. Some bankruptcy courts have taken the position that typing is the only thing they can do. Other courts have allowed services other than typing as long as they don't give legal advice.

Courts also disagree on how BPPs may handle the filing fee. All courts agree that BPPs may not accept cash for the filing fee. However, some courts allow BPPs to accept money orders from their customers where the money order is made out to the court while other courts have ruled that even money orders made out to the court violate Section 110(g). In those circumstances the customer must file the papers, not the BPP.

Corporations that prepare bankruptcy petitions are also considered to be BPPs. In such cases, the name of the individual who prepared the documents, as well as that person's social security number, must be disclosed on the documents along with the name and address of the corporation.

BPPs may not use the word 'legal' or similar terms in any advertising of bankruptcy document preparation services, or advertise such services under a heading containing such words. At least one court has ruled that use of the word 'paralegal' violates this prohibition. The use of such words can subject the petition preparer to the imposition of fines and the issuance of an injunction by the bankruptcy court.

Finally, the amount that a petition preparer can charge for the preparation of bankruptcy documents is generally fixed by the local office of the U.S. Trustee in consultation with the local bankruptcy court, although the court can award more on a case-by-case basis upon a showing of good cause. Since the amounts that bankruptcy courts permit BPPs to charge vary widely across the country, BPPs should consult their local office of the U.S. Trustee and local bankruptcy court decisions to determine what they can charge.

See Chapter 9, Section E, for more on BPP fees.

More information about bankruptcy. In Chapter 3, we discuss how an independent paralegal can run a bankruptcy form preparation service in a way that largely avoids the risk of being found guilty of the unauthorized practice of law. We discuss the regulation of fees charged by independent paralegals for preparing bankruptcy forms in Chapter 9.

E. Enforcement of Unauthorized Practice Rules

Is there a way to predict whether a UPL action is likely in a particular area? Not with any accuracy. This is because most UPL proceedings, civil and criminal, are triggered by an individual lawyer, bar association, or judge, often because the IP is perceived to be infringing on what many lawyers believe is their exclusive domain. In some states, bar associations are authorized to bring UPL actions in court against IPs. Often, the bar seeks an injunction to prohibit all or some activities of the paralegal service. Because of the uncertain definition of "practicing law," some courts will provide guidelines that the IP is directed to follow, and as long as the IP agrees to do this, he or she will usually be able to remain in business. Bar associations may also refer cases to the state or local prosecutor to demand that UPL charges be filed against a particular IP. A prosecutor or court may also initiate UPL proceedings on their own.

What happens if you do run afoul of the enforcement division of your state supreme court, or a bar association committee that threatens to turn you in to a court or to the local prosecutor? Deborah Rhode, in her *Stanford Law Review* study,[14] finds that normally no formal action is taken. Typically, what happens is this:

- The bar association or court contacts the independent paralegal—often by letter, but sometimes personally—and asks her to cease what it considers the offending conduct.
- If the IP doesn't comply, the bar may subpoena her to appear before a bar association hearing, at which point she is likely to be formally told to stop preparing forms for nonlawyers. This sort of intimidation causes many people to close down.

But what happens if the independent paralegal politely but firmly insists on her constitutional right to continue helping nonlawyers do their own legal paperwork? Depending on the makeup of the particular bar committee or the attitude of the state supreme court, and on the law of the particular state, the bar association or court may:

- Do nothing.
- Initiate its own civil court proceeding to try to put the independent paralegal out of business. As touched on earlier, this generally takes the form of an action in a trial court to prevent the IP from engaging in whatever activity organized lawyerdom alleges constitutes the unauthorized practice of law. If a resulting injunction is violated, the IP is typically held in contempt of court and jailed or fined, or both. (This is basically what happened to Rosemary Furman in Florida.)
- In the approximately 36 states where UPL is a crime, the matter may potentially be referred to a criminal prosecutor. Prosecutors, who are normally overloaded with higher profile criminal cases, such as those involving drugs and violence, will generally only prosecute a UPL case when they think they have a good chance of winning. Practically, this means that they most often go after nonlawyers who either incompetently practice law or fraudulently misrepresent their skills or status, as when an unlicensed person claims to be a lawyer. In either of these situations, the prosecutor can legitimately claim that he is putting out of business someone who is a danger to the public.

1. Enforcement Through a Prosecutor

To see how a UPL complaint might be handled, let's take a fairly typical example. Suppose a prosecutor is told by a bar associate that Mary Smith, a nonlawyer, prepared divorce forms for Leroy Jackson. First, the prosecutor knows that acting as a public stenographer is not a crime. At the very least, the prosecutor understands that to prove a criminal case she will have to establish that Smith transferred some legal expertise to Jackson (remember that states differ somewhat as to amount and types of legal information that must be transferred to constitute UPL). Assuming the prosecutor believes that Smith did transfer enough legal expertise or advice to Jackson to constitute UPL, the prosecutor will next likely look to see if Smith's advice was inaccurate or resulted in any harm. Assuming this was not the case (Jackson was pleased with Smith's service, which resulted in his getting a divorce at low cost), the prosecutor will be faced with trying to convict a person who is providing a good service at a reasonable price. If Smith requests a jury trial, as she is almost sure to do, this sort of case can often be difficult for the prosecutor to win unless Smith was clearly holding herself out to be, or acting like, a lawyer.

Faced with this sort of situation, many prosecutors are likely to decide to wait until they have a stronger case, one where an independent paralegal misrepresented her credentials or services, or where her legal advice resulted in customer harm. Smith will probably not be prosecuted and her file will become inactive. An article in the *Wisconsin Lawyer* (September 1994), by David Tenenbaum, discusses just this point.

> *Although some Wisconsin lawyers think the UPL statute should be enforced as a matter of principle, in practical terms, few if any prosecutors will pursue a case unless somebody is harmed by the unauthorized activity. Says Assistant Attorney General Judith Schultz, "There's no question that Sage would not have been prosecuted if all we had was straight, unauthorized practice, without fraud."*

Sometimes, however, the prosecutor may try to work a case up a bit, especially if the complaint has come from lawyers or judges who have political clout. If the prosecutor does decide to pursue Smith further, the next step will probably be to contact her form preparation service, anonymously, and request legal information. Often this means that an investigator posing as a customer, and almost certainly carrying a concealed tape recorder, will ask Smith a number of broad questions designed to get her to give what the District Attorney's office considers to be legal advice.

Don't give legal advice. As we discuss in Chapter 3, the best way for an independent paralegal who fears being investigated by prosecutors to protect herself is to consistently avoid answering broad customer questions about substantive law. To stay out of legal hot water, the independent paralegal wants to present herself as a form preparation service and no more. Throughout this book, we discuss a number of techniques to avoid giving what organized lawyerdom considers to be legal advice. The best approach is to refer the customer to another information source, such as a self-help law book, an Internet site, or an audio tape. An obvious problem in this area, however, is that some lawyers define unauthorized practice so broadly that it includes almost any interaction between an independent paralegal and the public where money changes hands but doesn't end up in a lawyer's pockets. As we discuss later in this chapter, at least some of organized lawyerdom's efforts to characterize law practice so expansively have been rejected by courts.

Assuming a prosecutor decides to continue working up a UPL case against Smith, the next step, short of actually prosecuting, is usually to request a meeting. Normally, it happens something like this. Smith receives a letter (often called a "citation" or "cite" letter in the trade) asking her to show up at the prosecutor's office on a certain date to meet with deputy District Attorney so-and-so to discuss the allegation that she has engaged in illegal activities—to wit, practicing law without a license. The first thing Smith or any other IP should know about this sort of letter is that it is often part of a campaign to intimidate the IP into giving up her business, rather than the first step in a formal prosecution. A prosecutor who has already decided to prosecute an IP will probably not bother to write a cite letter.

The second thing Smith should understand about the citation letter process is that even though she is not required to show up, it's wise to do so. When a District Attorney is unsure of her legal ground (which is often the case if she sends a cite letter), she looks for a reason to either pursue a formal action or forget the matter. Smith's failure to show up may well be reason enough for her to decide to get tough. Of course, Smith is entitled, though not required, to have a lawyer present at any conference with law enforcement personnel.

At the meeting, a deputy District Attorney may try to scare Smith into voluntarily abandoning her business. In the past, many independent paralegals have done just that, concluding that even though they haven't done anything illegal, they don't have the resources to "fight city hall." Assuming Smith was operating a quality business and following the advice in this book on how to empower her customers without engaging in UPL, there is no reason for her to be intimidated into quitting. And surely she will be comforted to know that most people who have refused to close down haven't, in fact, been prosecuted. (See Virginia Simons's and Jolene Jacobs's interviews in the Appendix.)

What's Smith's best strategy at this point? First, she should try to get the prosecutor to talk about the issues she believes justify a prosecution. In this context, Smith should try to get the deputy prosecutor to agree that it's legal for nonlawyers to use self-help law books to carry out legal tasks. Next, Smith should try to get her to concede that the act of preparing forms for lay people doesn't constitute the practice of law. Finally, Smith should see if the prosecutor will agree that preparing forms following a customer's instructions gleaned from a self-help law book does not constitute unauthorized practice. Since this is now the legal view of many state courts (see Section E, below), it shouldn't be difficult, especially if Smith does some legal research and comes to the meeting armed with her state's court decisions.

Assuming Smith can get a prosecutor to concede that typing legal forms following the instructions of nonlawyers is not in and of itself illegal, she has laid the groundwork for a compromise that will allow her to continue her business without further hassle. Why do we say this? Because once the prosecutor concedes that her core form, word processing activity, is not illegal, her next step should be to cooperate with the prosecutor so that it's clear her future activities will be limited to this type of operation. In short, unless the prosecutor's requests are so outrageous that they will amount to Smith going out of business, she will be wise to try to find some common ground on which to compromise, even if she feels she is giving up important legal rights. The reason for this is that a compromise recognizes Smith's right to exist. It gets the prosecutor off her back and allows her crucial time to make the sort of alliances in the community that will make it difficult to prosecute her in the future. Later, once Smith feels she is sufficiently established and has the allies (for example, media people, prominent citizens, and maybe even judges and lawyers) necessary to fight back, she can always challenge what she feels are organized lawyerdom's illegal restrictions on her business.

As part of a settlement, Smith might agree to change her classified ads from "Divorce—$200" to "Self-Help Divorce Typing—$200." Or maybe, in an extreme situation, not to advertise in the local paper at all. (As we point out in Chapter 10, there are many other good ways to market your services.) Further, Smith might agree that all her customers will be given or sold a copy of a relevant self-help law book so each has the legal information necessary to make his own informed decisions.

But suppose no compromise with the prosecutor is possible and Smith is told flat out that if she doesn't close up shop in ten days, she will be charged with the crime of practicing law without a license. Based on the rarity of recent prosecutions in this area and our own conversations with a number of people faced with this sort of ultimatum, there is still a fairly good chance that she won't be prosecuted. Of course, we can't give her any such guarantee. But, if she feels that her business has been conducted with integrity and competence, and especially if she has some support from the media or the local legal community, she will probably want to keep operating at the same time that she makes the types of changes in her ads and operating policies discussed above to make her business as bulletproof as possible.

Finally, even if UPL charges are filed, Smith should know that this doesn't mean that either a trial or conviction will result. In many instances, she will again be given a chance to close her business in exchange for having the prosecution dropped at a pretrial conference or meeting. Why? Because, as we have emphasized repeatedly, organized lawyerdom is anxious not to create any more national anti-lawyer martyrs, as it did with Rosemary Furman in Florida. (See interview in the Appendix.) Unless Smith is plainly guilty of consumer fraud, lawyers will usually be almost as anxious to keep her out of the courtroom as she is to stay out.

2. Enforcement by State UPL Committees

Texas has yet another UPL enforcement model. There, the Supreme Court oversees a system of enforcement committees staffed almost completely by lawyers. There are several geographical UPL subcommittees and one statewide UPL committee. When a subcommittee receives a complaint—

almost always from a local attorney—that someone may be engaging in UPL, the subcommittee sends the paralegal a letter explaining that a complaint has been received and inviting the paralegal to attend a special meeting to explain his or her conduct. The source and nature of the complaint is not disclosed and the behavior alleged to be UPL is not described in advance.

When the paralegal shows up at the meeting, the subcommittee reviews the challenged behavior and attempts to work out an arrangement with the paralegal—usually that the paralegal go out of business, since there is no Texas law that specifically authorizes independent paralegal activity.

There is no way to know how often this happens, since the subcommittees do not issue reports of their activities. However, if the paralegal continues in his or her business in violation of the subcommittee's wishes, the subcommittee refers the matter to the statewide committee, which is authorized under Texas Supreme Court rules to file a lawsuit to shut the paralegal down. One such suit was filed in September, 2003 against the independent paralegal chain *We the People*.

Nolo was subjected to this Texas UPL process several years ago and ended up in court, litigating over both the rules governing the UPL process and the merits of whether the distribution of self-help law books and software in Texas constituted UPL. As we mentioned earlier, the case ended when the Texas legislature explicitly excluded books and software from its UPL statute. Especially if you expect to do business in Texas, spend some time at www.nolo.com/texas to get more details of Nolo's two-year struggle with the Texas UPL committees.

F.   A Review of Unauthorized Practice Litigation of the Past 30 Years

Before you can use the legal system to fight back, it's wise to learn what others in a similar situation have accomplished. To this end, let's go back a couple of decades and briefly outline how the unauthorized practice battle has unfolded. Note that while 30 years ago most judicial decisions involved the sale of self-help law books and kits, as we get closer to the present, this type of activity is much less subject to official question, and courts and prosecutors have become more concerned with IPs providing legal advice. The question of self-help law materials has most recently arisen in Texas and was only settled when the Texas legislature passed a special statute exempting self-help law books and software from the Texas UPL rules. See Section D, above. Also, see www.nolo.com/texas.

1967 The New York Court of Appeals (the highest N.Y. court) overturns the conviction of Norman Dacey, the nonlawyer author of *How to Avoid Probate* (Crown Books), holding that the publication and sale of a book about how a layperson can accomplish legal procedures did not constitute unauthorized practice. *N.Y. County Lawyers' Association v. Dacey*, 234 N.E.2d 459 (1967).

1973 The Florida Supreme Court holds that the inclusion of printed instructions along with legal forms constitutes the unlawful practice of law, but that the sale of naked forms by nonlawyers without instructions is okay. *Florida Bar v. American Legal and Business Forms, Inc.*, 274 So.2d 225 (1973).

1975 Advertisement, publication, and sale of legal forms and instructions was upheld as long as there was no personal contact between purchaser and seller. *Oregon State Bar v. Gilchrist*, 538 P.2d 913 (1975).

1976 The Michigan Supreme Court arrives at the same conclusion as *Gilchrist*, but several justices write extraordinary separate opinions. One of these cogently argues that offering personal help in filling out divorce forms, in addition to selling them, should not constitute unauthorized practice. *State Bar v. Cramer*, 399 Mich. 116 (1976).

1976 Colorado allows the preparation of divorce forms by an independent paralegal if the functions carried out are only those of a scrivener. In other words, if the form preparer sticks absolutely to the role of a public stenographer and takes down the customer's words verbatim, she is not guilty of practicing law without a license. While this case is worded conservatively, it basically allows independent paralegals to operate aboveground in Colorado. *Colorado Bar Assn. v. Miles*, 557 P.2d 1202 (1976).

1978 The Florida Supreme Court reverses its 1973 ruling discussed above and allows the sale of legal forms along with written instructions and personal contact between buyer and seller, provided the seller only copies information supplied by customers. *Florida Bar v. Brumbaugh*, 355 So.2d 1186 (1978).

1978 Missouri, Kansas, and New York courts refuse to allow personal contact between an independent paralegal and customers, although both say sale of forms and explanatory materials is okay. In *McGiffert v. State ex rel. Stowe*, 366 So.2d 680 (1978), an Alabama court holds that advertising services to obtain divorce "without attorney's fee" by a nonlicensed person is unauthorized practice.

1984 The Arizona state legislature repeals its statute that prohibits UPL. Although there is still a court rule prohibiting UPL, there has essentially been no UPL enforcement since 1984 and independent paralegals and publishers of self-help legal form books and kits have captured much of the business of preparing legal forms for divorce and other basic legal services.

1984 California disbands its state unauthorized practice office and leaves enforcement of unauthorized practice laws to local District Attorneys. Except in cases of fraud or misrepresentation, this means that in the years ahead, little enforcement of unauthorized practice will take place in California outside of a few counties where the local bar or an attorney is able to influence the District Attorney to initiate criminal prosecutions.

1984 Independent paralegal Rosemary Furman is held in contempt of court and sentenced to jail for violating an injunction ordering her not to engage in unauthorized practice, which among other things consisted of giving nonlawyers procedural advice and typing forms. Furman's request for a jury trial is denied. *Florida Bar v. Furman*, 451 So.2d 808 (1984). Giving up on Florida's outrageously pro-lawyer procedures, she takes her campaign against lawyers' monopolistic practices to a national audience via television, personal appearances, etc. (See Furman interview in the Appendix.) The Florida governor eventually commutes Furman's sentence on condition that she cease running her typing service.

1985 A number of states begin to follow the lead of California and enact simplified procedures for divorce, child support collections, will preparation, and other tasks, specifically designed to eliminate the need for lawyers. This trend towards state-sponsored self-help legal remedies, while still in its infancy, begins to give increased validity to the argument of independent paralegals that many routine legal services can be safely accomplished without lawyer help.

1985 The Washington State Supreme Court concludes that the drafting of contracts to buy and sell real estate by brokers does not constitute the unauthorized practice of law. The public, the court reasons, is better served by the freedom to choose from a range of providers, even if this means nonlawyers perform functions traditionally reserved by the legal profession. *Cultum v. Heritage House Realtors, Inc.*, 694 P.2d, 630 (1985).

1986 The American Bar Association's Commission on Professionalism recommends the limited licensing of paralegals to provide such services as real estate closings, simple wills, etc. Although there is little active follow-up, the fact that the ABA no longer seems interested in crusading against nonlawyer form preparers is important.

1987 Recognizing the huge, unmet need for moderately priced immigration counseling, California authorizes nonlawyer immigration consultants to operate as long as they disclose in writing that they are not lawyers. Cal. Bus. & Prof. Code § 27420.

1987 The Florida Supreme Court states that it is not UPL for IPs to engage in limited oral communications to help individuals complete court-approved legal forms.

1988 The California Public Protection Committee, appointed in 1986 by the state bar to investigate public harm from nonlawyer legal services and to determine if regulation of the nonlawyer providers would be appropriate, concluded that the state UPL laws should be repealed and that "legal technicians" (IPs) should be allowed to perform certain legal services provided that the IPs register and inform clients that they are not lawyers.

1990 In a Nevada case, the court states that it is not UPL for a legal scrivener service to offer forms and procedures that induce self-reliance by the customer. However, if the customer relies on the express or implied expertise of the IP form preparation service, it is unlawful practice. *State Bar of Nevada v. Johnson* et al., No.

CV89-5814 (Nev. 2nd Dist. Ct., April 12, 1990).

1991 The Florida Supreme Court (Rule 10-1.1(b)) approves a series of basic divorce and other legal forms specifically designed to be prepared by nonlawyers. [*Ed. note:* Since then, hundreds of additional forms have been approved.]

1993 The American Bar Association, in a publication entitled "Self-Representation in Divorce Cases," finds that in Maricopa County, Arizona, the area of the ABA study, at least one party was not represented by a lawyer in 90% of divorce cases. And in over half, both parties represented themselves.

1993 In a speech to the American Bar Association, U.S. Attorney General Janet Reno endorses the idea of nonlawyers providing basic legal information and form preparation.

1995 Robin Smith, longtime owner of People's Paralegal Service, of Beaverton, Oregon, and a past president of Oregon's statewide IP lobbying group (see interview in Appendix) is convicted of unauthorized practice and effectively enjoined from continuing her business. The trial court's decision is upheld by the Oregon Court of Appeal, and the Oregon and U.S. Supreme Courts decline to review the case.

1995 The American Bar Association report "Nonlawyer Activity in Law-Related Situations," concludes that "when adequate protections for the public are in place, nonlawyers have important roles to perform in providing affordable access to justice."

1995 In New York, the bar's Committee on Professional Responsibility publishes a much braver and more honest assessment of UPL. Its opinion, entitled "Prohibitions on Nonlawyer Practice: An Overview and Preliminary Assessment" (*The Record*, Vol. 50, No. 2), states, "...We give preliminary endorsement to a deregulated licensing approach that permits greater nonlawyer practice in specified areas but establishes minimal requirements in order to protect the public while simultaneously increasing the availability of low-cost accessible legal services to all."

1995 As the living trust grows in popularity, a number of enterprising souls engage in aggressive marketing practices designed to sell both living trusts and annuities to senior citizens. The bar associations in a number of states act to shut down what they call "living trust mills," and the courts in several leading cases rule that only lawyers may prepare living trusts. This is ironic, because the living trust was originally popularized by a nonlawyer (Norman Dacey) as a way to avoid the high attorney's fees commonly associated with probate.

1996   HALT—Americans for Legal Reform—hosts a national conference on independent paralegal issues that concludes that IPs should support doing away with all unauthorized practice of law rules at the same time they work together to develop self-regulatory programs designed to assure the public that IPs provide a safe and reliable service.

1998   The California legislature passes SB 1418 to become the first state in the country to specifically recognize a role for independent paralegals in the legal system. The statute becomes effective in January 2000 and by 2003, over 500 California independent paralegals (now called Legal Document Assistants) are registered to provide services to California consumers. Calif. Bus. and Prof. Code § 6400 and following.

1999   The Tennessee Court of Appeals rules that the preparation by a nonlawyer of a divorce petition on the basis of an informational questionnaire filled out by the customer, as well as asking for procedural information from the court clerk, constitute the unauthorized practice of law. *Fifteenth Judicial District Unified Bar Association v. Angie Glasgow*, No. M1996-00020-COA-R3-CV, 1999 WL 1128847 (Tenn.Ct.App. 12/10/1999).

2000   The Delaware Supreme Court rules that nonlawyers who provide real estate closing services and real estate and home equity loan settlement services are committing unauthorized practice of law. *In the Matter of Mid-Atlantic Settlement Services, Inc.* 755 A.2d 389 ("Table of Decisions Without Published Opinions")

2003   The Kentucky Supreme Court catches up to the 1985 Washington Supreme Court decision by authorizing nonlawyers to participate in real estate closings. *Countrywide Home Loans, Inc. v. Kentucky Bar Association*, No. 2000-SC-0206-KB (Ky. 08/21/2003).

2003 The Arizona Supreme Court issues rules authorizing independent paralegals (now called Legal Document Preparers) in Arizona to prepare forms and provide legal information to Arizona consumers without attorney supervision.

G. The Constitution and the Independent Paralegal[15]

This is not the place for a detailed scholarly treatise weighing all the constitutional theories that underlie the bar's efforts to proscribe the activities of nonlawyer competitors, including independent paralegals. The subject has already been ably covered by a number of law review articles. Again, one of the best of these is "Unauthorized Practice," by Deborah Rhode, in Vol. 34:1 of the *Stanford Law Review*.[16] In addition, what is ultimately judged to be constitutional in this area is almost sure to be influenced more by changing societal views about the right of the average person to gain affordable access to legal services than it will by the study of old cases.

Just the same, it's wise for all independent paralegals to understand a little about how the constitution relates to organized lawyerdom's continuing drive to protect its monopoly power over the legal system. Let's start our discussion by asking a basic question: Where does the United States Constitution say that only lawyers can legally help the public prepare their own legal paperwork or, for that matter, accomplish other "legal" tasks?

The answer, of course, is that the Constitution doesn't mention the subject. Why, then, haven't organized lawyerdom's activities long since been held to be an obvious restriction of the free-speech right of independent paralegals, or an unwarranted intrusion on the right of the public to petition their government by representing themselves in court?[17]

1. The Police Power Argument

Organized lawyerdom justifies its right to regulate independent paralegals under the rather vague umbrella of the Constitution's police power. Legislatures and courts, lawyers contend, have a legitimate interest in regulating the quality of legal services available to the public. This public interest rationale, it should be noted, has long been accepted as establishing a constitutional basis to regulate the First Amendment rights (freedom of speech, etc.) of all sorts of other groups, from teachers and bill collectors to operators of toxic waste dumps.

Specifically, when it comes to justifying their right to ban independent paralegals, lawyers claim that because independent paralegals are not subject to bar association rules of conduct, examinations for competence, educational standards, and the protections guaranteed clients by the lawyer-client relationship (whatever they are), there is a substantial risk that IPs will provide the public with an unacceptably low quality of service.

This rationale falls apart for two principal reasons. First, there is little evidence that existing unregulated IPs pose a greater threat to the public than do lawyers, as they are now regulated (loosely at best) by bar associations. Second, the fact that paralegals are not subject to regulation is an argument for regulation, not absolute prohibition of their entire business.

In addition, it is fair to ask whether the rules lawyers operate under are adequate to guarantee the public a competent level of service. After all, the rationale behind banning nonlawyers falls apart pretty quickly if lawyers themselves can't demonstrate competence. So the question becomes: Can they?

Given that lawyers do not learn basic form preparation skills in law school, are not tested on these skills on the multistate bar exam, and serve no apprenticeship to practicing lawyers, the answer is clearly no. There is absolutely no evidence that lawyers can competently deliver legal form preparation services. Indeed, with over 100,000 formal consumer complaints being filed against lawyers each year, it is reasonable to conclude that lawyers should be better trained and tested.

By contrast, attempts by bar investigators in several states to unearth complaints against IPs have been notably unsuccessful. Indeed, at several public hearings by the California bar's Public Protection Committee, and the Commission on Legal Technicians, far more members of the public showed up to complain about lack of lawyer competence than testified against IPs. In its report of April 1988, the Public Protection

Committee found that "there are a number of highly qualified and dedicated legal technicians [IPs] who deliver valuable assistance for fair consideration."

Similarly, a number of years ago, when title insurance companies began to fill out real estate documents, the Colorado Supreme Court found "no convincing evidence that the massive changeover in the performance of this service from attorneys to title companies has been accompanied by any great loss, detriment or inconvenience to the public. The uncontroverted evidence was that lawyers for this simple operation considerably slowed the loan closings and cost the persons involved a great deal of money."[18]

Barlow Christensen, in his study of unauthorized practice published in the American Bar Foundation's *Research Journal* (Spring 1980) concludes:

> *Suppression of the practice of law by nonlawyers has been proclaimed to be in the public interest, a necessary protection against incompetence, divided loyalties, and other evils. But this interest of the public is one that has been defined, articulated, promulgated, and enforced not by the public but by the legal profession. And nowhere, in all of the literature or in any of the court decisions, is there evidence of a public voice with respect to this supposed public interest.*

Even if we assume that the independent paralegal movement does present a threat to American consumers because an occasional paralegal might provide poor service, is this a sufficient constitutional justification for the prohibition against all independent paralegal activity currently advocated by organized lawyerdom? Probably not. More reasonably, it supports regulating paralegals with legitimate and fair rules that really do protect the public, not the legal profession.

2. The Void for Vagueness Argument

There are at least four reasons why current unauthorized practice regulations, as typically applied, are unconstitutional and should have been adjudged to be so long ago. The first has to do with the vague and self-serving nature of the basic statutory definition of the unauthorized practice of law. As noted earlier in this chapter, most states define the practice of law as either being something lawyers customarily do, or something it takes a lawyer's knowledge to do, or something it takes more than ordinary intelligence and knowledge to do, or something you have to get a license to do, or all four. These definitions are so hopelessly circular, vague, and ambiguous that they fail to fairly inform either the IP or the general public as to what conduct is prohibited.[19] Indeed, even bar groups that have studied this legal area conclude that, with the exception of appearing in court—something IPs don't usually want to do—defining what the practice of law consists of is impossible. For one example, see the article "The Authorized Practice of Legal Reference Service," by Madison Mosley, Jr. (*The Law Library Journal*, Vol. 87 N.I., Winter 1995), where the author concludes that case law simply doesn't provide a "workable definition of the practice of law" and therefore "provides little, if any, guidance to reference librarians [worried about UPL]."

No matter how persuasive the "void for vagueness" argument is, no appellate court has ever bought it. In 2000, a lower Florida court ruled that the Florida statute was void for vagueness but a higher Florida court overturned it. *State of Florida v. Scott Edward Foster, Jr.*, Case Nos 95-1200 & 95-2312 (2-28-96).

3. The Freedom of Speech Argument

A second and even more powerful reason why most restrictions on IP activities are unconstitutional involves their violation of the U.S. Constitution's First Amendment guarantee of freedom of speech.

This argument was persuasively advanced in the late 1990s by co-author Stephen Elias in another Nolo book entitled *"Fed Up With the Legal System: What's Wrong and How to Fix It."* Since that book was published, various state and federal government entities have put up websites containing large amounts of quality legal information about how to use and access the U.S. legal system. For instance, the federal Administrative Office of the Courts publishes Bankruptcy Basics www.uscourts.gov/bankruptcycourts.html (click the link to "bankruptcy basics"), providing would-be bankruptcy filers with information about the process and advice on how to access the bankruptcy court. The California Judicial Council's self-help website at www.courtinfo.ca.gov provides detailed information on how to get a divorce in California. Since these and other government websites intend that nonlawyers will be reading and acting on this information, it could be argued that the First Amendment allows IPs to impart the same information to their customers. All together, these materials provide a strong basis for the argument that legal *information* should be treated differently than legal *advice*. Elias writes in Fed Up:

> *Information—especially information about how to approach and use the organs of our government—is the lifeblood of a democracy. The more freely such information flows, the better the democracy works. Blockages tend to unfairly concentrate power in the hands of the privileged.*
>
> *Today we face a legal access crisis precisely because information about how to approach and use our courts moves sluggishly if at all. It is dammed up by a class of professionals known as lawyers. In all states except Arizona, lawyers have used their power to enact statutes restricting to lawyers the right to provide legal information designed to solve an individual's legal needs. And in all but a few states, the laws go on to provide that a nonlawyer who gives legal advice has committed a crime punishable by imprisonment.*
>
> *Almost no other type of speech has ever been similarly forbidden in advance to the public. The reason is clear. Prohibitions on disseminating information are almost always ruled to be unconstitutional violations of the First Amendment, which forbids any law that abridges the freedom of speech. This is especially true when it comes to speech about how to deal with public bodies such as Congress, state legislatures, and administrative agencies. There is no good reason to treat the courts differently than any other organ of government.*
>
> *Courts have allowed only a handful of narrow exceptions to this near-absolute rule prohibiting advance restrictions to free speech. Obscenity, incitement to violence, and false speech (libel, slander, fraud) are examples of the kinds of speech that the government may legally abridge. The government also may restrict commercial speech, such as*

advertising, if the restriction directly serves substantial state interests and the restriction is in reasonable proportion to the interests served.

If speech does not fall within these types of exceptions, it is fully protected under the First Amendment. It may be restricted only if the government has a compelling interest for doing so and the restriction is as narrowly tailored as possible to satisfy the compelling interest.

The U.S. Supreme Court has ruled that legal advice is fully protected speech rather than commercial speech, even though the legal advice is given for a fee. (Board of Trustees, State University of New York v. Fox, *492 U.S. 469 (1989).) That means that the government must have a compelling interest in stopping nonlawyers from giving legal advice. It's a tough standard to meet.*

Consumer protection is the reason usually advanced by the legal profession to justify handing it the exclusive right to give legal advice. According to this view, poor legal advice can cause such serious harm that a license should be required of those who provide it. Numerous studies of this issue, however, have shown that this fear is unwarranted. No study has produced concrete evidence that legal advice from nonlawyers causes more harm than that sold by licensed lawyers.

Most recently, a well-funded two-year national study conducted by the American Bar Association Committee on Nonlawyer Practices (May 1996) confirmed what earlier studies have found: occasional instances of fraud by nonlawyers but very little evidence of problems caused by bad legal advice. The study also found that nonlawyers function quite competently in the many areas where they are authorized to deliver complex legal information and services, including Social Security, disability, and real estate transactions.

When you think about it, denying consumers who can't afford a lawyer the right to purchase legal advice from more affordable sources is a ridiculous way to protect them. The argument put forth by lawyers' groups seems to be that it is better for most consumers to have no legal advice than for some to receive advice that may be wrong. Interestingly, this argument is raised by lawyers, almost never by consumers, and lawyers persist in making it even though there have been very few complaints about existing nonlawyer legal form preparation businesses. It's as if accountants and tax lawyers could put H&R Block and other tax preparers out of business because they didn't approve of their training or level of advice.

Thus there seems to be no compelling reason to deny nonlawyers the right to offer the public information about our laws and courts. But even if there were a compelling interest, the method of regulation—barring everyone but lawyers from giving legal advice—is much broader than it needs to be. For example, the term "legal advice" is never clearly defined in the laws that forbid nonlawyers from giving it. This means that when a complaint against a nonlawyer is made, a judge (also a lawyer, of course) has no reasonable standard to use when deciding whether or not legal advice was given. As a result, unauthorized practice laws make criminals out of anyone who utters words that might, even after the fact, be interpreted as legal advice by a court. This sort of blanket censorship of all unlicensed legal advice is surely as blatant a violation of the First Amendment as you'll ever find.

So the question becomes, is there an alternative approach to regulating who provides legal information to the public, that doesn't violate the First Amendment, but still provides a reasonable level of consumer protection? The answer is yes.

States can and should continue to regulate the legal profession even as they decriminalize legal advice by nonlawyers. People who wish to call themselves lawyers and represent others in court would still have to qualify for this privilege. However, people who choose not to go this route would not be prosecuted for giving legal advice.

This is a workable, sensible system; it is exactly the way most states now regulate the accounting profession. You may call yourself a Certified Public Accountant if you meet the state's qualifications; otherwise you are free to give tax preparation, bookkeeping, or accounting advice as long as you don't use the CPA label. Consumers are free to choose a CPA, and pay a higher rate for the expertise the label carries with it, or consult someone without the CPA credential who probably charges less.

But what happens if a nonlawyer provides poor services or gives bad advice? If a customer loses money because of wrong legal advice given by a nonlawyer, the complaint could and should be addressed under the same consumer protection rules that are applied to other similar businesses. Dissatisfied customers could sue in small claims or regular court for damages, or ask local prosecutors—or a more specialized regulatory agency if one becomes appropriate—to shut down businesses that make a practice of dispensing shoddy legal advice. Incidentally, this is exactly what happens if you are wronged by a lawyer.

MARYLAND TRIES TO DISTINGUISH LEGAL INFORMATION
FROM LEGAL ADVICE

In 1995, the Attorney General's office for the state of Maryland was asked whether IPs, or "lay advocates," who help victims of domestic violence are guilty of UPL. In opinion 95-056 (December 1995), the Attorney General said the following:

1. *A lay advocate may:*
(i) *provide victims with basic information about the existence of legal rights and remedies;*
(ii) *provide victims with basic information about the manner in which judicial proceedings are conducted;*
(iii) *assist a victim to prepare a legal pleading or other legal document on her own behalf by defining unfamiliar terms on a form, explaining where on a form the victim is to provide certain information, and if necessary transcribing or otherwise recording the victim's own words verbatim;*
(iv) *sit with a victim at trial table, if permitted by the court; and*
(v) *engage in the general advocacy of the rights of battered women as a group.*
2. *Except under the supervision of an attorney, a lay advocate may not:*
(i) *provide any advice relating to a victim's rights or remedies, including whether a victim's particular circumstances suggest that she should pursue a particular remedy;*
(ii) *provide information about the legal aspects of judicial proceedings, such as how to present a case, call witnesses, introduce evidence, and the like;*
(iii) *use the advocate's own language in preparing or filling out form pleadings or other legal documents; or*
(iv) *engage in advocacy before any governmental representative on behalf of an individual victim.*

4. The Due Process Argument

A third powerful reason why traditional unauthorized practice regulations are unconstitutional has to do with the manner in which bar associations prosecute people who they believe are guilty of the unauthorized practice of law. Even assuming that legislatures, and in some circumstances courts, are entitled to reasonably regulate how IPs fill out legal forms, organized lawyerdom must still meet a reasonable standard of fairness (due process) when it comes to enforcing its rules. This is not being done anywhere today.

As outlined above, actions against independent paralegals are commonly instituted not in a criminal proceeding in which the IP has the right to a jury trial, but by bar committees made up primarily or exclusively of lawyers or, more typically, by judicial officials acting on bar association complaints. This was the situation faced by Rosemary Furman in Florida. (See Rosemary Furman interview in Appendix.) In either instance, the complaint leading to bar or court action is almost always from a member of the legal profession angry at low-cost competition, not from a consumer with a legitimate gripe. And in some situations, especially where bar associations try to order IPs out of business on their own initiative, everyone involved in the process of investigating and sanctioning the independent paralegal (a decision usually made in secret) is an attorney with a pecuniary interest in suppressing nonlawyer competition. In other professions, courts have not allowed such interested parties to have absolute regulatory power. For example, in *Gibson v. Berryhill*, 331 F.Supp. 122 (1971) aff'd, 411 U.S. 564 (1973), a federal court held that a board made up of optometrists in private practice wasn't sufficiently impartial to be allowed to prohibit another optometrist from working for a corporation.

Also, as noted earlier, in many instances, before official action to go after an IP is taken, a bar committee or court first threatens the independent paralegal in an "informal" proceeding. Thus, the independent paralegal often finds herself in the surreal situation of being called to account by a group of lawyers, told to stay off their turf, and threatened with a fine and jail, all as part of an extra-judicial proceeding in which the independent paralegal has no fair way to defend her conduct. It's worthy of note that in other areas of American life, including the regulation of books claimed to be pornographic, where First Amendment rights were being restricted by quasi-official, but essentially private, review boards, the U.S. Supreme Court has found a constitutional violation.[20] See Section E2, above, where we explain how this aproach works in Texas and refer you to www.nolo.com/texas.

5. The Discriminatory Prosecution Argument

And finally, there is the issue of selective or discriminatory prosecution. This term applies when a state singles out for criminal prosecution one or a few people in a certain regulated group while ignoring others who may be guilty of the same conduct. It is most commonly used to dismiss prosecutions against defendants in regulated businesses (taxicabs or taverns, for example), where a prosecutor picks out a political or personal enemy for harsh treatment. Given that many prosecutions of IPs take place only because a locally prominent lawyer (or lawyers) uses her personal clout with the DA's office to insist that the IP competitor be forced out of business, at the same time that other IPs doing much the same type of legal form preparation are not targeted, it's reasonable to expect that more and more IPs will raise this "selective or discriminatory prosecution" defense.

If actions by lawyers to suppress nonlawyer competition are so obviously biased, why aren't there court decisions saying they are unconstitutional? Partly because lawyers' groups are adept at backing off in situations when a court case might produce a bad precedent, and partly because very few independent paralegals have had enough financial resources to fully litigate the issue. But mostly because judges, blinded by their claim of absolute power over the legal system based on the "inherent powers" doctrine (see Section D above), have so far applied a biased standard of what constitutes fair procedure. Indeed, the current legal standards and procedures applied to people who compete with lawyers are so unfair that, sooner or later, they are bound to be ruled in violation of both First Amendment guarantees of free speech and the U.S. Constitution's due process clause.

6. The Antitrust Argument

When looking at the system under which lawyers regulate their legal monopoly, it's hard not to think about the federal and state antitrust laws—the laws that prohibit big business from ganging up on little business or acting "in restraint of trade." At first blush, a professional group that jails paralegals and/or forces them out of business, simply because the professionals don't like the competition, appears to be in clear violation of the antitrust laws. However, it ain't necessarily so.

The U.S. Supreme Court ruled in *Parker v. Brown*, 317 U.S. 341 (1943), that official state entities may engage in antitrust activity in furtherance of their police powers and as part of their regulatory activity. This loophole lets state bar associations regulate nonlawyers as long as they do so under the auspices of state law. However, to the extent that bar associations are acting purely in their own interests, rather than in the interest of the state's citizens as a whole, they may still be guilty of antitrust violations.

In comments made December 20, 2002, the Federal Trade Commission and the Attorney General's Office had this to say about antitrust practices by bar associations:

The DOJ and the FTC are entrusted with enforcing the federal antitrust laws. Both agencies work to promote free and unfettered competition in all sectors of the American economy. The United States Supreme Court has observed that, "ultimately, competition will produce not only lower prices but also better goods and services. The heart of our national economic policy long has been faith in the value of competition'" [footnote omitted] Competition benefits consumers of both traditional manufacturing industries and services offered by the learned professions. [footnote omitted] Restraining competition, in turn, can force consumers to pay increased prices or to accept goods and services of poorer quality.

Together, the DOJ and the FTC have become increasingly concerned about efforts to prevent nonlawyers from competing with attorneys in the provision of certain services through the adoption of Unauthorized Practice of Law opinions and laws by state bar agencies, courts, and legislatures. In addressing these concerns, the DOJ and the FTC encourage competition through advocacy letters such as this one. The DOJ and the FTC have been concerned particularly about attempts to restrict nonlawyer competition in real estate closings, and have urged the states of Kentucky, Virginia, Rhode Island, and North Carolina to reject such restrictions, through letters to their State Bars (state agencies) and legislatures, and through an amicus curiae brief filed with the Kentucky Supreme Court in 2000. [footnote omitted] In addition, the DOJ has challenged in court attempts by bar associations to restrain competition from nonlawyers, [footnote omitted] and the FTC has challenged anticompetitive restrictions on certain business practices of lawyers. [footnote omitted] Our ongoing concern has led us to submit these comments.

7. What Constitutional Regulation Might Look Like

Let's shift gears now and assume for a moment that to be constitutional, regulation of paralegals must be strictly limited to rules necessary to protect American people from incompetent work done by untrained people and that these rules must be both fairly and impartially administered. What might such a regulation scheme look like?

- Legal recognition of the fact that every citizen's right to self-representation and reasonable access to the courts necessarily includes the right to get competent help from reasonably priced service providers.

- State unauthorized practice of law regulations should be eliminated entirely or strictly limited so that they do not prohibit the preparation of routine legal forms or the giving of common-sense procedural and factual information needed to prepare and file such forms.

- For form preparation in more complicated legal areas where there is a higher possibility of consumer harm, registration and licensure of IPs may make some sense as it does in California and Texas. But all state-imposed requirements should have a clear logical relationship between the task to be performed and the requirements needed to perform it. For example, if an IP must pass a test as a condition of qualifying for a license, the test should be tightly based on the skill the IP needs to carry out the particular form preparation task. (This means an IP who applies for a license to help customers prepare probate papers should be tested on that skill and not on general legal knowledge or principles.) No educational qualifications should be required as prerequisite to taking a skills-based test.

- Administration of any regulatory system dealing with independent paralegals should not be left in the hands of bar associations, state supreme courts, or other lawyers' groups who not only have a clear bias in favor of suppressing competition, but regularly target for prosecution IPs such as Oregon's Robin Smith, who prominently advocate for legislation allowing and sensibly regulating IP practice. Instead, any regulations should be administered by a consumer agency in the public interest. Adding a minority of lay people to existing bar association unauthorized practice committees or turning enforcement power over to the judiciary does not accomplish this goal.

As we've mentioned, in 1998 a bill to regulate California's independent paralegals was enacted into law; it became effective in 2000. The bill allows paralegals to prepare forms under the direction and control of the customer, and to provide the customer with materials written or approved by a California attorney. The new law requires independent paralegals to post a bond and to meet certain training and/or experience qualifications. See Chapter 14, Section A, where we discuss this new law in more detail.

In 2003, the Arizona legislature passed a bill authorizing IPs (called Legal Document Preparers) to provide legal information and forms to their customers.

endnotes

[1] You will find tips for doing legal research throughout this chapter. For a thorough guide, see Elias and Levinkind, *Legal Research: How to Find and Understand the Law* (Nolo). Also check out Nolo's Legal Research Center at www.nolo.com.

[2] Fla. St. Bar Rule 10-2.1.

[3] 215 Cal.App.3d 1599 (4th Dist., 1989).

[4] *Cultum v. Heritage House Realtors, Inc.,* 103 Wash. 2d 623 (1985). This decision was affirmed in *Perkins v. CTX Mortgage Co.,* 969 P.2d 93 (1999) 137 Wash. 2d 93.

[5] Cal. Bus. & Prof. Code § 6126.

[6] For a more in-depth discussion, see Wolfram, "Lawyer Turf and Lawyer Regulation—The Role of the Inherent-Powers Doctrine," *University of Arkansas at Little Rock Law Journal*, Vol. 12, No. 1 (1989-90).

[7] *Florida Bar Re: Advisory Opinion HRS Nonlawyer Counselor,* 547 So.2d 909 (1989).

[8] *Unauthorized Practice of Law Committee v. State of Rhode Island, Department of Workers' Compensation*, 543 A.2d 662 (1988).

[9] "The Proper Scope of Nonlawyer Representation in State Administrative Proceedings: A State Specific Balancing Approach," *Vand. L. Rev.*, Vol. 43:245 (January 1990).

[10] For example, see *UPL Comm. v. Employers Unity, Inc.*, 716 P.2d 460 (Colo. 1986); *UPL Comm. v. State Dept. of Workers' Comp.*, 543 A.2d 662 (RI 1988).

[11] *Sperry v. U.S.*, 373 U.S. 379 (1963).

[12] *The Florida Bar Re: Advisory Opinion—Nonlawyer Preparation of Pension Plans*, 571 So.2d 430 (1990).

[13] One court has held that the use of the word "paralegal" violated this provision of the Act. *In Re Burdick* (Northern Dist. of N.Y. 1996).

[14] Rhode, "Policing the Professional Monopoly: A Constitutional and Empirical Analysis of Unauthorized Practice Prohibitions," *Stanford Law Rev.*, Vol. 34:1 (1981). Although this study is dated, it is the only one of its kind that is currently available. See also Rhode, "The Delivery of Legal Services by Nonlawyers," *Georgetown Journal of Legal Ethics*, Vol. 4:209 (1990).

[15] A number of legal commentators believe that direct enforcement actions by state and local bar associations also violate the Sherman Antitrust Act. We do not discuss this here because of the rapid move by most bar associations to back off from direct enforcement of unauthorized practice actions, instead referring these proceedings to state supreme courts or to the local prosecutor. However, at least one state supreme court has held that there is no antitrust violation. *The Florida Bar Re: Advisory Opinion—Nonlawyer Preparation of Pension Plans*, 571 So.2d 430 (1990).

[16] Another excellent general article challenging the bar's assertion that it needs to regulate independent paralegals is Christensen, "The Unauthorized Practice of Law: Do Good Fences Really Make Good Neighbors—or Even Good Sense?," *American Bar Foundation Research Journal* (Spring 1980).

[17] In this context, the United States Supreme Court has ruled that if prisoners are denied the right to legal help in preparing habeas corpus petitions, they must be afforded a reasonable alternative. *Johnson v. Avery*, 393 U.S. 483 (1969). Shouldn't ordinary citizens who can't afford the high prices charged by lawyers be allowed to take advantage of low-cost alternatives to gain access to the legal forum their tax dollars support? For more on this access argument, see

"On Letting the Laity Litigate: The Petition Clause and Unauthorized Practice Rules," *Univ. of Penn. Law Review*, Vol. 132 (1984).

[18]*Conway-Bogue Realty Investment Co. v. Denver Bar Association*, 312 P.2d 998 (1957).

[19]To illustrate, consider that in some states (let's call them "Type A" states), real estate brokers have traditionally prepared property deeds, while in others ("Type B" states) this task has customarily been accomplished by lawyers. Does this mean Type B states can constitutionally charge a real estate broker who prepares a deed with unauthorized practice because lawyers normally do this work, but Type A states can't, because lawyers haven't traditionally handled it?

[20]*Bantam Books Inc. v. Sullivan*, 372 U.S. 58 (1963). ■

How to Do Your Job and Stay Out of Trouble

Given the fuzzy boundaries of what constitutes the "unauthorized practice of law," how do you protect yourself? There are no foolproof ways to avoid attacks by organized lawyerdom, but you can greatly reduce your vulnerability if you consistently do four things:

1. Tell the world you are not a lawyer.
2. Make sure your advertising and marketing copy doesn't imply that you are a lawyer.
3. Provide your customers access to the basic legal information necessary to make their own decisions, including how to choose necessary legal forms and paperwork, and
4. Limit yourself to legal form preparation—don't give legal advice or select forms.

A. Tell the World You Are Not a Lawyer

Making it clear that you are not licensed to practice law is not only an honest way to run your business, it protects you from the charge that you have fraudulently misrepresented your services. A strong statement making it clear that you are an IP typing service or legal technician, not a lawyer, will establish one essential part of your defense should you ever be charged with unauthorized practice.

California Note: In California, Legal Document Assistants are required to provide their customers with a standard contract in which they disclose that they are not lawyers and cannot provide legal advice. They also must provide this same information orally when soliciting customers and upon their first contact with the customer. This is probably a good idea no matter where you live.

If organized lawyerdom, through a bar association, public prosecutor, state court, or a state regulatory body, such as the Department of Consumer Affairs or Bureau of Professional Standards, ever scrutinizes your business, the first thing it will look at is whether you make it absolutely clear you are not a lawyer. In this context, it's not enough that you don't use the word "lawyer" or "attorney" in your advertisements. The thing organized lawyerdom will look for is whether a potential customer reading your promotional material, or coming to your place of business, is clearly and unequivocally put on notice that you are not a lawyer, and that you do not provide legal advice.[1]

When you think about it, making sure you are squeaky clean when it comes to informing the public that you help consumers prepare legal forms, but are not an attorney and do not give legal advice, is reasonable. Incidentally, this isn't a big hardship from a business point of view either, since the majority of your customers will seek you out precisely because you don't charge lawyer prices or have lawyer attitudes.

Think of it this way. If you consult a person who claims to be a CPA, or a chef "trained in Paris," or a "juggler" who used to work for the Ringling Brothers Circus, you expect that person to tell the truth about his background. If the "CPA" in fact turns out to be a tax preparer who has taken a few accounting courses, the "chef" worked for a week washing dishes at a fast food place in Paris, Illinois, and the "juggler's" job at Ringling Brothers involved following an elephant with a shovel, you are likely to feel ripped off, and justifiably so. This isn't to say that you might not choose a non-CPA tax preparer in the first place. You well might. But you're entitled to the information that lets you make the choice knowingly.

⚠ Special rules for bankruptcy. Federal law 11 U.S.C. § 110(g)(1) prohibits IPs who prepare bankruptcy paperwork (bankruptcy form preparers) from using the word "legal" or any similar word in advertising or promotions. See Chapter 2, Section C3.

Here are some detailed suggestions about how to tell the world you are not a lawyer:

Business name. We present a detailed discussion of good and bad business names in Chapter 5. For now, the main point is to choose a name for your business that cannot possibly be read to imply that you are a lawyer. The best way to do this is to emphasize "self-help" in your title.

Promotional materials. All brochures and flyers you distribute should clearly state that you are not a lawyer. This message should not be buried in the text, but set out, near the top, in at least 10-point boldface type. Something like this works well: "The ABC Self-Help Typing Service is not staffed by lawyers and does not give legal advice."

Logos and stationery. Your stationery and, if you use one, your logo, should reinforce the message that you are a self-help form preparation service. Prominent use of the term "self-help" is an excellent way to do this. Thus, The Jefferson County Form Preparation Service might add to its stationery a line such as this: "Quality Nonlawyer Form Preparation for Self-Help Divorce and Bankruptcy."

In choosing a logo, avoid using the scales of justice or similar symbols associated with lawyers. Instead, why not choose a graphic image that reinforces the idea of people helping themselves.

Advertisements and circulars. If you use print, radio, or TV ads (see Chapter 10), you will probably not be able to afford to include a lengthy statement that you are not a lawyer and do not provide legal expertise. Fortunately, there are several cost-efficient ways to get your point across. One is to emphasize the self-help aspect of your service. For example, instead of titling an ad "Divorce" or "Bankruptcy," you might say "Divorce Yourself" or "Do Your Own Bankruptcy," incorporating the concept of self-help directly into your sales message. If your business name already embodies this concept, so much the better.

Here is a newspaper advertisement for an independent paralegal business that does a poor job of notifying the public that no lawyers are involved, and probably violates federal law regulating bankruptcy petition preparers.

LEGAL ALTERNATIVE, INC.

BANKRUPTCY
Overwhelmed by Debts & Unsympathetic Creditors?

WE CAN HELP!

BANKRUPTCY...**$175.00**
- Complete preparation of all legal documents
- Aid in establishing new credit
- Few filers lose any personal possessions, only their debts

DIVORCE..**$180.00**

INCORPORATION...**$250.00**
Satisfaction Guaranteed   (503) 255-3420

The problem with this ad is that it does not inform the public that it is a nonlawyer typing service. Although it can be argued that the name "Legal Alternatives, Inc." informs the public that no lawyers are involved, this is far from obvious (there are lots of alternatives in the world, including alternative lawyers). A prosecutor or bar association would probably contend that the prominent use of the word "legal" is likely to confuse the public.

Here is an excerpt from a flyer that does a much better job of informing the public that the paralegal business doesn't involve attorney services:

SELF-HELP DIVORCE CENTER

A sensible nonlawyer alternative since 1972

You Make the Decisions, We Do the Paperwork

■ We type forms for: Legal divorce, annulment, and legal separation
■ Our fees are reasonable: our basic charge is $90–$225 (+ court filing fee)
■ Our typing service is efficient and reliable

If you have already decided on divorce and have a good grasp of the legal and practical rules and procedures you face, you do not necessarily need the services of an attorney. If you can make your own decisions about property, custody, support; and if your spouse does not hire an attorney to contest the divorce, you can sensibly get your own legal divorce without a lawyer.

Employees at the Self-Help Divorce Center are trained to record your decisions on the proper divorce forms. Taking it step-by-step, we type your divorce papers under your guidance and instruction and send them to you as you need them. We rely on the book *How to Do Your Own Divorce in California,* by Attorney Ed Sherman, and recommend that you carefully read it. It explains what forms you'll need to file and provides easy-to-understand information about all aspects of your divorce.

SELF-HELP DIVORCE CENTER

870 Main Street, Suite 10

Lexington, CA 94450

(In the Bradley Building across from Macy's Park at Eighth and Main)

Monday-Friday • Evening and Saturday appointments available

904-5757   •   432-4485

Office signs. It is essential that you prominently display a sign in your office making it clear who you are and what you do. A straightforward plaque mounted on your waiting room or office wall that says something like the following will do the job.

ACME TYPING
A Nonlawyer Form Preparation Service

The Acme Typing Service is designed to help nonlawyers prepare their own paperwork to file their own bankruptcy, divorce, stepparent adoption, and other uncontested legal actions. You make all legal and practical decisions and select the necessary legal forms. Our role is to prepare the paperwork under your direction. We are not lawyers and do not give legal advice. If you are unsure about any of the legal aspects of your case, please take a look at the excellent self-help legal information published by Nolo.com and other self-help law publishers, available at your nearest bookstore or library, or see a lawyer.

Why is it necessary to display a sign if your ads and flyers make it clear that you are not a lawyer? Because it is an extremely convenient way to document that you've made every effort to tell the public that you are not a lawyer and do not provide legal services. If you still aren't convinced, think of it this way: lawyers, who after all are past masters at elevating form over substance, truly believe in the power of disclaimers. Remember, they are the ones who get paid to write all those little warnings on the back of everything from parking lot tickets to new car purchase agreements by which customers must disclaim all sorts of rights and accept dozens of unpalatable responsibilities. Again, the point is simple—lawyers will have a difficult time claiming (and more important, a judge will have even more trouble concluding) that you are misleading the public if you constantly and obviously emphasize that you aren't a lawyer and that your customers must accept the responsibility that comes with doing their own legal work.

Signed statements. While office signs, truth in advertising, and promotional materials emphasizing that you are not a lawyer are important, they are not a substitute for your most important self-protection device. This is a written statement signed by all your customers clearly acknowledging three things:

1. You aren't a lawyer,

2. Your customers are representing themselves and have access to the legal materials necessary to make their own informed decisions, and

3. Your role is limited to preparing legal forms selected by your customers under your customers' direction.

Each statement should be signed in duplicate (or immediately photocopied) during the initial customer interview, with one copy given to the customer and the other retained in your permanent file. If you deal with customers who aren't fluent in English, all statements, signs, information, and disclaimers should also be available in Spanish, Chinese, Vietnamese, and/or other relevant languages or dialects. You may find it convenient to make this signed statement part of a more detailed information sheet that establishes the price of your services and some details about how your business works. As we mentioned earlier, California Legal Document Assistants are required to provide their customers with a sample contract, and with oral notice upon first contacting their client, both of which tell their customers that they are not lawyers and can't provide legal advice. Whatever state you are in, we recommend that you use both the contract and the oral notice in your own practice as a model for informing your customers that you aren't a lawyer and can't practice law.

Below is a sample cover sheet for a customer contract.

For a copy of the California LDA contract, go to the CALDA website at www.calda.org. You can download the contract that contains the statutory language. If you are working in California, you must use the contract as is. If you are in another state that doesn't have a required form for the contract, you can use it as a template.

SAMPLE CONTRACT COVER FOR LEGAL DOCUMENT ASSISTANTS
Recommended for Independent Paralegals Everywhere

_____

(Name of Your Business)

WELCOME

Thank you for choosing us as your Legal Document Preparation Service. We look forward to working with you to achieve your self-help legal solution.

Our service uses a standard contract prepared by the National Self-Help Law Project. We would like you to review this contract before our interview with you.

The most important part of the contract—a description of the services we will provide you and the fees we will charge for them—will be completed during your appointment. In addition, the Contract includes a number of disclosures about the nature and scope of our services.

These disclosures:

- Remind you that we are not attorneys.
- Affirm that we don't engage in the practice of law.
- Describe the type of services we can and do provide.
- Explain our policies regarding your original documents.
- Explain our twenty-four hour cancellation and refund policy.
- Tell you who to contact for free legal services, or if you want to file a complaint against us.

We believe that this contract will provide a good working basis for our future relationship. We will be happy to answer any questions you have about it.

If you are in California, you should add two more bullets to the list in the Welcome sheet: one stating that the contract will advise the customer of the counties in which you have registered and filed a bond, and one stating that the contract will inform the customer that the county clerk does not vouch for the LDA services to be provided.

Get information in the customer's own handwriting. In Chapter 8, we discuss many of the techniques necessary to running a quality legal typing business. One of these is either to get all factual information in the customer's own handwriting or, if it's necessary to employ an oral interview technique, to have your customer check all the information you collect and sign a statement that it is correct. Also, in Section D below, we provide some additional suggestions for preparing a questionnaire.

Why is it best to have your customers provide information in their own handwriting? Because if you are ever charged with unauthorized practice, your best line of defense will be that you prepared legal forms under the direction of your customer. Being able to produce all key information in your customer's handwriting will make it far easier to document that your customer, not you, supplied the necessary information.

B. Provide Your Customers Access to the Basic Legal Information Necessary to Make Their Own Decisions

Legal form preparers who run afoul of organized lawyerdom usually do so because they directly transfer legal expertise to their customers. Or put another way, they act like junior lawyers. Fortunately, because of the wealth of good quality self-help legal information currently on the market, there is no need to do this. The IP's role should be to identify and make available the independently published legal material customers will need to make their own informed decisions. If the IP limits himself to preparing forms under his customers' directions, he should not be vulnerable to charges of UPL.

California, Florida, and Arizona Note: In California, Florida, and Arizona, special laws regulate how independent paralegals are required to interact with their customers. In California, Legal Document Assistants may provide their customers with legal information written or approved by an attorney, but aren't permitted to impart this information to clients orally. In Arizona and Florida, on the other hand, IPs may orally give their customers general factual and legal information about the law involved with the forms they are preparing, but are not allowed to provide their customers with advice about their options or possible legal strategies.

Your first job as an independent paralegal is to locate legal information that will answer the common substantive legal questions your customers ask. Once you do, it's best to keep this material in your office for your customers to look at or, if for some reason doing this is impossible, you will want to tell them where to get it. Sometimes even one or two good books will answer most questions in a particular field. For example *How to File for Chapter 7 Bankruptcy*, by Elias, Leonard & Renauer (Nolo), is a detailed "how-to" guide. It does not deal with every complication that can arise in a bankruptcy, but it does very thoroughly answer routine questions. Because it is such a good resource, it makes sense to require that every bankruptcy customer own it, even if you must supply the book yourself and include the cost in your fee.

But isn't referring customers to written materials more cumbersome than simply answering their questions in the first place? Perhaps, but it can be an essential survival strategy for an IP, especially in the parts of the country where organized lawyerdom is determined to suppress independent paralegals. Many of the self-help legal materials currently on the market are of good quality and will empower your customers to do better legal work. In other words, taking the little bit of extra trouble to help your customers use good self-help law materials as part of your business will not only provide you with a good measure of legal protection, it will enhance your customer satisfaction, and therefore your business.

As you take the time to help your customers educate themselves, consider that this approach can be markedly superior to that followed by most lawyers. Traditionally, lawyers have often preferred to tell their clients what to do, while simultaneously hoarding the basic legal information necessary to sensibly question the advice. For example, should a client ask how much spousal support is reasonable in a given situation, a typical lawyer will provide a dollar figure, with no explanation of the laws and practice that make that number (and often a whole range of alternative numbers) make sense. Even worse is the fact that the lawyer may have a financial incentive to choose a dollar figure high enough to inflame the other spouse and result in extended litigation (and therefore a higher lawyer fee). By contrast, an IP who answers the same question by providing the customer with an up-to-date written discussion of spousal support laws and practices provides a superior service. This is especially true if the written materials are keyed to a number of different fact situations and present a reasonable range of support amounts appropriate for each.

Okay, let's assume that we have convinced you of the desirability of making written materials available to your customers and that you have located the necessary books, articles, and software. The next question is, how do you get them into the hands of your customers? Here are several strategies:

Sell the product. If an excellent self-help product is available in a particular legal area, such as an up-to-date, easy-to-understand, small business incorporation manual designed specifically for your state, you will want to sell it. In fact, for your own self-protection, you will probably want to require every customer to buy it and to state in writing that they have read it. Because we have an economic interest in certain Nolo products, you may want to discount our advice as being self-interested and hence unreliable. We are convinced, however, that if you do, you are likely to regret your decision. Why? Because, again, at the risk of being repetitive, a self-help law product allows you not only to put solid information into the hands of your customers, but to lay the groundwork in advance for one of the few effective defenses to a prosecution for unauthorized practice. The defense is simply that a customer has the right to purchase an independently published self-help law product (whose publication is protected by the First Amendment) and, using the information it contains, tell you, the independent paralegal, what (legal) forms to use and what to put in them.

Nolo extends bookstore-type discounts to IPs who wish to stock and resell its books. For information, call customer service at 510-549-1976 or visit the Nolo website at nolo.com.

⚠ Consider sending customers to a bookstore. If you face a particularly uptight situation with a local prosecutor or court, you may not want to sell any legal material yourself on the theory that the more separate you are from the way in which your customer gets legal information, the better off you are. While this extra degree of care is no longer necessary in the many states where IPs are well established, it is still a good idea in states where stamping out unauthorized practice is a maniacal concern of organized lawyerdom. Following this approach, you would arrange for a local bookstore or office supply store (many already carry legal forms), or another nearby merchant, to stock the books in volume, and then refer your customers to that store.

Use the Internet. Although your customers may prefer to visit the bookstore the old fashioned way, by walking through the doors, the Internet provides a wonderful alternative. With very little trouble, your customers can purchase legal self-help books from a website such as amazon.com, barnesandnoble.com, or, if the book is a Nolo book, nolo.com. Also, if the customer wants, you can order it yourself as a convenience and pass the cost on to the customer. See Chapter 11 for a discussion of how the Internet is likely to affect the independent paralegal business in coming years.

Set up your own small library. Most IPs report that they hear the same legal questions over and over again. For example, people who are filing for divorce, and who have minor children, will often ask what rules govern child custody. If there are self-help law books available that detail these rules, you should have them in your own library. In addition, you may want to gather other legal materials and have them available to be read by your customers. For example, you might have available publications printing your state supreme court's most recent court decision on child custody rules.

Get together with other IPs and create materials. The California Association of Legal Document Assistants (CALDA) has published a set of pamphlets that set out the laws governing various procedures and the forms to be used for each procedure. CALDA distributes these pamphlets at its annual conference for a nominal fee. The LDAs attending the conference distribute them to their customers. Since the materials have been written and approved by an attorney, they meet the criteria established for such materials under the California Legal Document Assistant Act. See www.calda.org for more about CALDA's services.

Use legal information phone lines. A number of companies have established legal information phone services. For two or three dollars per minute, charged to a credit card, a caller can have a lawyer answer legal questions. In theory, these services are a wonderful resource for the independent paralegal as they provide a ready source of legal information for confused customers and free the independent paralegal from the temptation of providing legal information. Sadly, a number of these phone answer services are essentially scams run by lawyers who profit not by answering questions, but by talking clients into buying their services or referring them to other lawyers for a fee. When a self-helper calls, the service tries to talk them out of handling their own action.

Incidentally, many independent paralegals not only recommend that customers who have legal questions call these services, they arrange for them to do so from their office so they can listen in and use the information as part of their own continuing education effort.

Use the law library. In states with smaller populations there may be few, if any, published self-help law materials. If you face this situation, you may have no book to sell unless you work in legal areas such as bankruptcy, copyright, patent, or Social Security appeals, which are under federal jurisdiction, or a publisher has published a good book tracking the laws of all 50 states. And even in states where there are self-help materials available, some may be procedure-oriented, and not deal in sufficient detail with substantive law.

Law libraries are located in most county courthouses and are open to the public. Many law school libraries, especially those at publicly funded universities, are similarly open to all. Your main goal will be to locate the practice books or court decisions lawyers rely on to answer the same routine questions your customers will ask. The reference librarian, if so disposed, can surely direct you to the best materials. In this context, it's worthy of note that the American Association of Law Librarians has been working hard to make law libraries more accessible to the public, and some law librarians have already collected and organized materials of interest to nonlawyers.

Use the Internet for research. The Internet offers a wide array of legal resources. See Chapter 11, where we describe the basics of doing legal research on the Web. Those of you who have already learned traditional legal research methods may still prefer to use the law library. Nothing wrong with that, especially since most law libraries also provide fast connections to the Internet for free.

HOW TO IMPROVE LEGAL RESEARCH SKILLS

Independent paralegals who have attended a formal paralegal school already know basic legal research skills. For others, it's an essential skill that should be promptly mastered. Because legal materials are organized in unique ways, it's almost essential that you either take a course or spend time with good self-help teaching tools. Here is an excellent one:

- *Legal Research: How to Find and Understand the Law,* by Stephen Elias and Susan Levinkind (Nolo): A basic text, designed for paralegals, which follows a step-by-step approach to mastering legal research techniques both on the Internet and in the law library.

Once you have located the materials you know your customers will want to refer to, create a short reading list. A list for people doing their own divorce should contain five to ten entries that focus on substantive law, such as rules governing child support and child custody and visitation. You may also want to include these information sources on your customer information sheet along with basic information, such as the amount of court filing fees.

Let's now look at an example of how this approach to helping your customers educate themselves might work in practice.

EXAMPLE: Cathy P. is a resident of Red Bluff, California. She has been employed on a temporary basis by several lawyers as a typist and has prepared several dozen sets of divorce forms. Recently she got her own divorce, handling the whole thing herself without problem. She then helped her boyfriend prepare his own divorce papers. She has just decided to set up a part-time typing service to prepare divorce papers for others.

To deepen her knowledge, Cathy first attends courses in family law and how to organize an independent paralegal business, sponsored by the California Association of Legal Document Assistants. (See Chapter 10, Section K.) In addition, she follows a number of the learning techniques discussed in Chapter 8, Section B. As part of preparing herself to deal with customers' questions about divorce, Cathy checks several local bookstores. She finds several books on self-help divorce in California. One, *How to Do Your Own Divorce in California*, by Ed Sherman, contains all the forms and instructions necessary for a person to represent herself in an uncontested divorce, as well as the background information necessary to make sensible decisions about how to divide property and debts. Cathy decides to require every customer to purchase and read this book. To make this clear, she adds a sentence to her general disclaimer form that tells people that she is not a lawyer. It looks like this:

"I agree to obtain a copy of *How to Do Your Own Divorce in California*, by Attorney Ed Sherman, and to read it carefully."

Date_____ Signature_____

Cathy then locates additional books on divorce, especially those pertaining to California. These include:

- *Using Divorce Mediation* by Katherine Stoner (Nolo), a step-by-step guide to choosing and using mediation to lessen the pain and cost of divorce.

- *California Family Law: Practice and Procedure*, by Kirkland, Wisey, and Richmond, editorial consultants, (Matthew Bender), a thorough multivolume treatise on California divorce law, complete with forms. Probably the best comprehensive source of information for both lawyers and laypersons.

- *California Practice Guide*, by William P. Hogoboom (The Rutter Group), a two-volume set that is excellent when it comes to explaining the procedures and paperwork requirements of divorce.

- *Child Custody: Building Parenting Agreements That Work*, by Mimi Lyster (Nolo). An excellent hands-on guide that shows divorcing parents how to craft their own win-win child custody agreements. The author sets out the 40-plus issues that most typically divide divorcing parents and the range of legal and practical options available for resolving each.

- *Divorce Solutions: How to Make Any Divorce Better,* by Ed Sherman (Nolo Occidental), deals with the practical, financial, and emotional aspects of a divorce.
- *Divorce and Money,* by Violet Woodhouse with Dale Fetherling (Nolo), explains how to evaluate such major assets as pensions, investments, family homes and businesses, and how to arrive at a division of property that is fair to both sides.
- *Second Chances: Men, Women & Children a Decade After Divorce,* by Judith Wallerstein and Sandra Blakeslee (Mariner Books). Contains a great chapter on joint custody and how children are negatively affected by their parents' squabbles.
- *The Joint Custody Handbook,* by Miriam Galper Cohen (Running Press). Good advice on the practical aspects of making joint custody work.
- *The Divorced Parent: Success Strategies for Raising Your Children After Separation,* by Stephanie Marston (Morrow). How to raise well-adjusted kids after a divorce.

C. Limit Yourself to Legal Form Preparation: Don't Give Legal Advice

Even if you include a dozen disclaimers in your promotional material and wallpaper your office with signs stating that you don't practice law and are not a lawyer, you must live up to your statements or you may end up in legal hot water. In other words, if despite your assurances that you don't give legal advice, you in fact advise people on strategies for dealing with complicated legal problems or help them with problems arising out of contested lawsuits, you face the possibility of criminal UPL charges or being cited by a court in a civil contempt or unfair business practices proceeding involving the same charge.

This raises the question of what types of transactions risk triggering a charge of unauthorized practice of law. There is no definitive answer. The difference between explaining general consumer information and transferring legal expertise is an extremely fine one. Depending on the geographical location, the factual context, and perhaps even on the sophistication of the customer, communicating a particular type of information may be judged to be the practice of law in one enforcement proceeding and not to be in another. For example, many judges would say that telling a customer who is getting a divorce that a judge will decide which parent is to be the primary custodian of the children, based on "the best interests of the children," is general consumer information, which is widely available and hence should not be considered the practice of law. However, a few judges might still claim this information is legal in nature, and therefore, a nonlawyer explaining it to a customer is impermissible.

A few years ago, if an independent paralegal was prosecuted (this was rare for other reasons—see Chapter 2), a judge would normally rule that explaining any information about the law to a consumer (for example, "You file the long white form and fill it out with black ink") constituted UPL. By contrast, today it is becoming increasingly recognized that explaining basic legal facts widely known in the community (for example, "It's a crime to lie on tax forms" or, "The speed limit is 55 mph") does not constitute the practice of law and therefore won't result in an unauthorized practice charge. We call this the "general knowledge" exception to the rule that only lawyers can give legal advice and we believe that in coming years, the rule will be greatly expanded to cover wide areas of information. Logically, any information widely available to the public through government websites, self-help law books, videos, software, consumer information packets, and magazines will fall into this category.

The Internet has caused a quantum leap in what legal information falls into the general information category. Hundreds of websites offer tutorials and articles about laws pertaining to business operations, bankruptcy, and family law. Since there are no meaningful barriers to creating a website with legal content, legal information of all types is already generally available. It's hard to see how the organized bar will be able to maintain its monopoly over the delivery of "legal information" when this information is available in plain English at the click of a mouse. See Chapter 11 for a discussion of how the Internet is likely to affect the independent paralegal movement as a whole.

Family law is the area where this "general knowledge" rule has already expanded the types of information an IP can transfer to a customer. In large part, this is because state court websites, consumer reporters, consumer action columns, and self-help books, to mention but a few information sources, routinely explain the basics of divorce, adoption, change of name, and guardianship. For example, it's possible to learn that a consumer is, in most states, eligible for a divorce on a "no fault" basis, or that all parents who have the ability to do so must pay child support, from literally dozens of nonlawyer sources. Even lawyers' groups have begun to recognize the value of the public getting this information, to the extent that they often bestow community service awards on the reporters who prepare or present these materials.

And now for a face full of cold water. Despite the trend towards liberating the law from lawyers, there is no way to know for sure what information a local bar association, prosecutor, or judge will regard as being general public knowledge as opposed to legal information. In short, despite the broad national trend towards allowing IPs to communicate basic consumer law information to their customers, particular individuals who do so are still vulnerable.

Given this, what general guidelines should an independent paralegal follow to be in the best position to defend herself should organized lawyerdom strike? As we emphasize throughout this book, the conservative answer is to do nothing but prepare forms in uncontested actions under the customer's direction. This is best accomplished by following the customer's instructions as to which forms to prepare and what to put on them, after first providing the customer with the self-help law information materials necessary to make informed choices. If the customer still has substantive legal questions, even routine ones, the independent paralegal should always refer them back to the self-help law materials that discuss the areas of their concern, or to a lawyer-staffed law phone service or directly to a lawyer.

Alternatively, you can alert your customers to some of the excellent self-help websites that are now available. These sites are sponsored by state and federal courts and provide excellent guidelines on how to handle many different court procedures without a lawyer. See, for example, www.courtinfo.ca.gov.

What about very routine questions about subjects that are common knowledge in the community, such as, "Is a parent legally responsible to support his or her minor child?" IPs who work in parts of the country where the likelihood of prosecution is low may conclude that they can safely provide answers. But before an IP, even one who feels legally secure, goes too far down the road of personally providing customers with legal information, we believe she should take a hard, critical look not only at what she is doing, but why she is doing it. Is she really answering legal questions and providing legal information because this is the only efficient way to legally inform the customer, or is it because she enjoys being an authority figure and secretly yearns to be a "junior lawyer?" In our experience, it is often for this latter reason.

Again, a good compromise between never giving oral information or answering a customer's sensible questions, on the one hand, and acting like a lawyer on the other, is to back all oral information you give with high-quality self-help legal materials published by someone other than yourself. For example, if you are typing articles and bylaws for profit and nonprofit corporations in Houston, Texas, and provide the books *How to Form Your Own Texas Corporation* and *How to Form a Nonprofit Corporation*, both by Anthony Mancuso (Nolo), as part of doing every corporation, you can sensibly argue that the information you are giving orally is simply a summary of independently published materials.

California Note: In California, IPs can distribute materials written or approved by an attorney. See Chapter 14, Section A, for more on the California legislation.

Arizona Note: Under the new Arizona legislation, IPs can distribute materials written or approved by an attorney. See Chapter 14, Section A, for more on the new Arizona legislation.

D. Create a Good Questionnaire

As we suggest elsewhere in this book, an integral aspect of the independent paralegal business is using questionnaires to acquire and preserve information from the customer and to document decisions made by the customer. It is possible, and even a common practice, to design questionnaires so that they simply track the forms that will ultimately be produced from the information. But two additional steps can greatly reduce the risk of a UPL charge.

1. Whenever a question on your questionnaire calls for a decision or for information that requires some type of legal knowledge, the question should include a reference to the legal materials that you sell or recommend to the customer. For instance, assume that you are going to do divorces and your questionnaire asks customers with children whether they want sole or joint custody. Since this question calls for a decision, you would want to specifically refer the customer to where she can get help in making this decision. Assuming you are selling a self-help divorce book as a necessary part of your services, the question on custody would also contain a chapter and section reference to the book's discussion on custody. Just the fact that the reference is on the questionnaire will effectively demonstrate to would-be prosecutors how your customers get their legal information, and will likely dispel any notion that they are getting their information from you personally (which is the primary no-no when operating an independent paralegal business). Of course, these references won't be necessary for the bulk of the questions, most of which will be seeking facts in the customer's possession. For example, questions about the customer's name, age, children, property, and place of residence usually should not require references to legal materials.

2.   Another addition to the questionnaire that will come in handy if
     you are ever investigated for UPL is a preliminary Question and
     Answer page about the legal issues that commonly arise in the
     procedure.

          As with other written materials, you will want these questions
     and answers to be written or approved by an attorney.

          Set out below are the first three pages of a sample bankruptcy
     questionnaire prepared by the authors. The first page sets out the rules
     for using the questionnaire. The second page gives the customer a
     place to list questions about the book that the IP has provided. The
     third page is an example of how you can lay out a questionnaire to get
     the answers you need in a format appropriate for transferring them to
     the bankruptcy petition form.

INSTRUCTIONS FOR BANKRUPTCY

Questionnaire

Follow these general guidelines when completing the questionnaire:

1. Carefully read the instructions at the beginning of each part.
2. **Completely answer every question** on each page. For instance, where the name and address of a person or firm is requested, give the full name and address, including zip code, city, and state.
3. Be thorough. The only wrong answer is one that leaves information out. If in doubt, provide more information, not less.
4. Where you are given a choice of yes or no, check the correct answer. If the question does not apply, indicate with an **N/A** (not applicable).
5. Print clearly or **type.** We must be able to read your answers in order to enter them in your bankruptcy papers accurately.
6. Be scrupulously honest. Dishonesty has no place in the bankruptcy process. You must declare under penalty of perjury that all your answers are true. If you think an honest answer to a question will hurt you, see our bankruptcy attorney before proceeding further.

Except when otherwise indicated, the book referred to in this questionnaire is *How to File for Chapter 7 Bankruptcy*, 10th edition (Nolo). The notation [book, Ch. 3/11] means Chapter 3, page 11 of *How to File for Chapter 7 Bankruptcy*. You may purchase this reference book for an additional $25 or borrow a used copy if available. If you have questions or need assistance please call us at 707-263-7200.

The minimum cost is $375 legal fee plus $200 Court Filing Fee.

BANKRUPTCY QUESTIONNAIRE
Preliminary Matters

You may have one or more concerns that you wish to address before completing your bankruptcy. Please read the **Understanding Bankruptcy Green Sheet** that we have provided you. It is a reference to the specific chapters and sections of *How to File for Chapter 7 Bankruptcy* where you can find relevant information that will help guide your decisions. Use the space below to list any additional questions you may have about the issues raised in each section of the book.

Chapter   **Page**   **Question**

_____

_____

_____

_____

_____

_____

_____

_____

_____

_____

_____

_____

_____

_____

_____

_____

_____

Comments:

SECTION 1: BASIC INFORMATION

Part A. Name and Address

Name:_____
                Last   *First*   *Middle*

Telephone Number   Home: _____   Work: _____
Have you used any other names in the past six years? __ No __ Yes ***If yes, list***
   other names: _____   _____
Social Security Number: __ __ __ - __ __ - __ __ __ __
Address: _____
City: _____ State: _____ Zip: _____
County: _____ Have you lived at this address for at least 180 days?
   __ No __ Yes
If you have a different mailing address, please list:
Mailing Address: _____
City:_____ State: _____ Zip: _____

Part B. Name and Address of Spouse

If you are filing *jointly* with your spouse, fill in the following information about your
   spouse:
Name:_____
                Last   *First*   *Middle*

Has your spouse used any other names in the past six years? __ No __ Yes ***If yes, list***
   other names: _____   _____
Social Security Number: __ __ __ - __ __ - __ __ __ __
Address: *(if different from your address):*
City: _____ State: _____ Zip: _____
   County: _____
If your spouse has a different mailing address, please list:
Mailing Address:
City: _____ State: _____ Zip: _____

Part C. Prior/Pending Bankruptcy Cases

Has a bankruptcy case been filed by you or against you in the last 6 years? __ No __Yes
If yes, in which district of which state was the case filed?
Case Number: _____ Date filed: _____
Are there currently any bankruptcy cases pending against you, your business, your
   spouse, or your spouse's business? __ No __Yes
If yes, name of debtor: _____ Relationship to you: _____
Case Number: _____ Date filed: _____ Judge: _____
   District _____

■

Legal Areas Open to Independent Paralegals

Most people who open businesses as independent paralegals have a good idea of the type of legal paperwork they want to help people with. Often they just want to continue doing what they did when they worked for a private attorney, a legal clinic, or a court clerk's office. Or, occasionally the independent paralegal has become interested in a particular area because of a personal experience with the legal system. For example, we know two IPs who got involved with handling landlord problems after several of their own tenants refused to pay the rent. It is also fairly common for people to get started in the divorce typing business after successfully handling their own divorce.

California and Arizona Note: In California and Arizona, state law restricts entry into the IP field. In California, you can't be an IP unless you attended paralegal school or worked for a lawyer for a number of years (existing paralegals were grandfathered in). In Arizona you must take a test and also meet educational requirements. See Chapter 14 for more detail on the California and Arizona regulatory schemes.

Because so many uncontested divorces and bankruptcies are processed each year, and because independent paralegals have been successfully preparing paperwork in these fields for some time, the majority of fledgling IPs initially choose these legal areas. This makes sense, unless the geographical area where the new IP wishes to work is already saturated with divorce and bankruptcy typing services, as is the case in a number of West Coast communities.

However, just because a number of independent paralegals have done well preparing divorces and bankruptcies, don't be fooled into thinking that you must do the same in order to succeed. There are, in fact, dozens of legal areas open to you. Before listing a number of these, let's take a moment to understand why some types of legal tasks offer great potential to independent paralegals, while others do not.

A. Avoid Contested Cases

A basic rule for survival as an independent paralegal is to refrain from working with customers who have contested disputes or whose disputes are likely to become contested. Legal literacy in the U.S. is so miserably low that the average citizen doesn't know enough about the law or legal procedures to handle a contested dispute without considerable help. If, as an independent paralegal, you are the nearest thing to a legal expert in the life of a person who is confused, and perhaps intimidated, by a contested lawsuit, she will almost inevitably ask you for legal advice and information. This in turn will put you in an awkward position. Unlike uncontested actions, such as applying for a patent or trademark, where there are high-quality self-help law materials to which you can refer your customers, there are few, if any, reliable materials to help nonlawyers cope with a contested lawsuit, especially if the other party is represented by a lawyer. (An exception is *Represent Yourself in Court: How to Prepare & Try a Winning Case*, by Paul Bergman & Sara J. Berman-Barrett (Nolo), which does an excellent job of showing the reader how to handle a contested civil court case.)

Now here's the fix you may find yourself in if you take on contested cases: If in attempting to respond to your customers' anxious questions you provide legal information, you may be charged with practicing law without a license. On the other hand, if you refuse to provide customers with the information they think they need to deal with an immediate problem, they are likely to become demanding and perhaps angry. At the very least, trying to deal with this will be a drag on your business. And, of course, there is always the risk that the lawyer representing the other side will report you to the UPL enforcement agency, or an unhappy customer will complain to the bar association or a consumer agency.

The best and probably the only way to avoid this sort of problem is to limit your work strictly to uncontested actions. An exception would be if you work in a cause-related, nonprofit setting, such as advising women on how to collect child support. IPs who work in a nonprofit setting, even one that involves contested cases, are at less risk of being challenged by the bar, at least in part because lawyers don't get much in the way of fees from these areas and so are less concerned about nonlawyers getting involved.

Fortunately, deciding to limit your work to uncontested matters does not involve much sacrifice, as the great majority (surely over 80%) of all legal matters presented to American courts and administrative tribunals do not involve a dispute. For example, despite the impression you may have gained from watching daytime TV dramas, where every divorcing couple has a small mansion, two BMWs, and a herd of lawyers who make house calls, the great majority of modern divorces are not contested and do not require expensive lawyers or, for that matter, in most instances, any lawyer at all. This makes sense when you remember that the majority of people who divorce are relatively young, don't have much property, and often don't have children. With little to fight about, most avail themselves of the opportunity that no-fault divorce laws and standardized divorce forms offer to end their legal relationship with as little hassle as possible.

This isn't to say that every divorce is uncontested. Obviously, the trauma of a couple separating can occasionally be so powerful that it spills over into the legal arena. Indeed, several established divorce typing services report that about 5% of the seemingly uncontested divorces they prepare end up being contested, at least to some degree. This points up the need for independent paralegals working in the divorce area to emphasize in their promotional material that they only handle uncontested actions. Even more important, it indicates the necessity for tight customer screening at the initial customer interview, designed to weed out cases that are likely to become contested. Finally, the IP should plan in advance to deal efficiently with those few customers who, despite good screening, end up involved in a fight. (See Chapter 7, Section A.) For example, here is an excerpt from a flyer used by one divorce typing service.

DIVORCE YOURSELF
A NONLAWYER DIVORCE TYPING SERVICE!

With our form preparation help, you can file your own uncontested divorce. To be uncontested, you and your spouse must agree on the main issues of divorce, including:

- Custody of the Children
- Visitation Rights
- Child Support
- Spousal Support
- Division of Property

Important: We do not work with people involved in contested divorces. If you believe that your divorce is likely to be contested, please see a lawyer. If, after you engage our services to help you prepare your uncontested divorce, your spouse files court papers to contest it, we reserve the right to refer you to a lawyer.

In addition to adopting written policies stating that you don't handle contested actions, it's important that you learn to recognize and respect the warning signals that will alert you when a contest is likely. For example, if a potential divorce customer tells you he doesn't plan to pay child support, wants to make his spouse pay all the bills, and that if she gives him any trouble, he will find a way to get her to toe the line, you will want to decline his business. In this situation, the couple obviously hasn't agreed on anything, and the other spouse is almost sure to end up with a lawyer to protect her interests.

Turning away customers can be a tough task for the new businessperson who is understandably anxious to develop business quickly. The danger is, of course, that a business-hungry IP will talk himself into helping a customer prepare paperwork in situations in which a later contest is likely. There is no more detailed advice we can give you except to pay attention to any warning signals your customers give. You will lose much more than you gain if you take on a customer who has a messy contested problem.

Consumer bankruptcies are another area in which most filings are not contested. In bankruptcy, the underlying problem is normally painfully simple—the debtor owes a lot of money and has very little. Because there isn't much to discuss, except the holes in the debtor's pocket, few creditors are likely to challenge the bankruptcy. Very occasionally a creditor will surface with a claim that must be defended. One that is not too unusual is a creditor's assertion that the debtor submitted a fraudulent financial statement to get credit in the first place. If this occurs, or indeed, if a similar legal hassle develops in any other area in which you are working, whether it be divorce, incorporation, or probate, you will want to be able to refer your customer to a lawyer.

B. Type Legal Forms in High Demand

In addition to avoiding contested actions, you obviously want to work in areas of legal form preparation for which there is steady consumer demand. Fortunately, there is an added benefit in doing this for legal areas where the volume of paperwork is high—the legal bureaucracy has almost always worked out step-by-step protocols for handling that paperwork. Think of it this way: If a state court gets one stepparent adoption filing per calendar quarter, they may informally make up at least some of the paperwork requirements as they go along. But if they receive 20 a week, you can be sure that rules for forms and procedures will be clearly defined. And once they are, it's not difficult for the IPs to help their customers conform.

At this point you may want to interrupt and ask something like this: "Doesn't each person's unique legal problem require a high degree of customization when it comes to filling out paperwork?" The simple answer is "No." Whenever a society has to deal with a great many people who need to accomplish the same task, whether it's applying for a driver's license, filing income tax, or applying for a business permit, the only cost-effective approach is to reduce the procedural steps to rote. This generally amounts to requiring the person who wants to accomplish the particular task (or their lawyer or typing service) to insert "magic words" in boxes and blanks on forms. And this is exactly the same approach courts use when it comes to filing for divorce or a change of name. The fact that lawyers think of divorce and name changes as "legal tasks" does not change the fact that, in uncontested situations, if you put the correct words in the correct boxes and blanks, you get the result you desire, and if you don't, you don't.

To sum up, in deciding whether a particular legal area is a good one for a paralegal approach, determine if:

- most filings are uncontested,
- volume is reasonably high,
- the paperwork is routine,
- you can charge enough to make a living (see Chapter 9), and
- resources are available for you to educate yourself as to how to do the particular task.

C.   Legal Areas Open to Independent Paralegals

Now let's examine some of the specific legal form preparation tasks that have worked well for independent paralegals. As mentioned, divorces and bankruptcies have long been popular with IPs because there are a lot of them and because many people who need one or the other can't afford to pay a lawyer. But these aren't the only areas where an IP can prosper. Consider that every year there are more than a quarter million evictions, at least half a million small business incorporations and, taken together, hundreds of thousands of stepparent adoptions, name changes, and conservatorships for people (most of them elderly) who aren't competent to manage their own financial affairs. In addition, hundreds of thousands of copyright applications are filed, millions of wills and living trusts are prepared, hundreds of thousands of Social Security disability appeals are filed, and the estates of the majority of people who die must be probated. All of these legal areas and many more are suitable for the independent paralegal because, for the most part, they involve the preparation of routine, and usually fairly repetitive, paperwork.

Here is a list of areas in which paralegals currently practice.

- **Divorce (and annulment).** This is the big one, with the majority of IPs handling divorce petitions. Your clients might want to look at *Divorce & Money: How to Make the Best Financial Decisions During Divorce*, by Violet Woodhouse (Nolo).

- **Bankruptcy (Chapter 7 and Chapter 13).** Nationally, this is the fastest growing IP area. Over one million bankruptcies are filed in the U.S. each year, and preprinted forms and easily available self-help law books make doing the paperwork routine. As discussed in Chapter 2, the passage of the federal law 11 U.S.C. § 110(g)(1), which regulates and legalizes the activities of bankruptcy petition preparers, has made it easier to operate legally in this field, but has imposed strict rules and created tough and often unfair penalties for those who don't follow them.

- **Evictions and other landlord services.** This is a fast-growing, high-profit area that paralegals may well take over almost entirely.

- **Guardianships.** This usually routine legal action gives a grandparent or other relative or friend, who typically already has physical custody of a child who isn't their own, legal status that is often demanded by schools, hospitals, banks, and others. About 25% of IPs handle guardianships.

- **Civil paternity actions.** When unmarried couples separate, a judicial decree of paternity is a necessary part of getting a court order for support, visitation, and custody. Preparing the paperwork necessary to establish a parental relationship under the Uniform Parentage Act makes up a significant portion of the business of many IPs.

- **Conservatorships.** An action brought by family members when an older person can no longer handle their own business and financial affairs, or when any family member becomes incompetent.

- **Tenants' rights.** Most opportunity in this area is with nonprofit tenants' advocacy organizations, or public agencies such as rent boards or mediation services.

- **Probate.** Unless a decedent had a probate-avoiding living trust or other pre-established plan to avoid probate, probate is normally required to get necessary court approval to transfer titled assets from the deceased person to his inheritors. Particularly in California, where an excellent workbook on this subject is available (*How to Probate an Estate in California,* by Julia Nissley (Nolo)), many IPs have entered this field. Another useful Nolo book is *Estate Planning Basics,* by Denis Clifford.

- **Judgment collection.** In most states, bill collectors are regulated. Don't choose this field until you check out your state's rules. In some states, there are excellent opportunities to help clients collect judgments by using the state's judgment collection statutes. For example, in California there is an organization called California Association of Judgment Professionals. CAJP has several hundred members who meet annually and share tips on how to collect money judgments obtained in a court of law.

- **Immigration.** Using materials such as Nolo's *How to Get a Green Card: Legal Ways to Stay in the USA*, by Loida Nicolas Lewis and Len T. Madlansacay, many paralegals provide immigration information and form preparation services. In some states, such as California, providers must comply with regulatory laws. (Cal. Bus. & Prof. Code §§ 22440-22448.)

- **Business entity formation.** Helping small business people create business entities such as corporations, limited liability companies, and partnerships, is an area of almost unlimited potential for the independent paralegal who can afford to computerize the form preparation. (See Chapter 11.) Nolo has a number of useful titles in this area, including *Form Your Own Limited Liability Company*, *Nolo's Quick LLC*, and *Incorporate Your Business*, all by Anthony Mancuso. (Check the website for other titles relating to specific states.)

- **Deed and other real estate transfers.** In many states, real estate people, title companies, and other nonlawyers already control this business when residential and commercial property is bought or sold. However, consumers often need help in arranging private real estate transfers between friends and family, and this is a potential area for IP involvement.

- **Adoptions.** Many IPs prepare adoptions that occur when a parent with custody of children from a former marriage or living-together relationship remarries and the new spouse wants to legally adopt the children. If the absent natural parent consents, or is out of the picture, the paperwork is routine.

- **Small claims court procedures.** Many IPs who currently work in this area concentrate on running group seminars and classes aimed at small business people who use the court regularly. The idea is primarily to teach them how to use small claims court to sue customers who have failed to pay bills. But as small claims dollar limits increase in many states, the small claims counseling business is beginning to focus on helping individual consumers prepare their cases. Yes, this raises the issue of an IP helping a consumer prepare for a contested action, but since it's in the context of a court where people are encouraged to represent themselves, nonlawyers should be able to provide this information free of unauthorized practice of law charges. Nolo has a helpful book in this area, too: *Everybody's Guide to Small Claims Court in California*, by Ralph Warner.

- **Child support increases and decreases.** In many states, parents are entitled to petition for increases based on inflation or changed circumstances. In some states, court personnel and child support agencies will help with those petitions, and in many others, nonprofit organizations provide help. But in lots of communities, IPs prepare much of this mostly routine paperwork.

- **Grandparent visitation.** When parents divorce, grandparents are sometimes denied access to the kids. Especially in California, IPs help them prepare the paperwork necessary to get a court order allowing them visitation.

- **Restraining orders.** As with child support increases discussed just above, many women's groups provide this help. But especially when a customer is filing for divorce, IPs often prepare these protective orders in addition to typing divorce papers.

- **Simple wills.** Using *Nolo's Simple Will Book* (Nolo), or software such as *WillMaker* (Nolo), many IPs are helping customers prepare their own simple wills. (See Chapter 11 for more on using computerized legal form preparation software.)

- **Living trusts.** Lawyers advertise these probate avoidance devices for $1,500–$4,000. Many IPs will prepare them for $200–$400, often relying on books such as Denis Clifford's *Make Your Own Living Trust* (Nolo) or software such as *Quicken WillMaker* (Nolo) to inform the customer and protect the IP from charges of unauthorized practice. In recent years, organized lawyerdom has cracked down hard on what it considers to be "living trust mills." See Chapter 2, Section E.

- **Name changes.** These are truly routine and easy. There are lots more of them than you might expect—check the number with your State Department of Vital Statistics. If you are in California, you can use Nolo's *How to Change Your Name in California,* by Lisa Sedano and Emily Doskow.

- **Social Security disability appeals.** The federal government allows nonlawyers to handle these cases, so there are no worries about unauthorized practice. A number of nonprofit groups who work with seniors and the disabled do this work using paralegals. In addition, many IPs are establishing their own for-profit businesses in this area (see interview with Glynda Dixon in Appendix).

- **Copyright applications.** This is a routine, by-the-numbers job already handled by nonlawyers at most publishing companies. It's an area paralegals are sure to invade soon. A general guide is *Patent, Copyright & Trademark* by Stephen Elias and Richard Stim (Nolo).

- **Partnership agreements.** Nolo publishes a book entitled *The Partnership Book: How to Write a Partnership Agreement* that makes it easy for IPs to help small business people prepare their own partnership agreements.

- **Paternity petitions.** These come up in several contexts, one of the most common being where an unmarried father wants to assert his rights to visit and otherwise parent his child.

- **Securities industry arbitration.** This field involves claims by investors that they were ripped off by stockbrokers and other investment advisors. All claims must be mediated or arbitrated—court proceedings are rarely involved. Many thousands of cases are filed each year, and there is no requirement that advocates be lawyers.

- **Mediation.** Many disputes involving divorce, neighbors, small business ownership, child custody, and consumer issues are resolved through mediation and never end up in court. Generally, there is no requirement that mediators be lawyers. See Chapter 7, Section D, for more on mediation.

- **Nonprofit corporations.** Many people form nonprofit corporations for a variety of purposes. Anyone who learns the process should be able to make a good living helping others with their paperwork. Nolo has an excellent, nationwide book on forming this type of organization as well as a book specific to California: *How to Form a Nonprofit Corporation (National Edition)* and *How to Form a Nonprofit Corporation in California,* both by Anthony Mancuso

- **Trademarks.** This field involves searching trademark databases to see whether it's okay to use a proposed business or product name, logo, slogan, or other device intended to identify the business or product in the marketplace. Some trademark search firms go further and help their customers prepare federal trademark registration applications.

CAN INDEPENDENT PARALEGALS REPRESENT CUSTOMERS APPEARING BEFORE ADMINISTRATIVE AGENCIES?

The Federal Administrative Procedure Act (see Chapter 2, Section C) allows federal agencies to permit nonlawyers to appear before them. Many do. For example, Social Security disability appeals, Medicare appeals, Veterans' programs, and federal housing programs can be handled by nonlawyers. State UPL laws can apply to federal agencies and programs. If the agency has not explicitly stated that nonlawyers may appear before it, check in your state to see what the situation is.

At the state agency level, things are more confused. In some states, nonlawyers have the right under state law to appear before many types of administrative agencies. In others, only lawyers can appear before most agencies. In a few, state courts have used the inherent powers doctrine (see Chapter 2) to restrict the right of the state legislature to empower nonlawyers to appear before agencies. This means you will have to check with each agency you are interested in to see if nonlawyers are allowed.

After reading this list you may be tempted to prepare several types of paperwork. There is nothing wrong with this, as long as you have the detailed knowledge to handle each and you don't spread yourself too thin. Especially if you are new to the business, however, it's best to concentrate on one area at first, learn it thoroughly, and then branch out.

When you are ready to expand, look for areas that are a natural extension of the one you already handle. Not only does this facilitate your learning process, but it makes it much easier to market your services as a coherent package. For example, the late Virginia Simons, a longtime paralegal in Bakersfield, California, defined her form preparation business around family problems. Thus, she typed guardianships, conservatorships, stepparent adoptions, name changes, minors' emancipation petitions, child custody and support modifications, and paperwork to establish a parental relationship for unmarried couples, as well as divorces. She took pleasure in this diversity, both because her work became more varied and interesting, and because, with lots of competing IPs working in Bakersfield, there wasn't enough divorce typing to go around.

At a glance, it sounds as if Simons took on a lot. But since all her work was family-related, and California has adopted easy-to-use pre-printed forms, there were (and are) many similarities and procedural overlaps from one type of action to the next. ■

5

Naming Your Business

Naming a new business is fun. You free your imagination, let your creative juices flow, and come up with a name that tells the world exactly who you are. Right? Unfortunately, things are usually not that simple, especially when it comes to naming an independent paralegal business.

If you choose a name that describes the services your business offers (for example, "Probate Form Typing Service"), people will know what you do. However, since the name uses common and descriptive terms, you may have difficulty preventing a competing business with a similar name from opening up in the next town. If your name sounds too much like a lawyer's ("Divorce Law Consultants") you are likely to have the organized bar on your case in a hurry. If you pick a creative name that has nothing to do with lawyers ("Unicorn Enterprises" or "XYBOR Services"), your name will be easy to protect from use by competitors and will probably not trigger hostility from organized lawyerdom, but most people won't have a clue as to what you do. As we'll see, the best approach is to pick a name that suggests your services without describing them outright.

HOW TO TRADEMARK YOUR NAME

In this chapter, and especially in Section G, we briefly discuss basic concepts of trademark law. We don't have the space here to show you how to protect a name under federal and state trademark law. Doing this involves a number of steps, including choosing a protectable name, conducting a trademark search, and formally registering your name. If you plan to operate in more than one state, you will probably want to register your name with the Federal Patent & Trademark Office. Nolo publishes a step-by-step guide for this purpose entitled *Trademark: Legal Care for Your Business & Product Name,* by Stephen Elias (Nolo).

As you can see, coming up with a good name for an independent paralegal business involves juggling a number of variables. Here are a few suggestions.

A. Avoid Buzz Words That May Antagonize Organized Lawyerdom

As you should now clearly appreciate, an IPs ability to survive depends in large part on the ability to avoid the wrath of organized lawyerdom. The first place to practice this skill is in the selection of your name. Choose a name that carefully avoids such lawyer buzz words as "lawyer," "attorney," "counsel," "counselor," "legal," "legal services," "legal information," "legal resource center," "legal clinic," "law," or "paralegal." There is an obvious reason for this advice. It amounts to illegal misrepresentation to use a name that suggests you are a lawyer if you are not.

In California, a Legal Document Assistant may not use the word "paralegal" to describe themselves or their business. (Cal. Bus. & Prof. Code §§ 6400 and following). In the United States a Bankruptcy Petition Preparer may not use the word "legal." At least one bankruptcy court has ruled that the term "paralegal" is also verboten to BPPs.

B. Choosing a Name That Emphasizes Self-Help Law

In our opinion, the best approach to naming your business is to adopt a name that emphasizes that you prepare paperwork for people who are handling their own legal affairs. In this context, some independent paralegals use the Latin terms for self-representation—*in pro per* (in one's own person) and *pro se* (on one's own behalf). Although technically accurate, we believe that using somewhat obscure terms such as these is counterproductive for three reasons. First, many potential customers don't know what these Latin phrases mean. Second, some wrongly believe such phrases have something to do with lawyers, and may even wrongly conclude that you provide legal advice. Third, and most important, because Latin gobbledygook is negatively associated with lawyers and their seeming addiction to jargon, at least some potential customers are likely to be turned off.

By pleasant contrast, however, the rough English equivalents of *in pro per* and *pro se,* such as "self-represented," "self-help," and "do your own," work well as names when combined with a description of the actual service offered. Thus, "Self-Help Bankruptcy Typing Service" and "Do Your Own Divorce Typing Center" are both relatively safe and informative names.

It is not wise to use the word "help" without further defining it by adding a word such as "self." Otherwise, names like "Divorce Help" or "Bankruptcy Help" make it sound as if you provide legal expertise and information in these areas. Since doing this risks a charge that you are practicing law without a license, these are counterproductive names.

C. Using Descriptive Names

We have suggested that names that accurately describe what you do have an advantage from a marketing point of view and also help keep you out of trouble with organized lawyerdom. Thus you might end up with "South Boston Divorce Typing Service" or "Quality Incorporation Form Typing Service." Rosemary Furman, the pioneering Florida paralegal (see interview in the Appendix), who did business for years in Jacksonville, Florida, under the nose of a hostile bar, called her business the "Northside Typing Service." The point of this approach is, of course, to let potential customers have some idea of what you do, but to avoid giving organized lawyerdom a convenient way to accuse you of UPL.

The downside of using a descriptive name is that, under trademark law, descriptive names can be difficult to protect from use by potential competitors. For example, terms such as "typing," "form preparation," "word processing," "stenographer," and "secretarial" are in such general use that they are considered to be in the "public domain," and can be used by anyone, except in a few limited situations in which they are likely to result in customer confusion. (We discuss this concept in more detail in Section G, below.)

D. Combining a Unique and Descriptive Name

A good approach to naming an IP business is to combine an unusual or fanciful name with descriptive terminology. This gets around the problem that a descriptive name is often hard to protect legally. Thus, White Rose Divorce Typing Service would be protectable as a trademark if no one else had previously claimed or used it, and at the same time it tells your customers what you do.

E. Using Your Own Name

Yet another approach to naming your business is to use your own name, perhaps combining it with a term that describes what you do. Thus, Kwan Lee might use "Lee Probate Form Preparation Services."

One advantage of using your own name is that, in many states, it eliminates the need to file a fictitious business name statement. On the other hand, a potential disadvantage is that you can't claim exclusive use of your name under the trademark laws should someone else with the same name also want to use it, unless over a period of time it has become so well known and identified with your business that it clearly defines it in the public mind. (See Section G, below.)

This means if your own name is a common one, you may wish to choose a more distinctive name for your business. However, if your name is somewhat unusual, using it as part of your business name is probably fairly safe, since the chances of another independent paralegal with the same name going into competition with you seems fairly remote. For the same reasons, you might call yourself the P & K Lee Probate Form Preparation Business, a name that would likely be distinctive even if another person named Lee opened a similar business.

What about using your own name along with a vague-sounding term such as "Associates," "Consultants," or "Organization"? We consider this a poor idea for two reasons. First, you are likely to end up with a name that sounds like a law firm, while at the same time it doesn't inform potential customers about what you do. For example, "Jones & Lee, Associates" may sound prestigious, but it is a lousy name for a form preparation service that helps people prepare their own wills and living trusts. Also, without a qualifier like "Jones & Lee Typing Service," or the addition of initials, you run the risk of infringing the trademark of some other business already using that name, especially if your name is similar to a famous one, like Firestone, Sears, or Champion.

If you are determined to use a vague term like associates, you can make it far more safe and effective by using it in conjunction with a term that describes what you do. Thus, if Jones and Lee, Associates, adds "A self-help typing service for wills and living trusts," their name fairly and accurately describes their business. Of course, they may find this a bit cumbersome and expensive when it comes to listing their services in classified ads.

F. Using "Paralegal" as Part of Your Name

Let's now briefly discuss the term many, if not most, nonlawyers who run legal form typing services use to describe themselves: "paralegal." Like "midwife," "computer consultant," and "financial planner," "paralegal" can mean almost anything. Because most states have no official certification programs for paralegals, people with all different kinds of training and experience quite properly and legally use this term. Some base their claim to be a paralegal on the fact that they took several paralegal courses at a business school. Others have a degree in paralegal studies from a university or college that requires several years of study and may or may not be accredited by the American Bar Association or some other group. Still others are former law firm employees who establish their own business to market specialized "freelance paralegal" services to lawyers. And, of course, there are also many "independent paralegals" who teach themselves how to type and market legal form preparation services directly to the public.

So far, so good, you are probably thinking. If the term paralegal can mean a variety of things, why shouldn't I use it to describe my independent typing service? Simply put, because the great majority of people who call themselves paralegals currently work for lawyers. This means that in the view of organized lawyerdom, paralegals are an extension of their empire. Your use of the term may give rise to their charge that you are representing yourself to the public as working under lawyer supervision. If this is hard to swallow, consider the parallel reality of the medical profession, where many doctors believe that "nurses" are people put on the earth to serve them, and the very word nurse conjures up, in the public mind, the image of a person who takes orders from a physician.

At least one trial court decision, *State Bar of Nevada v. Johnson,* (CV89-5814 (Nev. 2d Dist. Ct. 1990)), has specifically disapproved of the use of "paralegal" as a name for a legal typing service. In establishing guidelines for typing service operation, that court stated:

> *...The court probably cannot keep the defendants from appropriating a business name [Paralegal] which is not elsewhere prohibited in an as yet unregulated field. The court does feel, however, that it is within its power to limit advertising a status as "paralegals," as well as advertising the firm's ability to furnish "paralegal" services, because the term misleads the public into believing that the defendants are in the business of providing legal and non-scrivener services.*

What about attempting to define the term paralegal with a second term, such as "Everyone's," "People's" or "Public," to eliminate the suggestion that lawyers are involved? This helps, but we would still advise avoiding a term that is likely to annoy lawyers. At this point, you may wonder what difference this makes, if lawyers are out to shut you down anyway. We don't have a definitive response to this query, except to suggest that whenever you deal with a large, unpredictable beast with long claws, it makes sense to avoid needlessly pulling its tail.

 California Note: You may not use the term "paralegal" to describe your legal document assistant business in California.

G. Legal Protection Against Copiers

So far we have briefly mentioned the legal concept of protecting your business name from use by competitors. Now let's look more thoroughly at the legal rules that are relevant to protecting the name of any business, including yours. As part of doing so, it will be necessary for you to read the following material on Internet domain names, trade names, and service marks.

1. Trade Names

The name that you select for your business is considered your "trade name." Trade names are subject to two major restrictions:

(1) Your trade name can't be so similar to another trade name used by the same type of business in your area as to cause customer confusion. For instance, if "Speedy Divorce Form Preparation Service" has been open down the street for a year or two, you cannot legally open your own business under this, or a very similar, name.

What this often means, in practice, is that if you form a corporation, your proposed trade name will be reviewed by the state agency in charge of corporate registrations to see whether it is too similar to existing corporate names. If it is, it will be rejected and you'll have to come up with another. Likewise, if you have a sole proprietorship or a partnership, you will have to file a fictitious business name statement with the county (or the state, in some places). Your proposed name usually will be checked against other names in your county and rejected if it is identical or too similar to an existing one.

In addition, unincorporated businesses can defend their trade names from use by others under state laws prohibiting unfair competition. These laws generally require only that businesses not engage in conduct that creates a likelihood of customer confusion. Thus, assuming you (or a competing business) aren't incorporated, if another "Speedy Divorce Form Preparation Service" opens up in another part of your county, or maybe even your state, you probably could challenge them under unfair competition laws if you could show it was likely that some of your customers would be confused by the new business's identical trade name. The same laws can be applied against you if you select a name identical (or too similar) to a rival's.

(2) Similar restrictions apply to your trade name, when used as a trademark or service mark (see Section 3, below). Your name cannot be so similar in look, sound, or meaning to an existing trademark that it creates the likelihood of customer confusion. Even though your trade name is approved by your state's Secretary of State (corporation, LLC) or your county's fictitious business name registrar (sole proprietor, partnership), it still may violate (infringe) an existing trademark. And in most states, your Secretary of State or county fictitious business name registrar won't check your name against the federal or state trademark lists. You'll have to do this for yourself.

2. Internet Domain Name

If you are planning on creating a website to market your services, you will also need to choose and register an Internet domain name, like yahoo.com or nolo.com. You can pick any name you want as your domain name if it is not previously taken by someone else. (You can also expand your name options by using a less common extension, like .biz, instead of the more common .com, .org, or .net.) But most businesses prefer, if possible, to use their business name as their domain name. The issues involved in choosing a domain name range from getting your hands on an available one to avoiding trademark lawsuits based on your choice of name.

A good domain name should be memorable, clever, and easily spelled. Unfortunately, many of the best names are already taken. To see if the name you have in mind has been registered, go to www.whois.com. This site allows you to search for a particular name. For example, if you are starting a speed typing business, you might check "speedy.com." If you find that speedy.com is already taken, the www.whois.com website offers a "brainstorming" function that allows you to peruse other possibilities. After you enter relevant keywords (such as quick, speedy, and typing), the site will return a list of related names that are still up for grabs.

Once you've found an available name, you'll need to make sure it doesn't conflict with someone else's trademark. If your choice will cause customer confusion between your company and another, you're safer choosing another name. This is true even if the other business is half-way across the country. Once you've established a Web presence, you are in competition with businesses around the globe, and must address trademark issues broadly. A generic name such as "coffee.com" will keep you safest from lawsuits, but will also leave you unable to protect your name from use by other businesses. In choosing your name, you'll need to strike a balance.

After you've chosen an appropriate domain name, you can register it online with a service such as Network Solutions, at the website mentioned above. Some businesses register under more than one name, or register common misspellings of their names.

For detailed and up-to-date information on choosing and registering domain names, as well as avoiding domain name conflicts, get a copy of *Trademark: Legal Care for Your Business & Product Name,* by Steve Elias and Richard Stim (Nolo). Also read *Domain Names: How to Choose & Protect a Great Name for Your Website,* by Stephen Elias and Patricia Gima (Nolo).

3. Trademarks or Service Marks

While trademarks refer to products and service marks refer to services, they mean the same thing for puposes of this discussion. Now suppose you chose a highly distinctive name, such as White Rose Divorce Typing Service. As a result of one of those sleights of hand for which the law is famous, a distinctive trade name such as this is entitled to much more protection than a merely descriptive trade name the instant it is used to identify the services being offered by the business. Why? Because when a trade name is used to identify services, it magically becomes a trademark, and distinctive trademarks, as we explain immediately below, are fairly easy to protect against use by others.

This need not be confusing, because your trade name (that is, the name you select for your business) will most likely be the same as your "trademark" (any name or symbol that is used to market a particular product or service). For instance, "Hyatt Legal Services," is both the name of the business and its trademark. Or, to take a more relevant example, if you use "South Bay Probate Typing Specialists" to market South Bay Probate Typing Specialists form preparation services, you have chosen both a trade name and a trademark.

In practice, your trade name becomes your trademark as soon as you use it to market your services. The only difference between them as far as you are concerned is that trade names are entitled to slightly less and different protections than are trademarks. So while trade names have protections under unfair competition laws, trademarks have both that and protection under trademark laws, which are stronger and provide stiffer penalties for infringement.

The wrinkle is that only trademarks that are distinctive or unique get meaningful protection from copiers under trademark laws. To return to the "Speedy Divorce Form" example, because Speedy is a common promotional term, and because Divorce Form says what the business does, the mark is too descriptive or not unusual enough to get much, if any, protection as a trademark. Other words that are not unique enough to act as trademarks are common surnames and geographic terms, unless they gain secondary meaning. (See "A Secondary Meaning Rule," below.)

On the other hand, White Rose Divorce Form Typing Service is distinctive because it applies a term not usually associated with such a business. That makes it unique, and therefore fully protectable as a trademark. Other ways to create a unique trademark are to make up a word (like Zoline Forms Preparation), or to use a term in a suggestive way (like Ethereal Probate Services), as long as it's not too close to the subject matter of the services to become descriptive. Distinctive or unique marks are registrable with the state trademark office (or the federal office, if you do business across state lines). Once registered, the mark is exclusively yours to use within the state (or the country).

A SECONDARY MEANING RULE: DESCRIPTIVE BUSINESS NAMES CAN EVENTUALLY BECOME PROTECTED AS TRADEMARKS

A trademark that starts out in the public domain because it is descriptive or already in common use, including surnames or geographic terms, can sometimes gain the right to legal protection later. Called the "secondary meaning" rule, this legal concept allows a business to gain exclusive use of a descriptive or other common mark once the business becomes so well known by that name that the name comes to signify the business in the public mind. For example, McDonald's is no longer a common surname to most people; instead, we all know it as a trademark for the fast food chain. Likewise, "Ace Hardware" is protectable as a trademark because it has become so famous that we know exactly what stores the mark refers to. But note: Proving that your mark has acquired secondary meaning can take years and cost lots, due to customer surveys and attorney fees. This concept is discussed in detail in Nolo's book, *Trademark: Legal Care for Your Business & Product Name,* by Stephen Elias and Rich Stim.

---

4. Improper Use of the Name of a Well-Known Business

There is one more factor to consider when you're thinking about trademarks: "dilution" of famous marks. For example, suppose that you decide to name your independent paralegal clinic "Tiffany Scriveners." As it happens, the trademark "Tiffany" is owned by the company selling Tiffany jewelry. Under general trademark/service mark law, you would only be prevented from using the Tiffany mark if customers would be likely to confuse your product or service with that attached to the mark. However, another legal rule allows the owner of a mark to prevent its use by another if the qualities associated with the mark would be diminished in some significant way. For instance, if a company called "Tiffany Chimney Cleaners," or "Tiffany Bankruptcy Form Preparation Service," opened its doors, the first person through them would probably be a lawyer representing the Tiffany jewelry company, with court papers alleging dilution of the Tiffany mark. In short, our advice on this one is simple: don't use or play on the unique trade name or trademark of a large business. For example, Godiva Chocolates made Dogiva Dog Biscuits change its name under this rule.

5. Summing Up the Law of Trade Names and Service Marks

Suppose Speedy Divorce Form, a sole proprietorship, was the first to use this name in connection with a divorce-form typing business that only operates within one state. If it used its name locally and just filed a fictitious business name statement, Speedy Divorce Form would be entitled to protection only against other businesses operating in the same area because of the likelihood of consumer confusion. If Speedy Divorce Form were able to register its name as a trademark with the proper state agency, it might be able to prevent a rival business from using the same mark anywhere in that state. However, this would depend on the law of the particular state. The term might be viewed as too descriptive to gain even statewide protection.

If Speedy Divorce Form operated in at least two states, then it might be entitled to some national protection for the mark by registering it with the U.S. Patent and Trademark Office. Again, because this name is so descriptive, courts would be much less willing to protect it against use by others than if it were highly distinctive, such as, say, "Klingon Divorce Typing Service" or "White Rose Self-Help Bankruptcy Typing Service."

H. Summing Up: Names You Shouldn't Use

So far, we've covered factors you should try to incorporate into a business name—the degrees of distinctiveness and descriptiveness. We have also discussed why it's a good idea to identify your business in a way that prevents lawyers from claiming you are misleading the public into thinking you are a law office or that you provide legal advice or help. Now, let's summarize this information in a list of "don'ts." Remember, it's worth the time it takes to choose a name carefully, because if your business becomes a success, your name will be one of your most valuable assets, and you won't want to have to change it.

- Do not use a name that uses words like "law," "legal services," or "paralegal." (See Section A for other words to avoid.)

- Do not use the same name as an existing business that operates in your area.

- Do not use a name that can be easily confused with that used by any business in your area.

- Don't use a name other than your own (or, if you are incorporated, other than the name your corporation is registered under) without first filing a fictitious name statement (in most states). Contact your county clerk's office for information.

- If you plan to incorporate, don't use a name without first checking with your state's corporation commissioner or secretary of state. If the state finds your name is the same or confusingly similar to one already used by another corporation, you will probably be required to choose another.

- Do not use the name of a large national corporation, even if incorporated in another state.

- Do not use a name that could easily be confused with a trademark that you have reason to believe is federally registered (you can tell by the "®" that accompanies the mark) or registered in your state.

- Don't forget to register your name with your state's trademark office or, if you will use it across state lines, with the Federal Patent and Trademark Office.

For additional information about trademark law and how to register your name with the patent and trademark office, see the book, *Trademark: Legal Care for Your Business & Product Name*, by Stephen Elias and Rich Stim (Nolo). ■

CHAPTER

6

Establishing an Office

P eople have successfully begun businesses from all sorts of places. For some businesses *location* is very important, but for others it may be a lot less important, and for virtual businesses (such as those run 100% from an Internet site) location may be irrelevant. The two basic issues to consider when choosing the location for your independent paralegal business are the economics of the location and zoning laws related to your business operation. Although we believe on balance that it's usually easiest to rent a modest office as opposed to operating from your living space, this may not be always practical. There is nothing wrong with starting small, even if this means operating out of a spare bedroom or converted garage—unless you are in an area in which zoning laws prohibit home-based businesses that involve customer visits. This chapter will help you figure out how to find a suitable location that meets the needs of your independent paralegal business and complies with your state and local laws and regulations.

A. Should You Open a Home-Based Independent Paralegal Business?

It may sound wonderful to save time and money if you just set up your independent paralegal business in your home. However, the savings from not paying commercial rent or commuting cost may not be enough to offset the requirements that affect the operation of an independent paralegal business. In addition, legal and paralegal services usually are not considered "home occupations" and may be prevented from operating in a residence altogether. There are zoning enforcement authorities (usually the Planning or Building Department) in a few places that don't allow home businesses of any kind. You should check locally to find out what your rules are.

If your independent paralegal business can be declared a "home occupation," the next step is to find out what the zoning requirements are for such businesses in your city and county. You will want to know what your home-office restrictions are, and what permits and fees are required. Home office restrictions commonly include:

- the employees must be residents of the home
- the business may not use more than one room in the home

- the business may not use space outside the main home structure (for instance, no business activities in the garage)
- the business must only be conducted between 8 a.m. and 5 p.m. Monday through Friday
- no business signs may be visible outside the home, and
- no customers are allowed on the premises (this is the most troublesome one).

Home occupation permit fees commonly range from $1 to $25 per year in some places in California and $750 in parts of New York. Other places have a zoning clearance fee of $10 or more. Check with your zoning agency for further information. Contact any other appropriate city or county department for other permits or registration requirements.

If you plan to operate out of your home, here are a few suggestions that should go far towards reassuring your customers that you run a quality business:

- Set up a defined work area separate from your living space. A good-sized room is best, but a corner of a larger room will do in a pinch if it is carefully screened or partitioned. Furnish your workspace like an office and, if possible, provide a small waiting area for customers should appointments overlap. You will need a desk, a couple of sturdy chairs for customers (so you don't have to bring one in from the kitchen), a file cabinet, computer (or typewriter), and standard office supplies. It will help greatly if you can also afford a small photocopier and a fax machine.
- If you live with others, absolutely insist that they respect this work area. This not only means that it's kept free of personal belongings, but that it's quiet and private when you are working with customers.
- See customers only by appointment. When you talk to them by phone to make an appointment, inform them you operate from a home environment so they won't be surprised when they arrive. Some home-based independent paralegals often add that they do this in order to keep overhead, and therefore prices, down.

- Establish a business phone with an answering machine—preferably one that lets a caller talk for as long as he wants. Having a separate line allows you to instantly distinguish between business and personal calls. Answer your office phone only during working hours and always state your business name.
- If your situation allows, establish a separate business entrance.
- Have your office and waiting area reflect what you do. Displaying framed copies of newspaper articles about you and your business is one way to do this. For example, display newspaper articles about self-help law clinics on your wall, or display a collection of self-help law materials. Also, as discussed in Chapter 3, you should provide customers with printed information making it clear that they are representing themselves and that you are not an attorney. A description of your basic self-help philosophy would also be helpful. Here is an edited version of one used by the Superior California Legal Clinic:

DIVORCE HELP

DO YOU NEED LEGAL ASSISTANCE
OR A NONLAWYER TYPING SERVICE?

An alternative to hiring a lawyer to do your divorce is to "do it yourself." SUPERIOR CALIFORNIA LEGAL CLINIC'S trained nonlawyer personnel will help you prepare all forms necessary to do your own divorce.

- You can handle your own legal form preparation needs with a little help from us.
- Many people already know the basic information necessary to obtain their own divorce or accomplish other basic legal procedures. What they don't know is how to complete the necessary forms.
- Our service is based on the idea that everyone should have the opportunity to handle their own case efficiently, simply, and at an affordable price.

CAUTION:

Representing yourself can work well for routine uncontested actions. However, if you expect a legal battle, you should not do your own divorce without attorney representation or assistance.

- If you live with others, discuss your needs in detail and make sure they are supportive of your home business. If your family or housemates have doubts about your enterprise, don't embark on it until all their concerns have been positively resolved. For example, if your spouse is concerned about how you will cope with your customer's children or about customers who smoke, or perhaps about who will care for your own child while you are interviewing customers, don't brush these worries aside. Your business may be negatively affected if you don't come up with mutually acceptable solutions to these problems.
- Consider the needs of neighbors. In many areas where home-based businesses are technically illegal, municipal officials won't hassle you unless a complaint is filed. This usually occurs because neigh-

bors are angered over losing their parking space or fearful because they don't know why so many people are coming and going. A little communication (for example, "I type divorces, I don't deal drugs") and courtesy can work wonders. For example, if you have a driveway, keep your own car in the garage and ask customers to park in your driveway rather than in front of your neighbors' homes.

GOOD INFORMATION ABOUT RUNNING A HOME-BASED BUSINESS

For more information about running a business from your home, we recommend the following books:

- *Working From Home*, by Paul and Sarah Edwards (Jeremy Tarcher): This book offers a good overview and sound advice about living and working under the same roof. We particularly like the discussions on how to keep your personal and business lives separate and avoid loneliness.
- *The Home Office: How to Set Up and Use Efficient Personal Workspace in the Computer Age*, by Mark Alvar (Goodwood Press): As the subtitle indicates, this book focuses on the physical details of establishing a home office. Issues covered include choosing a suitable space, selecting furniture, and buying office equipment—including computer hardware and software.
- The Internet is a great place to find information about running a home business. Visit www.nolo.com. Go to the Small Business section and check out Nolo's collection of articles, resources, and links to other websites.

Despite the advantages of a home-based business, all independent paralegals we know who started this way eventually moved to a formal office setting. Many, of course, were glad they started at home, because it allowed them both to hide their existence from organized lawyerdom and test the financial waters of their new business without feeling that they were betting their whole economic future on its immediate success. Indeed, many held on to their jobs until their independent paralegal business (operated from home mostly during evening hours and on weekends) started generating enough money to allow it to be a full-time occupation.

People's reasons for eventually moving their business to a commercial office space vary, but an important one is often the realization that the cost of office space is significantly less than that for living space. The fact that it was initially cheaper to start at home (you already own or rent it), becomes less important as your business expands and you require more room. Then it usually becomes cheaper to find commercial office space, as opposed to getting a bigger living/work space.

Wanting to get away from living with a business is another important reason why many home-based IPs eventually move to an office setting. Several paralegals mentioned that it's one thing to share hearth and home with a little start-up business, but quite another—and much less desirable—to cohabit with a growing one.

Finally, some IPs report that the patience and support of family members, housemates, and neighbors can eventually wear thin. The fact that they are willing to cooperate with your needs for a few months or years while you are getting started doesn't mean they will do it forever.

B. Running an IP Business in a Commercial Space

If you do decide to operate from a commercial space, you have some choices to make. One option is to rent an office and put your name on the door. Another is to share space with an established business. Doing this can be a sensible halfway measure between moving your business out of your living space and opening your own office. This can be particularly desirable if you are on a tight budget, since sharing a business space costs a lot less than opening your own office.

It's not hard to find space to share. All sorts of businesses, including real estate and insurance agencies, business consultants, financial planners, and tax preparers, commonly have extra room. For a modest monthly rental, you can often arrange to put your desk, computer, or typewriter in a partitioned-off corner of a big office, or better yet, a small separate room. A big advantage to this sort of arrangement is that you gain the respectability an existing business provides without either the trouble or expense of renting your own place.

Another space-sharing alternative is to work out a cooperative arrangement with a nonprofit or other group that works in the same field that you do. For example, in exchange for free or low-cost space at a local women's organization, you might, in addition to typing divorces for a reasonable fee, agree to help low-income women prepare the paperwork for restraining orders for free. Similarly, if you want to do work for landlords, you might discuss your space needs with the county apartment house owners' association. In exchange for your offering members your services at a discounted fee, the association might be willing to provide you with free or low-rent space. (We discuss in more detail how IPs can work with nonprofits in Chapter 13.)

Sooner or later, however, you'll probably want to rent your own office space. There are loads of different types of office settings available, many of which are discussed in our interviews with Glynda Dixon, Robin Smith, and Jolene Jacobs in the Appendix. Here are some considerations about locating an IP business:

• You don't need or want a fancy office in a posh location, so it's fine to keep your rent budget relatively low.

- Location is important, but not nearly as critical as it can be to a retail store or restaurant. Most of your customers will be referred to you by others, so any easy-to-reach location will work. There is no need to locate in a high-rent district or an area with lots of pedestrian traffic.
- Access is important. Always ask yourself where customers will park. Also, check out public transit routes. Yours is not an affluent clientele and you'll do better if you're near a bus stop.
- Safety is important. Don't locate in an area people will think twice about coming to. Your customers will be working folks, many of whom will want to come by in the evening. If your neighborhood is scary after dark, a good number of people won't come.
- Older but still respectable business buildings like those recently abandoned by lawyers and doctors for fancy new office complexes are often a good choice, especially if they're located near courts and other city services. (See Glynda Dixon's interview.)
- Older shopping centers and strip malls often have offices upstairs, over the shops, that are available at very reasonable rates. Since these areas are usually located on busy streets, have parking lots, and are near public transportation, they can be a good choice.

In addition to location, you will need to think about how much space you'll need. It's our experience that working out of one room is difficult. Customers who are being interviewed or filling out paperwork appreciate a private area away from your reception space, which will often double as a child's play area. So rent at least two small offices, or a room big enough to be divided. If you can afford it, renting three work areas is even better: one for reception, one for customer interviews, and one for form preparation. We recommend a separate area for form preparation, not only because your computer, typewriter, photocopy, and fax machines take up space, but because you will want easy access to them at all times, something that may be difficult if interviews are being conducted in the same location.

C.   Negotiating a Good Lease or Rental Agreement

When you rent an office, you not only must worry about the amount of rent and the location and size of the space, you also must negotiate a lease or month-to-month rental agreement. Do you want to try and lock in a space for years or choose the shortest time period possible? There are no right answers—it depends on how established your business is, how fast it is growing, and whether you are likely to be challenged by organized lawyerdom, among a host of other factors. Here are some general, and at times conflicting, factors you will want to consider:

• Renting office space is easy in areas where the market is glutted. This means there is little need to lease a particular space for a long time. In these areas, in the unlikely event you are asked by the landlord to move, there will be a wide choice of other available locations.

• When you first open, you'll be doing many things to get your business known in the community. One of these will be to inform people where you are located. It follows, then, that assuming it turns out you have picked a good location, you will want to stay put for a while. If you do, you may want the security that comes with a long-term lease.

• If your business prospers, you may want more (or perhaps better-located) space. Unless it's likely to be available at your first location, this means you won't want a long lease that will make it difficult or expensive for you to move.

Fortunately, there is a way to at least partially resolve the conflict between wanting the security of knowing you can stay put and the freedom to move on. This involves renting an office space for a relatively short period with an option to renew for a longer period. For example, you might lease two rooms in a business building for six months or a year, with an option to renew at the end of the tenth month for an additional year or two at a pre-established rental amount. This allows you to see how things work out and make your decision accordingly. Because granting you an option potentially ties up a landlord's property, she may ask you for an extra payment in exchange.

As long as the amount is modest, this request is reasonable and you may want to go along. But suppose a landlord refuses to consider a short lease period with an option to renew and demands a lease for two or three years? Unless your business is well-established and you are absolutely sure you will stay there for that period, just say "no."

For more information about commercial leasing, you can consult *Leasing Space for Your Small Business*, by Janet Portman and Fred Steingold (Nolo).

D. Running a Small Business on the Internet

Here we provide a brief discussion of what running your business over the Internet might entail. Chances are you are already familiar with the Internet and the point-and-click interface known as the World Wide Web. But in case you aren't, in Chapter 11 we provide a brief overview of the Internet and what it means for independent paralegals.

It will come as no surprise that the Internet is rapidly becoming the location of choice for many businesses, especially those that are service oriented. It's certainly far easier, and often cheaper, to establish a site on the World Wide Web than it is to find and maintain office space in the physical realm. A website can explain what the business does, who its owners and operators are, the prices it charges, and its methods for delivering its services, all in an appealing way. Documents can be emailed to and from the site, questionnaires can be downloaded or even filled out online, legal materials can be included on the site or provided through a series of links to other sites. The fact is, many small businesses show great promise of making money on the Internet. But for most, it ain't happened yet, and the dot.com bust in recent years provides a cautionary tale.

Unlike some other types of service providers, independent paralegals may find that the Web is not a good substitute for an actual office. One of the most important roles of the independent paralegal is to provide a friendly human face to folks who are under great stress, especially when a divorce is involved. You may not get much business if your customers can't visit you in person.

Also, despite a current dramatic increase in folks hooking up to the Web, these folks may not be the same as your customer base. It may be that the customer base traditionally served by the independent paralegal (folks at the lower end of the income spectrum) will be the last to join the Internet revolution and will therefore not be able to find you on your spiffy new website.

Of course, as we mention in Chapter 11, where we go into the Internet in more detail, you might still want to have a website even if your primary business is conducted in real space. This is because the Internet is rapidly taking the place of the Yellow Pages as a method for consumers to locate desired services. Just as most independent paralegals find advertising in the Yellow Pages irresistible, so too will most IPs want their business to pop up when somebody enters "paralegal or typing service" into an Internet search engine.

As with other subjects, a picture is worth a thousand words. If you are already connected to the Internet, get out there and see how other IPs are using the Web. Use your favorite search engine to call up the electronic "Yellow Pages" for your area, enter the term "paralegals" in the search engine box, and visit the paralegal services that have websites (usually grouped near the top of the listing).

For more information on doing business on the Web, see *How to Get Your Business on the Web: A Legal Guide to E-Commerce*, by Fred Steingold (Nolo).

1. What's Involved in Setting Up a Business on the World Wide Web?

First, as a practical matter, you need to get attached to the Internet. You can do this through any number of Internet Service Providers (ISPs). In most instances, you will want your ISP to also host your Internet site. Hosting a site means that the site "lives" on the ISP's computer (called a server). The ISP's staff usually will work with you to get your site up and running, and provide some level of tech support for you to maintain it.

Second, you need to choose a name for your site. For more on this, see Chapter 5, Part G2.

Next, you register your domain name with a domain name registrar. The domain name typically costs $35 per year, although you can get a discount if you register for more than one year.

Now that you have the domain name, you'll need to create a website. While this is something that you can do yourself, many folks prefer to spend some money to have it done by someone else. Depending on how elaborate and "professional" you want your site to be, this can cost you from several hundreds to several thousands of dollars. If you want to do true commerce on your website, such as taking credit card orders, you'll need to spend even more. On the other hand, if you are willing to have your website serve only as a brochure, the functional equivalent of the Yellow Pages, you can get up and running with very little expense. For legal and practical information about doing business on the Web, see *How to Get Your Business on the Web: A Legal Guide to E-Commerce*, by Fred Steingold (Nolo).

Fortunately or unfortunately, a large number of website creation services are now trolling for potential customers. The chances are great that shortly after you register your domain name you'll be bombarded with solicitations for your business. As with all business-creation services, you'll need to do some comparative shopping. And before you lay out a lot of money, we suggest you get a good book (there are dozens) and see what's involved. You may decide to do it yourself after all.

E. Good Information on Small Business Operations

This book is primarily about how to run an independent paralegal business, not about small business skills generally. Just the same, when your thoughts turn to establishing an office, it's a good time to consider lots of other details of running a quality small business. Some of these are fairly mundane, such as getting a business license, buying appropriate equipment, and establishing a good bookkeeping system. Others are more complicated, such as creating realistic financial projections and a sound marketing plan.

There are several excellent books on how to accomplish these (and many more) small business tasks. We highly recommend the following:

- *Legal Guide for Starting & Running a Small Business*, by Fred S. Steingold (Nolo). The legal ins and outs that every business owner needs to know to establish and run a small business. Topics include: deciding whether to form a sole proprietorship, partnership, or corporation; buying a franchise or existing business; negotiating a favorable lease; hiring and firing employees; working with independent contractors; creating good contracts; and resolving business disputes.

- *The Small Business Start-Up Kit* and *The Small Business Start-Up Kit for California*, both by Peri Pakroo (Nolo). These well-written and organized books take you through the legal basics of starting a business—either in California or in another state. The books cover the issues involved in choosing a name, getting an office, obtaining permits, and setting up the proper tax and employee records.

- *Small Time Operator*, by Bernard Kamoroff (Bell Springs Publishing). This handy guide, which is updated yearly, has been popular for over 20 years for excellent reasons. It gives you essential information about the paperwork you'll have to deal with, including keeping books, paying taxes, becoming an employer, etc. The book also contains excellent information on how to use computers and other electronic equipment in your business. In fact, it is so detailed, it even tells you the type of calculator to buy. If you never buy another business book, buy this one.

- *How to Write a Business Plan*, by Mike McKeever (Nolo). This easy-to-use guide shows you how to raise money for your new business, including tips on how to arrange loans from both family members and conventional lenders. As part of doing this, it helps you prepare a detailed financial plan for your proposed business. In my experience, doing this may demonstrate that even using your best-case assumptions, your proposed business won't produce the financial rewards you expect. In short, this book not only will help you prepare to borrow money to get a business started, it gives you the financial tools necessary to assess your business idea realistically.

- *Honest Business*, by Michael Phillips and Salli Rasberry (Random House). This book might as well be entitled, Zen and the Art of Small Business Success. Although it's now a few years old, this remarkable book, which focuses on the personal and psychological qualities it takes to succeed in a small business, fills a niche occupied by no other. Much of Phillips's and Rasberry's advice stands conventional small business wisdom on its head. For example, they explain why having plenty of capital can be much worse for a new business person than not having enough.

- *Marketing Without Advertising*, by Michael Phillips and Salli Rasberry (Nolo). The same authors demolish the myth of advertising effectiveness and outline practical alternative ways for a small business to market its products and services. As we further develop in Chapter 10, creating a marketing plan that does not rely on expensive advertising is usually a key to success as an independent paralegal.

- *Running a One-Person Business*, by Whitmyer, Rasberry & Phillips (Ten Speed Press). A thoughtful book that covers the nuts and bolts: finances, time management, marketing, and more, plus interviews with successful entrepreneurs.

The Internet is loaded with information about small business operations. Visit Nolo's site at www.nolo.com. There you will find dozens of informative articles, FAQs, and helpful links to other small business sites on the Internet. ■

CHAPTER

7

How to Establish a Good Relationship
With Lawyers, Mediators, and Judges

There is no need to elaborate on the fact that organized lawyerdom has done a miserable job of providing routine legal services at a reasonable price to the American public, and that this is one reason for widespread public frustration with the profession. Indeed, many paralegals enter the legal form preparation business at least in part because of their own hostile feelings toward lawyers. Even though antipathy to the legal profession by IPs is reasonable, especially when you consider you must compete with a group that commonly wants to put you in jail, paradoxically, it is often to the advantage of both you and your customers that you work closely with one or more lawyers.

A. Working With Lawyers

Think of it this way—should you ever need to ask for help or advice, wouldn't it be nice to have access to a sympathetic legal expert supportive of the idea of self-help law and your role in it? And wouldn't it be great to be able to refer customers who need legal expertise you can't safely provide to a lawyer who is both reasonably priced and competent? And, while we are playing a fantasy game, wouldn't it also be terrific to know one or more lawyers willing to go to bat for you and your business should their less flexible brethren accuse you of unauthorized practice?

If your answer to any one of these questions is "yes," you're ready for the big question: "How do you find supportive lawyers, or at least one of them?"

Before we suggest ways to do this, a few more words about lawyers are appropriate. Throughout most of this book, we have pictured organized lawyerdom as a monolithic group almost universally hostile to the idea of nonlawyer competition. While viewing the legal profession as a monolith serves to focus your attention on survival techniques, it is also an oversimplification.

If, instead of looking at the entire legal profession with what amounts to a wide-angle camera lens, you instead employ a zoom lens to focus on individuals, you will immediately see that lawyers don't have a monolithic view of anything—even their own right to dominate the delivery of legal services. Put another way, many individual lawyers understand that their profession is out of touch with the legal needs of millions of ordinary Americans and are embarrassed by it. While the traditional view that lawyers should preserve their monopoly at all costs still dominates many state and local bar associations and county courthouses, even in these places, the notion that independent paralegals should be squelched under all circumstances is slowly receding. For instance, throughout the book, we refer to the Arizona, California, and Florida models of IP services, and also to the increasing number of states that are allowing nonlawyers to handle real estate closings without a lawyer. And once you get away from lawyers associated with the delivery of personal legal services and instead canvass those who work for big firms and public agencies, you'll find a good number who are actually supportive of efforts to make high-quality, low-cost legal form preparation services widely available. The fact that not all lawyers buy into the traditional views of organized lawyerdom should not be surprising when you consider that one-third of American lawyers have been admitted to practice in the last decade. And of course, it's also true that many of these younger lawyers are anxious to build up their businesses and so are open to working with IPs who will be a good source of referrals.

If you still doubt that fair-minded lawyers exist, consider the views of Bob Anderson, an attorney in Berkeley, California, who operated a divorce typing service as a paralegal prior to becoming an attorney:

While running the Divorce Center, I developed a list of friendly attorneys for advice and referral (whenever I made a referral I attempted to name at least two attorneys, so that the customer could make a choice). A number of positive effects flowed from this relationship as far as I was concerned. First, by referring questions to attorneys I greatly reduced the risk of my practicing law without a license. Second, I provided a better service to the customer in that s/he had questions answered that were beyond my knowledge. And third, I was able to refer people who called but could not use a self-help service for one reason or another to attorneys who were less likely to rip them off, but who would provide the required service. Now, as an attorney, I refer qualified cases to self-help typing centers. I get satisfaction from seeing that the self-help movement is continuing because (especially in California divorces) there is increasing recognition among us (attorneys) that we cannot properly service the typical self-help case because of the dollars involved versus the fees we have to charge.

Sylvia Cherry, a highly skilled IP who works in San Mateo, California, reports she works regularly with two lawyers—one who specializes in bankruptcy and the other divorce. She has gotten them to agree to see people she refers for a very reasonable fixed fee in the $50–$100 range for a half-hour consultation. When a customer has a question Sylvia can't answer or a problem she knows involves serious legal consequences—for example, dividing a valuable piece of real estate as part of a divorce—Sylvia refers the customer to the appropriate lawyer.

"But I don't just send a person over with a bunch of vague questions," Sylvia emphasizes. "I help my customer understand exactly what she needs to know to make good decisions. Then I have her write the key questions down. Following this approach, the lawyer's time isn't wasted and my customer really does come back with the answers she needs, so that I can finish preparing the paperwork. It's a great system, and my customers get the exact legal help they need at a reasonable price and I avoid the unauthorized practice of law."

B. How to Find Supportive Lawyers

Locating a lawyer or lawyers who will support what you are doing can also be a huge help when it comes to dealing with (or fending off) those who don't. Remarkably, if even one or two lawyers in your community know what you are about and approve your work, you are less likely to be prosecuted. Indeed, just one friendly lawyer may even be able to stop a prosecution that is in the works. We have seen this happen on at least three occasions. In each instance, after either one or several local attorneys quietly let it be known that they would go to bat for a particular independent paralegal who was threatened with an unauthorized practice charge, the planned prosecution was dropped. How can one, two, or even a small group of lawyers stop organized lawyerdom so easily? Because prosecutors know they are less likely to win the battle for public opinion if local lawyers are willing to take the witness stand or make public statements saying that the particular independent paralegal is not practicing law and is an asset to the community.

In addition to making contact with sympathetic lawyers for self-preservation reasons, you will also benefit from an alliance with at least one lawyer familiar with the legal subject or subjects you deal with, for a few reasons. First, if you pick a truly experienced lawyer, this person will probably know more than you do about the legal paperwork you are preparing. If you can occasionally call this person for advice when you face a difficult problem, it will be a big help.

Second, a relationship with a local lawyer will mean you have someone to whom you can refer customers who need formal legal advice, or whose problem changes from uncontested to contested before your horrified eyes. If you don't have the ability to do this, you may be tempted to try to help your customer solve a problem that you are not equipped or trained to deal with. Aside from the risk of being charged with the unauthorized practice of law, you also assume the risk (to your customers, at least) of giving bad or incomplete advice.

But, suppose you are just starting your business in a section of America where most lawyers are still maniacal about defending their monopoly. How do you find lawyer allies without making yourself so visible to organized lawyerdom that you do yourself more harm than good? There is no one right way to do this, but here are some hints. Please realize that like most general rules, each of these has its exceptions, and it will be up to you to apply them creatively to your situation:

- Avoid attorneys closely associated with local bar associations and bar referral panels. They tend to attract just the sort of small office traditionalists who will feel most threatened by your business and will want to close you down.
- Attorneys with strong pro-consumer records are good people to feel out. Also, lawyers who work in the emerging field of mediation often tend to be predisposed to helping people help themselves.
- Lawyers in private practice who have worked for federally funded legal services (often called "legal aid") programs can also be good

bets, as they have already worked in a clinic-like context where the same sorts of legal tasks you handle are accomplished by parale- gals. In addition, many lawyers who are attracted by legal aid work in the first place are sympathetic to the needs of the legally underserved. Current legal services intake workers, secretaries, and paralegals should be able to suggest some likely former legal ser- vices lawyers.

- Do not assume that a progressive political stance on social issues, such as the environment, women's rights, minority hiring, or disar- mament means a lawyer will be sympathetic with what you are doing. To the contrary, in our experience, it is often people who are fairly conservative politically who are the most pro-self-help law. This isn't so surprising when you realize that many conserva- tives take seriously the traditional right of every American to have good access to the legal system at a reasonable cost. Paradoxically, many personal injury, criminal defense, and other lawyers who often favor all sorts of reforms for society typically oppose long- needed legal reforms such as adopting no-fault automobile insur- ance, abolishing probate, and licensing independent paralegals. They fear change in these areas because it will negatively affect their monopoly over the legal system and, as a result, the girth of their wallets. Again, the point is, do not bare your soul to a lawyer just because you respect the stance that person took on an unrelated social issue.

- Personal friends and acquaintances (or, if necessary, friends of friends) can be a good source of possibly helpful lawyers. If you worked previously at a court clerk's office, or a local law firm, you probably know at least a few lawyers you respect. If you don't have these contacts, think about whether you know anyone whose judgment you trust who can suggest lawyers who are likely to be sympathetic.

In an effort to create a network of lawyer supporters, start by locating one lawyer to whom you can refer customers with problems more complicated than you can handle. As a significant percentage of almost one million lawyers in the U.S. are underemployed, there are plenty of likely candidates. Some of these lawyers are likely to be interested in (and often threatened by) the growth of the self-help law movement and want to get in on the action. One way for a lawyer to do this is to set up a paralegal division within their own office; another is to work closely with one or more self-help legal typing services.

When you locate someone who you think is a potential supporter, approach her carefully. Start by soliciting her general views on the desirability of opening up the legal system to more participation by nonlawyers. If they are hostile or extremely worried, back off. If they express an openness to the independent paralegal movement, but seem tentative, go slowly and don't presume too much at the start. Always remember that all lawyers, even your friends, have undergone a remarkably homogeneous educational experience that has repeatedly emphasized the fact that only lawyers are competent to practice law. This is a hard burden for even the most enlightened lawyer to completely put down, and you are likely to find that even a genuinely supportive lawyer will experience moments when he doubts whether your profession should exist. Try to anticipate this and help your lawyer friend come to terms with and conquer these occasional attacks of professional paranoia. No matter how highly she was recommended, or how much you respect her for other reasons, go slowly when it comes to disclosing what you are doing or plan to do. Again, if you are greeted with hostility, or even a lot of obvious nervousness, don't argue—back off quickly.

Assuming the lawyer seems genuinely open to working with you, ask if it will be okay if you occasionally refer customers who wish to handle their own legal affairs, but need some legal advice as part of doing so. If the lawyer wants to know more about your business, be prepared to demonstrate that you really run a self-help legal typing service and do not provide legal advice. (The best way to do this is to follow the techniques we discuss in Chapter 3.)

Again, assuming all signs are go, send over a few people. Check back with your customers to find out how they were treated. If you find they got good service at a fair price, try to gradually establish a closer relationship with the lawyer. The best way to do this is to make yourself valuable to the lawyer by continuing to refer appropriate customers to his office. As the lawyer comes to see that you are a responsible business producer, you can begin to discuss some of your needs. Over time, you will want to work out an informal understanding with the lawyer that in exchange for the business you produce, he will answer your occasional questions and go to bat for you if you are accused of practicing law without a license.

In Bakersfield, California, a group of local independent paralegals has taken this sort of relationship a step further. At the request of Virginia Simons and other area IPs, a number of local lawyers who were worried that IPs may not always know enough about the law to do a good job volunteered their time to help train independent paralegals on how to type divorce and bankruptcy forms. One reason why this cooperative relationship has developed is that lawyers have begun to see that IPs, by preparing legal paperwork for working- and lower-middle-class people but referring more complicated legal work to lawyers, are actually creating new clients. (The total law business pie in Bakersfield is expanding.) One big reason for this phenomenon is that, traditionally, many working-class consumers simply don't know any lawyers and, in some instances, are even afraid of them. The result has been that lots of serious legal problems have been ignored. But now that affordable, accessible IPs are in the picture, the person with a legal problem calls them first and, if appropriate, is referred to a lawyer who does that type of work at a reasonable fee. (See Virginia Simons interview in the Appendix.)

C.   Make a Lawyer Your "Partner"

So far, we have assumed that you want to open your own business and relate to lawyers only as you need them. We have discussed the fact that operating independently makes you vulnerable to the charge that you are practicing law without a license. For some readers, beginning a new business (which is never easy), at the same time that you may be attacked by hostile lawyers, will be too much to cope with.

One way to reduce the fear that you will be prosecuted for unauthorized practice is to work directly for a lawyer as a freelance paralegal. Another is to have a lawyer work very closely with your business. In other words, instead of working for a lawyer, encourage a lawyer to work with you. Before you dismiss this idea as silly, consider the fact that bill collectors have used this approach for years, often working with one lawyer in a stable long-term relationship that in all but name amounts to a shared business. Major portions of the medical profession also seem to be heading in this direction with business people increasingly owning hospitals, clinics, and emergency treatment facilities, and hiring doctors and other professional care providers to work for them.

More to the point, we know of several divorce and landlord eviction services run by independent paralegals who have a lawyer directly associated with their practice. In exchange for having the lawyer available to provide reasonably priced legal advice to the paralegal's customers when necessary, the independent paralegal typically refers all customers with contested cases and legal questions to the lawyer. Again, the advantage to this sort of arrangement to the lawyer, the paralegal, and the customer is obvious.

The desirability of establishing an independent paralegal business that works very closely with a lawyer must, of course, be weighed against the fact that having a lawyer closely associated with your business may negatively affect the way you work. Remember, one reason why independent paralegal services are so popular is that they allow customers the right to simplify their legal problems. Lawyers, of course, commonly do the opposite, burdening even the most routine legal tasks with layers of often unneeded complexity—a process that, in the eyes of many legal reformers, all too often seems to continue exactly as long as the client's money holds out. In short, if you have a lawyer associated with your operation, you want to be sure that her lawyerly tendency toward high-cost obfuscation doesn't end up affecting your business in a negative way.

Another potential problem for independent paralegals and lawyers who work closely together are state laws and state supreme court opinions that state that every business offering legal services to the public must be owned and controlled exclusively by lawyers. Specifically, these statutes make it illegal for nonlawyers to participate in the ownership of a law practice (Washington, DC, and North Dakota are limited exceptions) or to split legal fees with lawyers. In 1999, a select committee of the American Bar Association studied this issue of "multidisciplinary practice" (widely known as MDP) and recommended a loosening of the traditional restrictions on fee sharing among lawyers and nonlawyer. However, the ABA as a whole has rejected the recommendation, at least for now.

In the long run, these laws may well be struck down as being illegal restraints of trade under the Sherman Antitrust Act, but as this edition goes to press, they are still firmly on the books. Fortunately, if you engage in a little creative business organization, they shouldn't prevent you from working closely with a lawyer. One good approach, which in fact is mandatory in most states, is to keep the two businesses structurally separate. This not only means you should not formally hire the lawyer or split fees, but that each business should be an independent legal entity (that is, if you occupy the same office, put both names on the door, get separate business licenses and don't treat the lawyer as an employee or independent contractor). If a customer uses the services of both you and the lawyer, she should pay with separate checks. Yes, when an IP and a lawyer work closely together on a regular basis, respecting this somewhat artificial business division can be cumbersome, but if you're investigated by organized lawyerdom, you'll both be glad you took the trouble.

D. Working With Mediators

In some legal areas, a certain percentage of an independent paralegal's customers are likely to have, or develop, a dispute about at least one issue with another party. Divorce is the most obvious, where arguments over property division, support, child custody, and visitation are fairly common.

If you are typing paperwork for a divorce or another domestic action, such as a stepparent adoption, and your customer tells you that he and his former mate are having a serious dispute about a specific matter, your best bet is to encourage them to see a mediator.

Mediation is a process by which a third party (the mediator) helps people with a dispute arrive at their own solutions. Precisely because it is non-coercive—the mediator, unlike a judge or arbitrator, has no power to impose a decision—mediation often works brilliantly to settle domestic disputes. The idea is for you to refer the disputing couple to the mediator, have them work out their dispute and write down the agreed-upon compromise, and then have your customer return to your office to complete the other paperwork.

What type of mediator should you work with? Here are some thoughts:

- Most of your customers will be on a tight budget. You'll need to find a mediator who charges a reasonable fee (often in the range of $75 per hour) and is result-oriented. A mediator who expects to help customers probe their psyches for many hours, at $200 per hour, may be fine for the BMW set, but would not be a good choice for most of your customers.

- In many states, mediated agreements to divide property as part of a divorce can be submitted directly to a court as part of the divorce paperwork you type. If so, you will want to work with a mediator who knows how to prepare the necessary forms.

- This raises the question of whether the mediator should be a lawyer. Our answer—perhaps surprisingly— is not necessarily. Although lawyer mediators will normally be adept at preparing necessary paperwork, they often aren't able to shed their "lawyer in control" attitudes and truly let the parties arrive at their own solutions. In addition, many charge more than most of your customers will be able to afford. In our experience, nonlawyer mediators, whose fees are often more modest, are typically more open to allowing disputants to find their own solutions.

For more on how divorce mediation works, see *Using Divorce Mediation,* by attorney-mediator Katherine E. Stoner (Nolo).

E.   Working With the Courts

In some parts of America, court clerks and judges are implacably opposed to the self-help law movement and, by logical extension, to IPs. However, in many states, including large portions of Arizona, California, Florida, Maryland, and Vermont, the legal profession's outright hostility is beginning to be replaced by grudging acceptance and, in some instances, guarded support for independent paralegals. For example, in Napa, California, Sharon Goetting, who formerly prepared forms for divorces, guardianships, stepparent adoptions, and child support and custody modification orders, was instrumental in getting the courts to hand out a free referral publication informing the public about the existence of IP services.

Whether judges and court clerks are hostile or friendly, you may as well get used to the idea that you'll have to work fairly closely with them. Even if you never set foot in the courthouse, they will quickly come to recognize your paperwork, even though your name appears nowhere on it. Given this, we recommend that you try to form as positive a relationship as possible with key people at the courthouse. Here are some suggestions:

• Court clerks are often burdened by nonlawyers (and more often than you would guess, lawyers) filing incorrect and incomplete paperwork. Assuming that you really do know what you are doing, the papers your customers file will likely come as a welcome relief. This may result in your getting positive feedback from a court clerk. If so, use this as an opportunity to better introduce yourself. Make it clear that you only type paperwork and don't practice law. Then ask the clerk if she can suggest ways your work can be improved. One opportunity for this type of contact to take place is at the filing window, assuming, of course, you occasionally file paperwork your-self. In fact, in many communities, contacts at the filing window have led to such a positive independent paralegal-court clerk rela-tionship, that the clerk actually starts referring customers to the IP.

• If possible, get to know one or more local judges, who often re-view your paperwork. Sometimes this can be done through a civic organization or, if the judge must run for reelection, as part of her campaign. In other instances, a judge who is genuinely concerned about legal access for a particular group, such as single mothers, older people, or minorities, may be willing to counsel you on ways to improve your work. If you are a member of an IP association, consider asking the judge to meet with your group. (See Glynda Dixon's and Rose Palmer's interviews in the Appendix.) Obviously, in all meetings with judges it pays for IPs to go to great lengths to indicate that they do not give legal advice to customers. ■

CHAPTER 8

How to Run a Quality Business

A ll of the advice in this book about how to prosper as an independent paralegal assumes one crucial point: that you operate an excellent business. It is appropriate, then, to take a minute to touch on some basic business practices and procedures.

Before you even open your doors, it is essential that you devote some time to planning for your business. This includes:

- doing some market research
- becoming thoroughly familiar with how to prepare all the legal forms you will use in your business
- understanding how to run your business without engaging in the unauthorized practice of law (see Chapter 3 for a thorough discussion), and
- establishing a number of ordered business procedures to ensure that every customer receives quality error-free help.

A. Planning

As with any other business, proper planning is the key to starting a successful independent paralegal business. Planning lets you work things out on paper or computer screen first, and enables you to handle efficiently those things that are routine for your paralegal business. Experts claim that about 85% of your business activities can be anticipated; therefore, you can have a plan in place to deal with them. The remaining 15% are the crises, the things you just have to address personally or right away. Because most of your business is running itself instead of running you, you have the time you need to give the proper amount of attention to the things that really matter and that you can do best.

Most successful people follow these basic planning steps to reach their objectives. First, determine your personal goals. Knowing who you are and what you want is essential in establishing these goals and in running a successful independent paralegal business. It is less difficult to achieve your goals if they are your own, are clear, concrete, attainable within a specific time frame, and are written down.

After deciding that running your own independent paralegal business is compatible with your personal goals, the next step is to determine your business objectives. This process includes defining the legal needs you want to address in your business and deciding exactly how you're going to address them. This process will generate a series of essential tasks. For instance, if you decided to operate a will and living trust preparation service; you would need to:

- Find out who your potential customers are.
- Find out where they are located.
- Find out what services would most please them.
- Find out how to get them to purchase their wills or trusts from you.
- Determine where to locate your office.
- Determine how to furnish, supply, and equip the office.
- Decide on all the other little things necessary to set up your operation.

B. Market Research

Market research is, very simply, a way to get particular information from certain consumers and other available resources. In addition to it telling you where your potential customers are located, it helps you deal with such important issues and decisions such as:

- Where to locate your office
- What to name your business
- The characteristics of your potential customers
- What specialized services to offer your customers—your niche
- How best to offer services without unauthorized practice issues arising
- Approximately how many customers you may attract
- How much to charge for your services
- Who are your competitors, their customers, and the services they offer, and
- What type of advertising will attract your customers and not the District Attorney.

The amount of market research you conduct will depend on how many questions you need to answer and whether or not you plan to get financing for your paralegal business. Essentially, you will determine what percentage of your service area population needing IP services is likely to purchase such services from you, and at what price.

Most cities and counties require independent paralegal business operators to obtain various licenses or permits to show compliance with local regulations. As part of your market research you should check with your city and county offices before opening or expanding your independent paralegal services.

Good research can be costly, but failing to do it can be even more costly. You must do enough research to determine that there is a market for your services. The results of your market research are the best indicators of your potential for success.

The next steps are to write your business plan, implement and evaluate it, and make changes as needed. The Small Business Administration provides assistance in developing your business plan as well as making direct loans to small businesses. See your telephone directory for their local number, or visit them at www.sba.gov. Nolo has a host of resources that make business planning a snap. You can reach Nolo by calling 800-922-NOLO or at www.nolo.com.

C. Training

Some readers, who have worked for lawyers for years typing the same forms they plan to prepare as an independent paralegal, will already have the technical form-preparation expertise they need. However, many others will need basic training on how to prepare legal paperwork. Co-author Catherine Elias-Jermany discusses this in the interview that appears in the Appendix.

Prospective independent paralegals typically need both skills training and practical experience. Let's use the preparation of probate forms as an example. Your first step would be to study all available materials on the subject that are relevant to your state. For example, Nolo publishes *How to Probate an Estate in California*, by Julia Nissley, a very accessible and easy-to-use resource. However, in most states, you won't find very many how-to books written for nonlawyers, which means you will have to rely on materials aimed at lawyers. To locate these, you must become familiar with the resources that are specifically designed to show lawyers and paralegals how to probate an estate. These are published for all populous states. To locate the lawyer-oriented probate materials for your state, you would either visit a good-sized law library at a non-busy time and ask the reference librarian for a list of the materials she considers most helpful in the probate area or learn how to find equivalent materials on the Internet. (See Chapter 11 for more on using the Internet.)

Once you are up to speed on the basics of probate form preparation, you will need some real-world experience before you market your services to the public. Here are several ways to get it:

- Find a lawyer (usually a sole practitioner or member of a small firm) who needs help preparing probate paperwork but doesn't have a lot of money. In exchange for your freelance help at a very reasonable hourly fee (or maybe even initially as a volunteer), she can supply you with the necessary paperwork to learn on, as well as the guidance to make sure you do the work correctly.

- Study probate files at your local courthouse. Court records are public and your courthouse will have a procedure for checking out files. You'll want to closely examine a good-sized pile. Court clerks may be hostile if you explain exactly what your purpose is, so if anyone asks, it may be best to state that you're doing a research project and leave it at that. (Glynda Dixon discusses how she used this learning technique in her interview in the Appendix.)

- Work with, or for, a freelance paralegal who already prepares probate forms for lawyers. Your county paralegal association may be able to supply a list of freelancers working in your area. Obviously, you'll have to convince any freelance paralegal you call that your plans to sell form preparation services to the public will not compete with their business.

- Take a paralegal course that deals with probate specifically. The problem with this approach is that many paralegal schools won't allow you to take just the courses you are interested in but will want you to enroll for their entire program. Don't take no for an answer. Visit schools that offer hands-on probate form preparation courses and explore different ways you can get the help you need. At a minimum, find out what books and other materials the teacher uses and purchase them directly from the publisher.

- If possible, join local paralegal organizations, especially those that offer hands-on training. Some paralegal groups may not let you join unless you have already worked in the field or had formal training, but others aren't so fussy. There is no universal definition of the term "paralegal," and in many areas, self-taught people are accepted.

- Investigate to see if computer programs exist in your state to facilitate probate form preparation. Increasingly, legal publishers are publishing these for lawyers and freelance paralegals. These programs are designed to complete forms, not as a teaching tool, but there is a lot you can learn by working with such a program.

INDEPENDENT PARALEGAL TRAINING COURSES

A few community colleges, adult education schools and private business schools are beginning to offer legal form preparation courses geared to the needs of IPs. Check locally to see what is available in your area. Most paralegal programs are intended to train paralegals to work for attorneys, so you will have to put some effort into finding one that is really useful for IPs.

HOW TO GET TRAINING TO APPEAR BEFORE ADMINISTRATIVE AGENCIES

As noted a number of times in this book, many independent paralegals are beginning to specialize in representing people before federal and state administrative agencies, such as the Social Security Administration, which does not require advocates to be lawyers. As a result, we are often asked how a prospective IP can learn to do this. To our knowledge, there are no available courses; most IPs who currently represent people before agencies have learned either by working for the particular agency or for organizations such as a Legal Services program, which regularly represents people who appear before the agency. (See the interview with Glynda Dixon in the Appendix.)

D. Avoid Unauthorized Practice of Law

This subject is thoroughly discussed in Chapter 3. Avoiding unauthorized practice of law problems means your business will provide high-quality service, and conduct its operations based on the following principles:

- Customers should be provided with reliable and understandable written legal or electronic materials to help them make informed choices when preparing legal documents. (See Chapter 11 for more on finding legal materials on the Internet.)
- Customers are willing and able to read and understand these materials, and to make their own legal decisions.
- Customers are often better off taking responsibility for their own legal affairs than handing them over to a lawyer, when it is feasible to do so.
- If customers do need a lawyer, they should have access to one who is familiar with the materials used by you, and who also will be sympathetic to the customer's self-help efforts.

E.   Good Office Management

The third attribute of a good paralegal operation requires that you run a topnotch business operation. At the very least this involves doing the following:

- Running a clean, well-organized office from a good location (see Chapter 6);
- Learning good telephone skills so you can screen out inappropriate customers;
- Providing your customers with accurate and thorough information so that they can make their own decisions about the legal task they are concerned with;
- Using a typewriter or computer to prepare all necessary forms promptly and accurately;
- Making sure your customers thoroughly check the documents you prepare to ensure their accuracy before they are submitted to a court; and
- Documenting that you have done all of the above.

Let's now briefly look at how to do this by tracking a customer from her first contact with your business through the preparation of all the necessary forms.

Step 1: Initial Contact With a Potential Customer

Assume that you prepare the forms necessary for small businesses to incorporate or form limited liability companies. You receive a phone call from Alexis Elmore, who wishes to incorporate her business, which consists of two children's shoe stores. Your first job is to tell Elmore what you do and find out whether her situation is appropriate for your incorporation typing service. Accomplishing both of these tasks efficiently is a real skill, especially given the fact that you are solely in the business of typing legal forms, not of transferring legal expertise.

Specifically, you would want to ask if Elmore has a pretty good idea of what a corporation is, what's involved in preparing the paperwork for a corporation, who's going to own it, and how many shares of stock will be issued. You need to be sure Elmore knows enough about incorporation, and its alternatives, to provide you with the information necessary to complete the incorporation forms. If Elmore replies that her accountant recommended that she incorporate and she has discussed the tax advantages with him and has read a self-help book on the subject, she is probably ready to go ahead. However, if she seems confused about what a corporation is, or is unsure that her decision to incorporate is wise, she has more work to do before she uses your typing service. You might suggest she read several good books on the subject and consult a tax or small business adviser before going ahead.

If Elmore's answers make sense to you, or she takes your advice, learns more, and then calls you back, you will want to briefly tell her how your form preparation service works and how much you charge. Assuming this sounds good to her, it's time to make an appointment.

California Note: In California, Legal Document Assistants must orally disclose at their first meeting or phone contact with a client that they are not attorneys and cannot provide legal advice. Here is a sample of the required disclosure: "I am not an attorney, and my business [if it is a partnership or a corporation, or uses a fictitious business name], Lake County Self-Help Law Center, is not a law firm. I cannot represent you in court, advise you about your legal rights or the law, or select legal forms for you." (Cal. Bus. & Prof. Code § 6410.5.)

Step 2: Initial Office Interview

When Elmore comes to your clean, well-organized office for her first appointment, she should first encounter a reception room or area that contains material about self-help law in general and your incorporation form preparation service in particular. Having a small library of good small-business operations books is also valuable. If Elmore must wait a few minutes, she will be surrounded by materials that tell her more about what you do. Not only will it make a good impression, but you'll have the materials close at hand should you want to refer Elmore to good sources of more information. And don't forget to keep a few toys on hand just in case Elmore brings little Barbara.

California Note: Again, in California, at the first in-person meeting with a customer, Legal Document Assistants must orally disclose that they are not attorneys and cannot provide legal advice. They also must offer their customers an official form contract to sign. If they wish, LDAs may ask the customer to sign another official form confirming that the required oral disclosure has been provided—which provides the LDA with a "safe harbor" in case the client reports them for UPL in the future. (Cal. Bus. & Prof. Code § 6410.5.)

Step 3: Open a File

Your first task at the interview is to open a file. First, have Elmore read and sign a statement that describes your self-help form preparation service and clearly states that you are not a lawyer. (This is discussed in detail in Chapter 3.) Assuming you have a computer, you will probably want to enter Elmore's biographical information and instruct the computer to generate the intake sheet. If you have the proper software, this will allow you to simultaneously add the customer's name to your master list for later use in keeping track of her file and communicating with her by phone and mail. At this stage, it is also appropriate to verify that your customer knows how much your service costs and to establish how she plans to pay. Many independent paralegals ask for a substantial portion of their fee at the first interview. As discussed in Chapter 3, we recommend setting your basic fee to cover the cost of necessary self-help law books or kits, rather than trying to sell them separately. If Elmore has already purchased the necessary material separately, you can offer her a small discount.

Step 4: Gather the Necessary Information From the Customer

Assuming that Elmore has done her homework and has a pretty good idea of what incorporation entails, your next task is to gather the information necessary to prepare the paperwork. The best way to do this is to have Elmore fill out a detailed information form or questionnaire. (See Chapter 3, Section D, for more on how to construct a questionnaire).

Step 5: Help Your Customer Fill In the Information Sheet

You'll want to get as much information as possible from Elmore in her own handwriting. This way, if you are ever investigated, it's easier to demonstrate that you were typing forms under her supervision, and not engaging in the practice of law. In addition, you will probably want to interview Elmore to be sure the information she has supplied is complete. For example, your questionnaire will probably ask how Elmore wants to be taxed. Ideally, this part of the questionnaire will also refer to legal materials that Elmore can use to make the decision regarding the LLC's tax status. But it's also possible that Elmore didn't read the material and just left this part of the form blank. In that event, you could redirect Elmore to the referenced materials or refer her to her tax advisor before proceeding further.

Step 6: Review the Information Form With Your Customer

After Elmore has carefully reviewed and completed the questionnaire, have her sign a statement at the bottom that says that the information in the questionnaire is complete, correct, and reflects her desires. Keep a signed copy of this form for your files. It is essential that you do this for two reasons. First, you need to protect yourself should Elmore, or any other customer, later claim that she gave you information that you forgot to include on the forms. For example, in the bankruptcy area, where all debts must be listed to be discharged and customers sometimes fail to provide a complete list, keeping a signed copy of the customer's worksheet or questionnaire is particularly important. Second, if a prosecutor or other attorney organization ever has questions about whether you are practicing law, you'll want to produce the worksheet, complete with the customer's signed statement that they (not you) provided the necessary information.

Step 7: Prepare the Legal Paperwork

Your next task is to prepare the necessary paperwork. For incorporation papers, which can run 60 or 70 pages, the only practical way to do this is by use of a computer or a typewriter with considerable memory capacity. Since most of the language you need is standard legal boilerplate, it's a waste of time, and hence money, to type them from scratch. In other areas of the law, such as filling out preprinted divorce forms, it is practical to either use a typewriter or, in many states, to purchase a computer form-generation package designed for use in law offices. If you begin with the typewritten approach, there is no reason you must bang all the keys yourself. With a good information sheet keyed directly to necessary legal forms, any competent typist should be able to prepare the forms quickly. Especially after your business becomes established, your time will be better spent dealing with customers or marketing your business.

Step 8: Review the Legal Paperwork With Your Customer

Review the completed paperwork with Elmore carefully. This will normally be done at a second or third appointment. When your joint review is complete, have Elmore sign a brief statement such as this:

I have carefully reviewed all forms prepared by the Pacific Rim Self-Help Incorporation Service according to my instruction and find them to be accurate and complete.

Date _____ Signature_____

When paperwork is complete and ready for filing, it's appropriate to ask for final payment. Most typing services prefer to be paid the balance on the spot to save the trouble of billing and collecting from slow payers. We think this approach makes sense.

Step 9: Tell Your Customer What to Do Next

Finally, you need to either file the paperwork for Elmore or give her a detailed, accurate, and up-to-date instruction sheet telling her how to accomplish this. There is no legal reason you can't file the papers, either in person or by mail. (Filing forms is not considered to be the practice of law.) However, we think it often makes sense to have your customer do the filing, to emphasize that it's her legal action and your role is simply that of a form preparer. Also, if your customer will have to make a court appearance, it makes sense for her to visit the courthouse first, to check out where and how this will occur.

Bankruptcy Petition Preparer Note: An exception to the rule that IPs are permitted to file their customers' paperwork is found in the Bankruptcy Petition Preparer Act (11 U.S. C. §§ 110 and following). In most places, BPPs are not allowed to handle their customers' filing fees and must therefore send their customers to the bankruptcy court to file their own paperwork.

In legal areas such as divorce, where a court appearance is still required in some states, customers will want you to coach them as to what to say and when to say it. Doing anything more than explaining how the particular procedure is normally structured comes perilously close to practicing law, unless your local court supports the idea of nonlawyers providing more extensive help (see the interview with Virginia Simons in the Appendix). Normally, your best bet is to refer them to the relevant parts of any self-help resource that discusses how to handle the appearance. Another good approach is to suggest that your customer stop by the court and watch how similar cases are presented.

Step 10: Maintain Accurate Records

Keep neat records of all work done. All information you get from Elmore or any other customer, particularly the signed statement that she recognizes you are not a lawyer, the signed customer information sheet, and the signed statement that she has read all completed paperwork and finds it to be accurate, should be kept indefinitely in a well-organized file system. In addition, all information maintained in your computer, such as mailing lists, agency referral sources, and customer demographic information, should be carefully maintained and regularly backed up.

■

How Much to Charge

If you are planning to go into business helping nonlawyers prepare legal forms, you probably already have some idea about how much is reasonable to charge in your community. This depends on a number of factors, including:

- How much lawyers charge to do the same task.
- How much other independent paralegals in your area charge for the task.
- How many hours it will take you on average to complete the legal paperwork.
- How much your overhead is, over and above paying yourself a reasonable salary. If you rent a nice office, hire an employee, and buy equipment such as a computer, this will be a significant amount.
- How much your customers are willing to pay; and
- Whether some or all of your motive to work as an independent paralegal is to further a cause you are personally involved in, such as men's, women's, or tenants' rights. If so, you may be willing to charge less than the market value for your services.

A. Establish How Much Money You and Your Business Need

One sensible approach to setting a price for typing a divorce or guardianship, or any other form preparation task is to work backwards—to first decide on the total amount you need to take in to run your business and pay yourself a decent wage, and then determine how much you must charge per form preparation job to meet this goal. As part of doing this, you will want to budget carefully, making sure to add in all your costs, from the telephone bill and office rent to computer paper, brochure printing, phone book ads, and office supplies. Also remember that if you will need to buy office equipment from your savings to get your business started, you should include in your budget an item to cover gradually reimbursing yourself before the equipment wears out.

And if you plan to hire part-time office help, don't forget to include these costs, plus any employer taxes you might be required to pay.

Once you arrive at a final overhead figure, increase it by at least 20% to cover things you haven't thought of. If you have never been in business for yourself before, increase your estimate by 30%.

Your next step is to decide how much you need to live on. Again, budget a little on the high side so that even if the business doesn't initially produce enough income to meet your goal, you won't starve.

TAKE TIME TO PREPARE A PROFIT-AND-LOSS FORECAST

To see if your proposed business will make money, given your cost assumptions and the number of customers you can realistically expect, it's wise to prepare a detailed profit-and-loss statement and cash flow forecast. It is particularly important to estimate cash flow accurately to determine whether money coming in will be adequate to cover your expenses. Remember, most of your expenses will be immediate, but at least some of your income will be delayed because customers will pay late. Fortunately, it is easy to create both a profit-and-loss forecast and a cash flow analysis following the detailed instructions in *How to Write a Business Plan*, by Mike McKeever (Nolo).

Now add the amount you'll need for personal living expenses to your estimate of the amount needed to cover business overhead. This is the grand total you'll need in order to prosper. For example, you might conclude that you and your business can both get by comfortably on a total income of $7,500 a month.

Your next task is to estimate realistically how many customers you can hope to attract in a month. For example, if you decide to type divorces and decide that, given a little time to develop your business, you should be able to attract and handle 50 per month, you must charge an average of $150 per customer to meet your $7,500 goal.

B.   Find Out What Competitors Charge

Let's continue to assume that, like most IPs, you plan to type divorces. If so, you'll want to determine what lawyers, including any large, heavily advertised legal clinics, charge for preparing divorce forms. In doing this, however, don't necessarily believe the lowest price quoted in ads; this is often a price for a bare bones service that very few customers qualify for. For example, if a customer asks a legal clinic for a widely advertised $700 divorce, she is likely to be told that if she owns property or has children, she must pay extra, usually a lot extra. This sort of "bait and switch" approach is the reason many customers find that heavily advertised legal clinics usually end up being no cheaper than your typical run-of-the-courthouse lawyer. In the divorce area, you will probably find that no matter what other legal clinics advertise, $750–$1,500 is the usual low-end lawyer rate for uncontested divorces. If so, you will be extremely competitive if you charge in the range of $150–$300.

You should also check what existing independent paralegals charge for the same services you plan to provide. For example, if there are already several independent paralegals in your city who type divorces for $175–$225, you will probably want to charge about the same, or perhaps a bit less, until you get established. As you gain experience, you will want to adjust those amounts up or down based on the average amount of time it takes you to prepare a divorce.

Special rules apply to bankruptcy. In many areas of the country, bankruptcy courts set a maximum fee that can be charged for preparing bankruptcy forms. These fees tend to be between $100 and $150, depending on the area. (See Chapter 2, Section C3, and Section E of this chapter for more on the Bankruptcy Petition Preparers.)

C.   Estimate How Long It Will Take to Prepare the Forms

If you're operating efficiently, you will probably find that a divorce takes you about two to four hours to prepare, depending mostly on how efficient your intake (fact gathering) procedures are and whether you use a computerized legal form generation package. The time it takes to type other legal forms varies greatly, depending on state law and the particular fact situation. For example, a bankruptcy often takes one-and-one-half to two-and-one-half hours to prepare, including meeting with the customer. An uncontested guardianship petition involving custody of minor children might typically take two to three hours of independent paralegal time in most states. Likewise, the formation of small business entities can be done very quickly if you have all the repetitious boilerplate information stored on a computer, or a typewriter with adequate memory. Preparing a living trust or a will using a computer program such as *Quicken WillMaker Plus* (see Chapter 11) may take no more than 90 minutes, including the time it takes to interview a customer who has already read the legal manual that comes with each program.

D. Draw Up a Price List

Once you have canvassed what the competition charges and considered this in light of how much you need to make and how many customers you believe you can attract, it's time to set your prices.

Some types of form preparation involve extra paperwork (for example, some divorces require a formal property settlement agreement), for which you will wish to charge extra. Doing this is fine, as long as you clearly state this in your ads and flyers and your initial meeting with the customer. In addition, be sure you indicate that your fees do not include court filing fees, fees for service of papers, and the like—unless, of course, they do. The point is to fully disclose all of your prices from the beginning. This honest business practice will be appreciated by your customers and will set you apart from other independent paralegal offices and especially lawyer-run legal clinics, which commonly use deceptive bait and switch advertising techniques.

In talking to a number of independent paralegals who face competition from other IPs, several have noted that they believe price is a major factor when customers choose one paralegal service over another. One good illustration of this point can be found in the San Francisco Bay Area, where the divorce form typing business has expanded to the extent that over 60% of divorces are now handled without a lawyer. As a result, a constant stream of new independent paralegals has been attracted to the business, often advertising low prices in an effort to build up volume. Jolene Jacobs, former owner of the Divorce Centers of California office in San Francisco, made these comments about pricing:

A lot of people just starting out are able to set a low price because they have another job, or other means of support, and they operate out of a house or very inexpensive office. Eventually, as they build a clientele and move out of the house, they are likely to conclude that it makes sense to raise their prices somewhat. For the most part, established typing services with reasonably competitive prices do not have to lower prices to meet every lowballer. As in lots of other businesses, consumers choose a typing service based both on price and their perception of the quality of the service offered, which often comes down to preferring an experienced over an inexperienced provider. In short, establishing a competitive price will be a factor in a typing service's success, but if you have a good reputation and sound marketing, you don't have to offer the lowest price in town.

(See Jolene Jacobs's interview in the Appendix for more about how this pioneer independent paralegal operated her business.)

Once you establish your prices, you should include them in your printed material for all to see and rely on. Here is a sample flyer:

Hours: 9:00-6:00: Mon-Sat   Phone: 416-555-1111

(evening appointments available)   Call for Appointment

QUALITY
SELF-HELP BANKRUPTCY CENTER
A Nonlawyer Typing Service

WE TYPE
Bankruptcy forms for Chapter 7 bankruptcy

* Our fee is $175 (this does not include the court filing fee)
* We provide all customers with a copy of *How to File for Chapter 7 Bankruptcy* and *Money Troubles,* published by Nolo. These excellent books provide comprehensive information about debt problems generally and bankruptcy specifically.
* All bankruptcy forms are prepared under the customer's direct supervision—we provide no legal advice.
* Our services are unconditionally guaranteed. If you are not satisfied, we will return your money immediately, with no ifs, ands, or buts.

950 Pelham Road (at 45th). Park at Racafrax Parking, Pelham and 44th

Parking validated

E. Fees for Preparing Bankruptcy Petitions

Unlike other legal areas, fees charged to help people file bankruptcy are subject to review by the bankruptcy judge. This review is done under a federal statute known as The Bankruptcy Petition Preparer's Act, passed by Congress in 1996. Logically enough, people who prepare bankruptcy petitions are labeled "bankruptcy petition preparers." The original purpose of the review was to prevent attorneys from ripping off both the debtor and the unsecured creditors, who might otherwise be entitled to the money used to pay the fees. In practice, few bankruptcy courts care how much lawyers charge. But under the BPP Act an increasing number of bankruptcy judges are using their authority over fees to push down the prices charged by BPPs who help people do their own bankruptcies.

Here is how this happens. Every bankruptcy filing includes a document, called a Statement of Affairs, that discloses the debtor's recent economic history. Among the items that must be disclosed is any money paid for help filing for bankruptcy. In addition, all attorneys must file a special form that discloses their fees, and the bankruptcy courts require BPPs to complete this form as well. A copy of the bankruptcy forms filed by the debtor goes directly to the U.S. Trustee's Office for that particular region. The U.S. Trustee is primarily charged with riding herd over the actual bankruptcy trustees in their region. However, the U.S. Trustee also systematically reviews work done by the local Bankruptcy Petition Preparers to make sure they are complying with the law and with the fee guidelines established by the local court. If the fees are more than the court allows, the U.S. Trustee hauls the BPP into court to show cause why he or she shouldn't disgorge the excess. Repeat overcharges are likely to result in the BPP being barred from working in that court.

If typing is all that is being done, this might be a reasonable approach by the bankruptcy powers that be. But BPPs often do a lot more than typing. Depending on the BPP, additional activities and costs might include:

- conducting an extensive customer interview using a questionnaire;
- sorting debts into the proper categories;
- alphabetizing the customer's list of creditors;
- negotiating with creditors;
- providing the customer with adequate written materials to explain how to make their own legal decisions;
- helping the customer to use and understand the written materials being used;
- preparing the customer to understand what will happen at the creditors' meeting; and
- making photocopies and filing the forms with the court.

While a few courts and U.S. trustees approve of all of these activities by BPPs, many wrongly believe that any activity other than typing constitutes the unauthorized practice of law and that no fees can be charged for illegal services.

If you are a new bankruptcy petition preparer, start by finding out what your local bankruptcy court and U.S. Trustee permit form preparation services to charge—some courts have reasonable limits—and stay within this limit. If there is no rule on fees, or you find the court has imposed a limit that is unfairly low, take the following steps:

- carefully itemize your activities (see above list) and costs;
- make these costs consistent with your overall business plan;
- restrict your activities to apparent clerical tasks;
- make sure that your customer gets all their basic bankruptcy legal expertise from publications or outside resources and not from you; and
- be prepared to present this information to any judge or trustee who inquires about how you set your fees.

F.   Get Cash Up Front

Another issue that always comes up when you run a small business is credit. Should you allow your customers to pay you in installments? Despite the fact that we know of several IPs who manage to do this successfully, our advice is not to give credit. Assuming your prices are primarily in the rock-bottom $150–$350 range, depending on the type of forms you prepare, it is reasonable to ask customers to pay your entire fee at your first meeting. It usually makes sense to charge low prices and collect all your fees right away, or to charge higher prices and bill people, but not to attempt both ways.

By not advancing credit, you may lose a little business to the competition, but in the long run you will come out far ahead both economically and psychologically. Why? Because the fact that you will always be paid up front will mean minimal bookkeeping and no need to send bills. And of intangible, but no less real, value, your peace of mind will never be disturbed by all those folks who promise to pay you later for typing their divorce and then patronize another typing service to get a bankruptcy, listing you as a creditor. Of course, one good way to allow people to be served now and pay later is to take credit cards. A number of IPs do this very successfully for all types of legal actions, except bankruptcies. If you have a good relationship with a bank, establishing a MasterCard/Visa account should not be difficult.

In fairness, many IPs find our "no-credit" approach a bit too strict. As an alternative, a number ask for full payment up front but are willing to take half when the customer comes in for the initial interview and the other half when the papers are picked up for filing. If the second half isn't forthcoming, neither are the papers. But don't let this approach get the better of you. If you take too firm a stand about returning the papers, you may find yourself on the other end of a UPL complaint.

G. Establish a Money-Back Guarantee

As noted in Chapter 12, "Customer Recourse," it is wise to establish a fast and generous recourse policy and to disclose it in advance. Obviously, you can't afford to include details in a small "penny saver" or phone book type listing, but you can and should put it in your general information sheet or brochure, or on your website. This should be given to all customers, available in your waiting room, and generally circulated in your community as part of your marketing efforts. ■

Chapter 10

Marketing Your Services

S uppose now you have done everything you think you need to do to open your doors to customers. Not so fast. First, you must figure out how you are going to attract your customers, get them to your open door, and then through it. This planning activity is called marketing. The importance of marketing to starting and operating your independent paralegal business cannot be overstated. Our statistics indicate that the failure rate of newly created businesses is directly related to marketing, or more precisely the lack of it. More than any other business function, marketing can help you to develop the goals and direction of your paralegal service. As legal consumers become increasingly aware of the various options available to them, only those paralegal services that are seen as *satisfying* their needs will draw them in.

Independent paralegal businesses require a special kind of marketing, one that combines the oldest techniques of persuasion with the newest methods of selling. Your marketing program must also proceed carefully—not only must you identify the customer's interests, convert these interests into a buying intention, and turn the buying intention into actual purchases—you must also avoid the unauthorized practice of law. You can think of this careful marketing strategy as "UPL-free target marketing"—advertising that does not violate the unauthorized practice rules of your state and follows local regulations governing the services you can provide. Target marketing for the independent paralegal is a simple, direct, and effective way of learning who and where your best customers are. It also helps you develop a plan to reach them and determine how to allocate your marketing dollars.

The first step in target marketing is to define your service. This should be easy. Legally, as a nonlawyer, what services can you provide directly to the public? In most states the answer will be: self-help services or assistance to self-represented legal consumers. Self-help services include giving a customer a detailed manual containing advice, making forms available for the customer's use, and filling in, filing, and serving the forms at the direction of the customer. This role is part tutor (helping someone learn how to learn), part cheerleader (assuring people that they really can "do it themselves,") part librarian (helping people get to the right information), and part legal secretary (preparing, organizing, and filing documents under someone else's direction—in this case the customer's).

The next step in your target marketing is to consider what needs of your self-help customers your services can satisfy. What will motivate consumers to select your service? The reasons customers choose self-help law should be expressed in your marketing message. The four factors that generally lead people to choose self-representation are the relative cost, the self-reliance of the customer, the customer's view of the necessity for an attorney, and distrust of lawyers. A closer look at these factors will show how they can be useful in targeting your market as well as in avoiding the unauthorized practice of law.

- **Cost.** To nobody's great surprise, it costs much less to use a legal form preparation service and a book than to use a lawyer. While lawyers are heard to argue that the costs associated with self-help law can be greater in the long run—assuming mistakes are made—this argument loses some credibility in the face of prevailing lawyers' fees. As with other purchasing decisions, only the wealthy can comfortably buy for the long run, and most of us learn to get by with the less expensive model—either because we must or because our spending priorities lie elsewhere.

- **Self-reliance.** People who view themselves as self-reliant are disinclined to turn their legal affairs over to others. They tend to believe that many law-related tasks can be handled without much, if any, help from a lawyer. As they do with their own taxes, life insurance, home repair, auto repair, and healthcare, these people buy books, software, and videotapes to educate themselves on the precise nature of the tasks, and then set out to accomplish as much as they can on their own. Only if they hit a dead end do they seek help from a professional.

- **Lack of necessity.** Many consumers firmly reject the notion that a lawyer is necessary for the all of the various tasks that lawyers define as legal services. For example, judges tend to define UPL as any task that is typically done by a lawyer. Not only is this definition circular in the extreme, but it no longer applies, given the growth of the self-help law and independent paralegal movement.

- **Distrust of Lawyers.** Attorneys will be the first to admit that many people flat-out detest all lawyers. The reason most often advanced by lawyers is that in every court case, somebody wins and somebody loses—and the losers take it out on their lawyers. Others might cite different reasons, but we won't go into that any more here.

Having looked at what you are offering and why people choose self-help law, the next step is for you to decide who you want as your customers—eligibility requirements for those who will use your business. Your customer will need to be able to:

- determine what the problem is
- determine their desired outcome, understand that you are not their lawyer or representative, gather sufficient information and facts to complete the paperwork
- understand and follow directions, assess the success of the assistance provided, and
- pay for the service.

Once you know the services you are offering, the need your business fills, the reasons people choose self-help, and what qualities you want in your customers, you are ready to develop your marketing plan. The following pages provide some tools and information to make your marketing efforts easier.

A. Marketing Methods and Objectives

You have determined who your potential customers are and exactly what legal form preparation services you are going to offer to them. You have also learned how to determine who your competition is and how to conduct an analysis of their service. You must now decide how to communicate effectively with your potential customers—your target market.

There are many methods and marketing tactics that you can utilize to convey your message to your customers. These tactics vary greatly in scope, cost, level of sophistication, and number of people reached. Marketing tactics are divided into two major groups: personal and impersonal. Personal tactics are those that place you in direct contact with the potential customer. Impersonal tactics are those that allow you to reach a far greater number of potential customers efficiently, if indirectly. Which tactic you choose depends on your strategy and your goals. *Who are you trying to reach?*

Having determined who your best potential customers are and defined your services in recognition of those customers' needs, you must decide which of the most common sources of customer information you wish to use in your marketing. Customers usually get their information from one of four sources:

- personal sources
- commercial sources
- public information, and
- personal experience.

You can maximize your marketing by attempting to impact all four.

B. Conventional Advertising Is Usually Not Cost-Effective

For a lot of people who are not experienced in small business economics, letting the general public know about your service means advertising. Indeed, if you are new to the independent paralegal business, you may have already considered getting together as much money as you can and running a series of splashy ads in local newspapers and perhaps even on radio or Cable TV.

If we do nothing else in this whole book, we want to convince you of one thing: spending a lot of money on advertising your services in conventional ways is unlikely to produce a profitable return. Or, put more directly, major advertising expenditures just plain will not work. There are two reasons for our dogmatism. The first is economic—the amount of business that conventional advertising will produce usually will not pay for its cost, assuming that you charge a reasonable amount for your services. The second reason that a major advertising campaign isn't a good idea for the independent paralegal is that it is almost sure to produce a negative reaction from the bar. As mentioned throughout this book, especially when your business is new, you are far better off maintaining a reasonably low profile. Of course, this may change in the years to come (and indeed, has already done so in parts of California, Florida, and Arizona) but in most places, it's unwise to run a lot of ads that will remind the tottering, but still powerful, legal establishment of your existence.

Before we discuss several cost-effective ways to market your paralegal services, here is a cogent excerpt from *Marketing Without Advertising,* by Michael Phillips and Salli Rasberry (Nolo):

A large and growing number of business people have become vividly aware that if they are to succeed in the long run, it is essential that they attract more loyal customers. Unfortunately, the mechanics of doing this are less obvious. After all, if you are already working eleven hours a day, you have no time to join a self-improvement club for the self-employed, no money to compete with major advertisers and probably no desire to turn yourself into a super salesperson.

· · · ·

And even if you can afford more advertising, many of you have probably begun to form the sneaking suspicion that despite conventional wisdom that dictates that advertising is essential, it is not cost effective in your business.

· · · ·

The truth, of course, is that very few of the 1,600 advertising messages we experience each day are effective in influencing our shopping or buying behavior and an even smaller amount of it is cost effective for the advertiser. When it comes to a small business trying to get its message heard against the babble of corporate America, the chances of people you want to reach really hearing or seeing your message is minuscule. And even worse than the cost involved, relying on advertising to improve your sales often stonewalls your imagination, keeping you from exploring the many superior methods available for promoting your business.

· · · ·

In fact, the best and most economical way to attract and hold customers is through personal recommendation. A customer who is pre-screened and prepared for what you have to offer is far more likely to appreciate you and use your business than is someone responding to an ad offering a low price. The essence of marketing without advertising then is to encourage "personal recommendation." How do you do this? Lots of ways, all of which start with creating an atmosphere of trust. Central to doing this is to run an honest business.

C. Understanding Advertising

Despite what is said in Section B, some advertising can help your business to develop a continuous stream of customers. This information is designed to help you understand how to use advertising effectively, assuming you plan to advertise at all.

Advertising can sometimes be important to a small business. Without it, you might not be able to tell prospective customers about your paralegal services—and you cannot sell to people who don't know about you. You may call advertising "clutter" during your favorite TV program, or "tacky" at its worst, but promotion can be critical to keeping your personal wheels of commerce turning.

With enough time and money, you are going to be able to experiment and find successful ads for your business. But a good ad, even a great ad, is not enough to make your advertising budget really effective. To do the most good, your advertising should be part of a complete promotion program. That is, advertising must be supported by other activities that will bring prospective customers into your office.

What is advertising? Advertising is any communication of a sales message. Advertising messages are usually non-personal; they say, "Hey, pay attention to me!" to everyone at once. These messages can be delivered via a wide range of media, including radio, newspaper, signs, calendars, and direct mail.

Advertising can promote ideas, goods, or services. Advertising messages are distinguishable from other types of communication and public relations messages because they attempt to *persuade* from the point of view of the advertiser, who must pay for the privilege.

Advertising is one-way communication sent by the seller to a group of prospective buyers. There's a lot of competition for the attention of prospective buyers, and only the best advertising will succeed in getting a message through. The "best" advertising works because it attracts favorable attention to your paralegal service and is remembered by those who see it. It is either especially clever, offers an outstanding value, or is otherwise memorable to the prospective purchasers of your services. If your advertising gets the public to remember you and *react* by purchasing from you, you've succeeded. Advertising strives to make a strong impression on the viewer or listener.

Advertising is the art of convincing people that debt is better than frustration.

—Robert Orben
American Legion Magazine

Advertising can do a lot, but it can't do everything. It can't make a better business person out of you; it can't get you organized; and it can't raise money miraculously over the weekend. It *can*:

- Promote your form preparation services and your business
- Stimulate demand and increase use of your paralegal service
- Offset competitors' advertising
- Make salespeople more effective
- Remind and reinforce customers
- Reduce sales fluctuations
- Promote goodwill.

Section K, below, lists 50 ways you can improve your business—including many advertising ideas. "Five Steps to Successful Advertising," below provides some specific advertising guidelines.

FIVE STEPS TO SUCCESSFUL ADVERTISING

There are five basic steps in developing an advertising budget and media plan. These five steps are:

1. Decide what you want to sell.

    This will be the core of your sales message, so think carefully. Do you want to get your customers excited about your new service? A special price? Your new location or grand opening? If you just want to sell your image, make sure you know what kind of image you want them to remember you for: Classy and well-priced? Special service? Once you have all these answers fixed in your mind, you can set out to establish your position in the market.

2. Determine the target audience for your sales message.

    Naturally, this should be the group of people who are your best prospects. What do you know about them? How would you describe them?

3. Determine why this group buys independent paralegal services.

    More to the point, why should they buy from you instead of your competitors? On Madison Avenue they call this your Unique Selling Proposition. And that's what your advertising should emphasize.

4. Determine how you plan to reach your potential customers.

    Now you have just about written the essence of your sales message. You still don't know the best way to deliver this message, but you're close. Your next step is to select the best communication media to use to reach your target audience with your sales message. In other words, how do your prospects usually get their information? Consider the major advertising options available in your market. Make a list of the media that appear to offer the audience, the costs, the format, and advantages that best fit your needs. To make your selection process easier, rank your advertising options from best to worst. Because you know that different customers respond to different types of media, you naturally want to cover your options as best you can afford. You are now developing your "media mix," which is simply a fancy way of saying you are not putting all of your advertising eggs into one basket.

5. Complete your media plan.

    Using the list you prepared in Step 4, assign some dollar amounts to these media. Using your best "educated guess" of where your advertising will be effective, write a percentage of your budget that you would like to see go to each media next to each item you listed above.

D. Getting Recommendations and Referrals

How do you encourage positive personal recommendations of your business? There are two ways. The first is to provide an excellent service and to let your satisfied customers spread the word for you. This will work, but it will take time to build to a level that will support you. In the meantime, you should make your services widely known to the people who are most likely to refer you customers. Ask yourself, who are the people who need the types of services you offer likely to be in contact with? For example, people in the armed services who need a divorce are likely to contact a military legal office (Judge Advocate General). Military lawyers don't handle divorce, but they can refer enlisted men and women to you if they know about your service. Similarly, lots of people who consider incorporating a small business talk to accountants or small business financial planners, both of whom are a good source of referrals if you prepare incorporation papers.

To tell referral sources about your business so they can tell others, you'll need good promotional material. See the following sample cover letter to referral agencies and the related flyer, "Lake County Self-Help Law Center, Inc."

Once you have designed a good packet of information, including listing your prices, location, general philosophy, disclaimer that you are not a lawyer, etc., make it available to as many referral sources as possible. Depending on the type of forms you prepare, you will want to communicate with some or all of the following:

- Accountants and tax preparers (especially if you prepare forms for bankruptcies)
- Legal services offices (legal aid)
- Battered women's shelters (especially if you handle restraining orders and divorces)
- Immigrants' help organizations
- Public library reference librarians
- Law school "pro per" assistance centers
- Law librarians (at courthouses and law school libraries)
- Community services referral agencies and directories
- Drug treatment centers
- Marriage counselors and family therapists
- Court clerks (this only works in areas where courts are open-minded about IPs)
- Mediation professionals (especially if you prepare divorce and other family law paperwork)
- Community mediation organizations
- Social services
- University and college student assistance offices
- Gray Panthers and other senior advocacy organizations (especially if you handle Social Security disability appeals)
- Local corporation personnel departments
- Parents Without Partners and other singles groups
- Law enforcement (including the Sheriff's Office, Probation Department, Parole Officers, and the County Jail)
- Consumer organizations
- The State Employment Office

- Women's organizations
- Collection agencies
- Child care centers
- Military bases, including all Judge Advocate General military law offices
- Local media (send it to reporters who care about consumer, legal, or family issues)
- Foreign language media and support groups (if you or an employee can speak the language)
- Any community group directly interested in your activity. (For example, if you do small business incorporations, you will want to contact a wide range of small business groups, accountants, and bookkeepers who work in this area, as well as the reference librarian at any public library with a large collection of business materials. Similarly, if you do evictions, you should work as closely as you can with the local apartment house owners' association, as well as real estate management groups and any other community organizations of interest to landlords.)

Sample Cover Letter to Referral Agencies

Here is a cover letter appropriate for communicating with guidance counselors. Modified slightly, it will also work well as a cover letter when you send marketing material to other groups.

Date _____

Dear _____ :

　　We know that as a guidance counselor you deal with difficult family concerns every day. Some of these involve counseling people who need basic legal services in areas such as divorce, child support modification, bankruptcy, stepparent adoption, and guardianship.

　　At Legal Forms, Inc., we offer high quality, low-cost legal form preparation in all these areas. We strive to create a relaxed, nonadversarial atmosphere in which our customers feel comfortable.

　　We are not attorneys and cannot give legal advice. But as part of our highly efficient legal form preparation service, we can, and do, stock a large selection of quality self-help law materials designed to help our customers inform themselves about the legal issues they face. These materials may be used free of charge at our office library and are also available for purchase at a very reasonable price.

　　As you can see from our enclosed pamphlet, we also offer a fairly wide array of other legal form preparation services, including conservatorships, wills, living trusts, and small business incorporations. If you have any questions, please feel free to call me at any time.

　　Sincerely,

　　John Kennedy

　　John Kennedy
　　Owner, Legal Forms, Inc.

Bob Mission of the Sacramento, California, Superior California Legal Clinic, reports that about 50% of his total referrals came from community agencies. Glynda Dixon, cofounder of CAIP and former owner of the Divorce Center in Oakland, California, emphasizes that you should not only send groups a flyer, but if possible, "follow up personally to see that it got to the right person and to convince them that you know your business and aren't a dingbat." For example, she occasionally spoke at luncheon meetings of groups interested in family matters and kept in close touch with a number of attorney mediators who work in the domestic law area, because she believed it was her responsibility to convince people who can refer customers that her office provided a really good service.

DEVELOPING AND DISTRIBUTING YOUR FLYER

An excellent and cost-effective way to get the word out is by the use of flyers. Design an eye-catching and informative one, clearly stating your services and prices.

Flyer Development Checklist

Completing the following activities will help you succeed in the development of your marketing flyer.

(Check off as completed)

__ Collect and review copies of your competitors' flyers
__ Brainstorm possible messages with associates
__ Evaluate messages for UPL/regulation violations
__ Develop rough draft and layout of copy
__ Have a graphic designer produce proof for your review
__ Finalize draft and have someone else proofread
__ Contact mailing list distributors for prices/schedule
__ Purchase mailing list(s) – arrange for delivery*
__ Determine printing process and provider
__ Review again for appropriateness and effectiveness
__ Take camera-ready copy to printer
__ 1Review printer's proof and have someone (not you) proofread
__ Prepare for bulk mailing through post office
__ Print out current customer list as mailing labels
__ Organize mailing party
__ Pick up flyers from printer
__ Prepare for mailing (mailing party)
__ Review flyer information with office staff
__ Take prepared flyers to the post office
__ Set up evaluation dates and telephone log
__ Start planning next flyer
__ Get everything ready to receive customers

*If you can't purchase a list, compile your own.

Post your flyer at appropriate places around town. Good locations include laundromats, food stores, factories and other larger employers, military bases and graduate schools, nonprofit helping agencies, and, if you are marketing to a particular ethnic group, appropriate social clubs and churches.

As a general rule, the closer to the courthouse you can get your material, the better, unless of course you are in an area where extreme hostility to IPs (on the part of organized lawyerdom) means you want to keep a low profile. Sharon Goetting, until recently the owner of Self-Help Paralegal Services in Napa, California, is one person who successfully learned how to work with court clerks and judges to get the word out. Sharon explains:

As part of starting my business, I went directly to the presiding judge and talked to him about the fact that over half the people who were trying to file papers were doing it without a lawyer and often experiencing great difficulty. I explained that I could help fix the problem by running a first-class form typing service. The judge said "Go for it" and allowed me to put my flyer right on the bulletin board in the Court lobby. The clerks aren't allowed to refer directly to a private business, but can and regularly do point out my flyer to frustrated pro pers. As a result, I get a steady stream of customers.

Especially in coastal states, such as New York, California, and Texas, where there are significant concentrations of non-English speakers, targeting your services to people who speak a language such as Spanish, Chinese, or Vietnamese can also make sense. To do this effectively, you will need to have all the promotional materials translated into the particular language. In addition, someone who is fluent in the language in question will need to be regularly available to handle your non-English speaking business. This will include telephone screening as well as customer interviews.

> **HOW TO GET HELP DESIGNING ADS AND FLYERS**
> * Contact a small, local, reasonably priced ad agency or, better yet, an independent reporter, freelance writer, English teacher, or someone else with truly excellent language skills. With their help, write, re-write, and proofread every word of every flyer, pamphlet, and other promotion piece you distribute at least five times.
> * Find a reasonably priced graphic artist. Usually you can get a referral from a local "instant printing" shop. Work with her, incorporating your written material into well-designed promotional material. And don't let her talk you into ultra-slick designs—instead, your materials should be a little on the conservative side, to reassure customers that your business is reliable and trustworthy.

E. Open Your Own Self-Help Law Store

A few years ago there were only a few self-help law books. Now there are hundreds of books and dozens of software programs—enough that in a number of places small business people are opening small self-help law book and software stores that occasionally also stock small business and consumer titles. For the IP, a small store can be a perfect sideline, since a significant percentage of the people who come to buy self-help materials will also need help preparing legal paperwork. And a store can also be a good place to run the occasional class or work-shop, thus generating even more business.

F. Build a Website

Without doubt, the World Wide Web is an outstanding way to market your independent paralegal business. In Chapter 6, Section D, we ex-plain that consumers are increasingly using the Web to find goods and services in the marketplace. The old standby, the Yellow Pages, is now available on the Web and with very little effort consumers can find you in a hurry. And if you aren't in the Yellow Pages, you may not be found at all.

As we also explain in Chapter 6, setting up a website can be easy or difficult, cheap or costly. As with other aspects of your business, the amount of money you choose to put into your website will depend on a number of variables, including the expectations of your customer base, your economic situation and, most importantly, how you plan to run your site. Some of you may wish to run your entire business from the website, which means you can pour as much money into it as you would into an office. On the other hand, some of you will just want to use your site as a marketing forum, an extended Yellow Pages ad. In that event, you'll have less of a need to add the bells and whistles that many full-bore commercial websites contain.

G. Keep a Good Mailing List

As part of contacting likely referral sources and your satisfied customers, it is essential that you collect, maintain, and regularly use a good mailing list. Keeping in touch with former customers, supporters, and others interested in your work provides these people with the necessary information to tell others about you. If you store your list on a personal computer and request the post office to supply you with all address changes (there is a small fee), you can easily and cheaply maintain and expand this marvelously effective, relatively low-cost marketing tool. Or if your list grows, you may want to work with a local mailing service that can show you how to most effectively use bulk mail.

You will want to use your mailing list in all sorts of contexts, including:

- To inform customers if you offer new services;
- To let people know about significant law changes that could affect them;
- To help organize potential supporters should you face a political fight, as will be the case if you introduce legislation (as discussed in Chapter 14) or are sued by organized lawyerdom;
- To remind customers to refer friends (a coupon offering a small discount often helps);

- To invite everyone to a party. Try this a couple of times a year—it allows you to market your services and have fun too.

H. List the Availability of Your Services

In addition to talking to community service organizations, it is essential to list the availability of your services widely in places where people are predisposed to look for them. Some types of listings are free, such as those maintained by public service organizations and agencies. More typically, you must pay a small fee to list, as is the case for business directories and phone books. But even where a fee is involved, costs are usually very reasonable when compared to your likely return. This is because, unlike display ads or electronic media spots, where you pay fairly large sums to aim your message at a very broad and mostly uninterested audience, listings are targeted at people who are looking for the particular service you offer. In addition, business listings have the advantage of being fairly inconspicuous, and thus are far less likely to come to the attention of organized lawyerdom than is a real advertising campaign. Here are a number of good places to list:

- Phone book Yellow Pages—you can't list under "Attorneys," but probably can list under headings such as "Document Preparation," "Divorce," "Legal Form Preparation," "Typing Services," and so on. The phone company makes up the headings; the best you can do is pick the available one that comes closest to describing what you do;
- Local business and community service directories, such as those put out by the Better Business Bureau and local trade groups;
- Self-help law books—several publishers of divorce, and other self-help law books charge IPs a modest fee to list right in the book. This, of course, is a great opportunity for IPs, as many book purchasers get disgusted in the middle of doing all their own paperwork and are likely to turn the whole thing over to an IP. One book that does this is *How to Do Your Own Divorce in California*, by Ed Sherman;

- Classified ads in newspapers. Most newspapers place these ads under "Business Personals." You need to leave the ad in for a month or two to begin to see results, since people will often find out about it when a friend says something like, "You know, I saw an ad for low-cost patent drafting services in the back of *Popular Invention* magazine";

- Classified or display ads that list your services in low-cost "penny saver" or "classified flea market" type papers. This, of course, is advertising of a sort, but is far different in general approach and cost than are large display ads. People who pick up classified ads are often looking for a specific service at a reasonable price. Again, these ads work best if you keep them in the publication over a long period of time in the same place;

- Directories and business listings aimed at people who don't speak English. In many communities, there is a large and growing need for IPs who work with Spanish and Chinese speakers, as well as those who know Southeast Asian languages.

Here is a small ad—essentially a listing of services—that would be appropriate for a free classified ad paper:

OREGON DIVORCE TYPING, INC.

Since 1978

UNCONTESTED DIVORCE............ $150–$250

We help you prepare your own divorce without an attorney.

1113 Melrose Street, Pullman, Oregon   441-5157

Monday - Saturday 10-6

And here is an ad that appeared in a classified ad publication in Portland, Oregon, called "Nickel Ads":

PLE'S PARALEGAL SERVICE, INC.

Legal Form Preparation Without a Lawyer

Wills • Name changes • Divorce • Bankruptcy
Probate • Incorporation • Stepparent adoption

High quality/Low cost

VISA   646-0990   MASTERCARD

I. Prepare Factual Information About the Areas You Specialize In

When telling people about the existence of your service, you usually want to keep your message short and to the point. After all, most people have more important things to think about than the details of your business. However, for those who ask for more information (and for helping agencies and others who are genuinely interested in your service) you'll want to develop material that goes into more detail. In Section D, above, we present a general flyer designed to accomplish this. In addition, you will want to prepare more in-depth material about each of the form preparation areas you specialize in. Your objectives in doing this are:

- Explain in detail what you do;
- Educate the potential customer or referral source about basic consumer information about the legal task (as long as you stick to basic widely available information about laws and procedures and do not give advice, this should not constitute UPL);
- Convince the potential customer that you offer a high-quality, reliable service;
- Present your message in a way that does not give organized lawyerdom an opportunity to charge you with unauthorized practice of law.

Here, by way of example, is a very informative flyer used by a Divorce Center of California office:

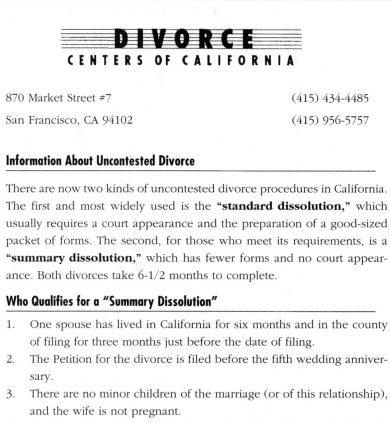

DIVORCE
CENTERS OF CALIFORNIA

870 Market Street #7   (415) 434-4485

San Francisco, CA 94102   (415) 956-5757

Information About Uncontested Divorce

There are now two kinds of uncontested divorce procedures in California. The first and most widely used is the **"standard dissolution,"** which usually requires a court appearance and the preparation of a good-sized packet of forms. The second, for those who meet its requirements, is a **"summary dissolution,"** which has fewer forms and no court appearance. Both divorces take 6-1/2 months to complete.

Who Qualifies for a "Summary Dissolution"

1. One spouse has lived in California for six months and in the county of filing for three months just before the date of filing.
2. The Petition for the divorce is filed before the fifth wedding anniversary.
3. There are no minor children of the marriage (or of this relationship), and the wife is not pregnant.
4. Neither spouse has any interest in real property (houses, land, etc.).
5. There is less than $4,000 in community obligations, not including car loans.
6. There is less than $25,000 in community property, not including cars.
7. Neither spouse owns more than $25,000 separately, not including cars.
8. Both spouses must sign the first papers.
9. Both spouses must read and understand the Summary Dissolution Booklet published by the State of California.

DIVORCE
CENTERS OF CALIFORNIA

870 Market Street #7   (415) 434-4485
San Francisco, CA 94102   (415) 956-5757

If for any reason you don't qualify for the Summary Dissolution, you must use the Standard Dissolution.

What Does It Cost?:

	Our Fee	Court Filing Fee
Summary Dissolution	$120	About $150 in many counties (it varies slightly)
Standard Dissolution	$220	About $170 in many counties (it varies slightly)

Please call for an appointment:
Monday-Friday, 9:00 a.m. to 5:30 p.m.
Telephone: 434-4485 or 956-5757

Thank you for your inquiry.

J.   Longer-Term Marketing Strategies

So far we have discussed several things you can do to get the word out about your business fairly quickly. This is crucial to the survival of a new business, of course. But taking a slightly longer view, it's also important that you plan now for the growth and expansion of your business in the years ahead. Again, to emphasize the point we made at the beginning of this chapter, the best way to do this is through the positive personal recommendations of satisfied customers. To encourage people to be enthusiastic about your business and tell others about you (and to report back favorably to referring agencies), it's essential that you do an excellent job. If your customers come to respect you and the service you offer, they will send others. If they don't, negative word will spread just as fast. To fully understand this point, ask yourself this: How often do you patronize a restaurant, service provider (carpenter, plumber, shoe repair shop), or buy a particular product or go to a movie because someone you know recommended it? Now ask yourself how often you engage in any of these transactions after a friend tells you the service or product is poor?

In *Marketing Without Advertising*, which we again heartily recommend, Phillips and Rasberry state that there are three essential elements to building the trust necessary to get the personal recommendation process going. They are:

- Providing a good service at a good price (see Chapter 9 for a discussion on price);

- Giving your customers a way to measure the quality of your service and reasonableness of your prices. Phillips and Rasberry discuss the general principles of how to do this. For independent paralegals, one good approach is to create office and waiting room displays and written material indicating exactly the services you perform, how much time it takes, how much the competition charges, and the like; and

- Offering your customers a money-back guarantee if they are unhappy with your service for any reason should be an essential part of your marketing strategy. Many public agencies and others may be reluctant to refer people to your somewhat controversial business unless they have confidence that any problems will be taken care of.

One good way to allow the community to see for itself that you are competent is to teach a course in your specialty. A number of legal typing service owners have done this. To reduce chances of being hassled for practicing law without a license, many charge no fee. Others charge a modest fee for the course but require students to own and read a good self-help law text and limit their oral presentation to the material in the book. The approach of reaching potential customers through courses works particularly well for typing service owners in specialized fields, such as those who prepare forms for landlords, nonprofit corporations, or people who want living trusts—areas where customers typically want a good deal of information about the subject before committing themselves.

Another good approach is to occasionally publish and distribute good consumer information about the subject areas in which you work. For example, if your state changes any aspect of its divorce, adoption, or landlord-tenant law and you type papers in any of these areas, you might prepare a flyer describing the details of the change. Of course, the circular should also remind people of how your business works. Do a nice job on the graphics (again, it often pays to work with a graphic artist) and make sure you proofread it at least three times to catch all errors in spelling and grammar. When you're satisfied, mail the flyer to all interested individuals, consumer groups, media organizations, former customers, and referral agencies.

K. More Tools You Can Use: 50 Ways to Leave Your Competition Behind

Before completing your marketing planning, take a little time to review your skills and values and make sure you have clearly defined your business goals, including the legal problem(s) you want to help people solve. It's important that you know exactly how you plan to offer assistance to the customer. *Fifty Ways to Leave Your Competition Behind* was designed by Catherine Elias-Jermany to help legal document preparation services achieve marketing success. We have compiled some of the favorite marketing methods and tips of the more successful independent paralegals throughout the United States. Some of these tips appear elsewhere in the book in somewhat different form, but here they are all set forth from a marketing perspective.

1. Additional Profit Centers

A paralegal business can add additional activities to serve as "profit centers." For example, you can add notary, copy, fax, mailbox, and answering or call-forwarding services. In addition, you can consider taking on new areas in your typing service, such as wills, name changes, divorces, living trusts, government benefit applications, and resumes.

2. Articles and Books

Increase your credibility with your customers by making pamphlets, articles, and books on relevant legal topics available to them. Put the materials on wall shelves in the waiting room, and enclose articles of interest with your regular customer mailings.

3. Association Memberships

Join as many community groups as possible, including the Chamber of Commerce and your local and state independent paralegal associations. Volunteer time and donate money and/or property in the name of your business. (Send out press releases each time your business makes a contribution.) Sponsor special community events.

4. Audiotapes / Videotapes

Prepare videotapes and audiotapes explaining what services you provide.

5. Better Pricing

Cost is the reason most customers choose a paralegal service. If you offer excellent service for a reasonable price, you will be far ahead of your competition. Develop your pricing strategy carefully. Every price change affects customer expectations. If you offer a rock bottom price, be prepared to explain how you can still provide quality service. If you charge more than your competition, explain why.

6. Better Brochures

A good-looking brochure will impart a feeling to the customer that your business offers high quality services. Remember to leave your brochures everywhere a potential customer may be found, including "take-one" boxes. However, don't leave them in places that will cause the customer to have bad associations with your business, such as in a seedy bar or liquor store. If you can't afford the brochure of your dreams right now, use your business cards, circulars, flyers, and other low-cost media until you've made a final decision about exactly what services you will provide. Customers are more likely to retain quality brochures, especially if they contain helpful hints and useful information related to your services.

7. Better Business Name

Your name should impart a strong sense of what you do, yet be uniquely yours (and pronounceable by your potential customers). A Legal Document Assistant's business name should not sound like a law firm, nor contain the word paralegal. (Jones, Smith, and Associates is a big no-no). For additional information or assistance in selecting an appropriate name, call the National Self-Help Law Center at 707-263-7200. They'll be happy to provide useful information about what IPs can call themselves.

8. Better Business Plan

Planning is the key to success. The more realistic and detailed your business plan, the more easily it can be used as an operation guide to keep your business on an even fiscal keel.

9. Better Customer Mailing List

Get and keep the name, address, and telephone number of every customer who contacts you; these are valuable resources. Ask for dates of birth on your intake forms. Send out birthday cards, flyers, and announcements of new services, as appropriate.

10. Better Customer Recourse

The best recourse policy for a legal document assistant business is a full refund for dissatisfied customers. Once offered, customers seldom require refunds. On the other hand, a lawyer for a fraud or UPL action instigated by an unhappy customer will cost you a bundle.

11. Better Customer Relationships

A satisfied customer is your most powerful marketing ally. If you always provide value and quality, you will have little trouble establishing credibility, a primary key to excellent customer relations. Disputes with customers should always be approached from a win-win perspective—and if both of you can't win, the customer should.

12. Better Distribution

When possible, offer your services in several outlets. Work the copy center near the courthouse on your slowest afternoon. Make home calls and use the mail. Trade shows are vehicles to get your name and specialty known—share a booth with another law-related organization or a copy service.

13. Better Follow-up

If you file papers for your customers, drop them a note to let them know their case is filed. Include the file number and close with a reminder: "if you have questions or need additional assistance don't hesitate to call me at . . ."

14. Better Forms

If your state has official, mandatory, or "approved" forms, make sure you use them and make sure the ones you use are up to date. Cultivate a good relationship with the people who distribute the forms so you will be informed when the forms change. Spend some time in the court records reviewing cases where the forms have been used, so you know which formats will and won't work.

15. Better Signage

Don't limit yourself to the inside sign "We are NOT lawyers and we DON'T give legal advice." Use creative and attractive signs as advertisements for your other "profit centers." A sign on your storefront is not the only place to let people know where you are. If you are in a large city, advertise in the subway, taxicabs, or buses. Avoid negative slogans and gimmicks.

16. Better Location

This is one of the most important factors to consider when opening a paralegal business. Access for your customer is the key to locating your business. In cities, public transportation is a must. In rural and suburban areas, parking is an important consideration. Heavy foot traffic is always desirable.

17. Better Logo

A clever logo will cause the public to think of your business when they see it. Sometimes a logo is a stylized way of presenting initials or a name. Other times the logo is purely a graphic image.

18. Better Niche

Be on the lookout for specific services that are needed but not provided by anyone else in your market area. The more unique your services are, the easier it will be to build your business. The degree of specialization required will depend on what other services exist in your market.

19. Better Phone Demeanor

Your first contact with a potential customer usually comes over the telephone. How that interaction is handled will often determine whether you or someone else gets the customer's business. Someone who understands and can articulate what your paralegal business can and cannot do should therefore answer your telephone promptly with a friendly, helpful, and professional greeting.

20. Better Presentation

Have several short (30-60 seconds) oral presentations about you and your paralegal business worked out in advance so you are ready to "sell" your business regardless of the context. Remember, everyone is either a potential customer or a good referral source.

21. Better Public Relations

Identify yourself as an advocate for the independent paralegal movement. Seize every possible opportunity to educate people about how paralegals can help them do many legal tasks without a lawyer. Writing an article for a local newspaper or giving a radio or television interview will get the name of your business out there while boosting your credibility. For instance, publicity in California newspapers about the State Bar's approval of legal technicians gave paralegal businesses an opportunity to produce follow-up pieces of their own.

22. Better Quality

Everything you do must be of exceptional quality. If you can't do it that way, don't do it. Taking on too many different areas at once can lead to confusion and error. Specialization, on the other hand, helps you achieve quality in increments. First master one task, and then move to the next.

23. Better Reputation

Most of your customers will come from two primary sources: referrals from the legal community (lawyers, judges, clerks) and referrals from satisfied customers. The extent to which these sources provide you with enough customers depends on your reputation, and your reputation will depend on the quality of your service and the way you treat people. You can build a reputation with the legal community through excellence in service and through the development of your own referral list for cases you cannot or should not accept. Your reputation in the community depends not only on how well you do the job, but also on your attitude towards the customer. Every contact with your business should be a positive experience for the customer. If you can't help them, get them to someone who can, or send them away with some useful information.

24. Better Customer Sources

Identify *all* possible sources of customers. In addition to the legal community and satisfied customers, your process server, notary, insurance salesperson, forms supplier, and other suppliers of goods and services are in a good position to send business your way. Be creative. You can think of many more.

25. Better Stationery

Classy stationery is essential for promoting your business. An expensive feel and look will make it a powerful tool. Standard lettering used on off white or light colored 24 lb. watermark bond is the best.

26. Better Theme

Your theme is a summary statement of benefits that you give to your prospective customers. It can be used to set you apart from your competition. Spend a significant amount of time drafting your theme so that it is clear and powerful. Show it to friends and associates. Consider each of their comments to be valid, and do your very best to work them into your theme while keeping it short and sweet. Remember the apology by C.K. Chesterton to his nephew: "I'm sorry this letter is so long; I didn't have time to write a shorter one."

27. Better Window Displays

Rent space where your windows have high visibility and can be used to interest passersby in your business. Keep the windows clean, neat, and changed often if you have displays. If you put a sign on the window, have it done professionally. Take the time to carefully choose the content of the sign and the form of lettering to be used. If your aesthetic sense falls a little short, get some help from someone who has a good eye for design and layout.

28. Better Business Cards

Your card should sell your service, and you should give it out at any opportunity. There are two approaches to business cards. One is to keep it simple but elegant, to impart a sense of quality and professionalism. The other is to load it up with information about your business, making your cards a type of advertisement. Regardless of your approach, your card should have, at a minimum, your business name, your name, your address, and your phone number, and should indicate that you are an independent paralegal. If you choose the advertising approach, consider identifying several of your services or including a sentence that summarizes what you do.

29. Better Circulars

This is the least expensive form of advertising for a paralegal business. Circulars can be placed on windshields, on counters, at homes, and in local businesses. Day workers will "bugle" an entire section of a community for a fee. Make sure the content is clear, concise, and attractive.

30. Classified, Display, and Magazine Ads

Analyze paid advertising for its cost-effectiveness and use it only when you think you can derive a clear benefit. As a general rule, paid advertising is not a particularly effective or desirable way to generate customers for a service business.

31. Column in Newspapers

A great way to get more business for your paralegal services is to write a regular column in a newspaper or magazine. You can write about wills, divorce, probate, and so on without giving legal advice, and many local newspapers are starved for good regular information for consumers. If you run into opposition because you're not a lawyer, search for a lawyer coauthor.

32. Competitiveness

To operate a successful paralegal business you must be willing to devote time, energy, and resources to marketing to get ahead. That's what the "Fifty Ways" are all about.

33. Better Computer

Every paralegal business needs a computer. If you don't already know how, learn how to use one right away. In our opinion, the easiest computers to use are Macintosh, from Apple, but PCs are, of course, in widespread use and are also a good choice. Both computers will allow you to turn out top-quality copy, and will run most of the currently available legal software. If you go with the Mac, make sure to check that the software you will need for your specific business area will be compatible with the Mac hardware, and if you plan to emphasize bankruptcy in your practice, you should get a PC. The best available bankruptcy software runs only on PCs.

34. Consultations

Offering consultations on how to use a specific self-help book is a good way to let people know you are there only to help them complete their legal forms. Only an attorney can conduct a paid legal consultation.

35. Credit Cards

If possible, accept credit cards. Making it easy for customers to pay for your services is well worth the small fee you will have to pay.

36. Direct-Marketing Coupons

Coupon services, like Coupon Spree®, will mail discount coupon books to selected residential areas, and you can advertise your services that way. The average cost to you is about three cents per household. Check your business directory for a local coupon service.

37. Gift Certificates

Offer gift certificates for self-help materials at face value, or at a discount for customers. This will identify you as a community resource for self-help law materials, and will encourage users of the materials to return to you if they need help.

38. Hours/Days of Operation

People who need the help of independent paralegals usually work during regular business hours. IPs who work evenings and weekends to accommodate these customers get a greater market share than competitors who are less flexible.

39. More Enthusiasm

Love what you are doing and show it all the time. Treat and pay your employees well so that they also will show enthusiasm. Enthusiasm is contagious and will make your customers eager to refer their friends and associates to you.

40. More Media Contacts

If you develop media contacts, you will be called upon to give your assistance and opinions about issues related to paralegals when those issues are in the news. It will also make it easier for you to get your press releases printed. The more your business is mentioned in the media, the greater your credibility will be in the community.

41. More Tie-Ins

Develop ties with local businesses that will display your posters, flyers, and brochures in exchange for you displaying theirs. It's a good idea if those businesses are at least marginally related to what you are doing— for example, it's probably better to have a reciprocal arrangement with a copy store, messenger service, or process server, than with a hairdresser.

42. Newsletter

A newsletter establishes your expertise and serves as a marketing tool. It provides you lots of space to sell without selling and to remind customers of their needs and your ability to assist them. Start small at first and don't promise too much. If later you find that the newsletter takes too much time, you will want the flexibility to discontinue it without winding up with egg on your face.

43. Posters

Adding visibility to your business identity will increase your customer base.

44. Parking

Unless you are located near good public transportation, parking is a very important consideration. If customers who drive can't park, they can't purchase. If you are downtown, rent several spaces for your customers' use.

45. Phone-Hold Messages

When your potential customer is on hold, a message about your paralegal services can impart useful information and sell your services.

46. Reprints

Reprints of your published news releases, articles you write, and advertisements can be used as newsletter fillers. You can also use blown-up posters and flyers in mailers to your customers.

47. Sales Training

The person(s) responsible for sales should have sales training.

48. Special Events

Hold special events at your office to bring the public in. An open house, a book signing, or a "meet the community leader" reception can help build up an awareness of your services in the public's mind.

49. Testimonials

Satisfied customers will often give written praise freely and these testimonials can be very impressive to potential customers. Put then in your brochure or get them in the form of a letter that you can then enlarge, frame, and place on your wall.

50. Yellow Pages

Paralegal businesses report that significant portions of their customers reach them through the yellow pages. It is expensive, but if your competition is there, you should be too. However, special yellow pages have not proven very useful for bringing in business and we don't recommend those.

We strongly recommend that you spend some time developing a written marketing strategy, incorporating your assessment of the target marketing information we discussed in the introduction to this chapter, and using the 50 tactics described above as part of your strategy. Appendix A contains a sample Marketing Strategy worksheet from Lake County Self-Help Law Center, Inc. Use this as a template to develop your own marketing strategy, and watch your business grow.

L. Where to Get Marketing Training

Throughout this book, we recommend the services offered by the California Association of Legal Documents Assistants (CALDA). Although CALDA is California-based, it offers out-of-state memberships. CALDA sponsors occasional educational activities for independent paralegals, as well as publishing an informative newsletter.

For more information on CALDA and how to become a member, go to www.calda.org.

M. Summing Up

To put the marketing suggestions made in this chapter in the context of the independent paralegal business, we discussed marketing strategy with Robin Smith, formally of People's Paralegal Service, in Beaverton, Oregon. Here is an excerpt of our discussion (see Appendix for a longer discussion with Robin):

Ralph Warner (RW): How important are referrals to People's Paralegal Service?

Robin Smith (RS): Crucial. It takes time and patience to develop a positive reputation with lots of community agencies. But once you do, and they trust you, they can really make a big difference. The power of 50 to 100 groups all occasionally referring you customers is amazing.

RW: *How do you develop good contacts at places that are likely to send you customers?*

RS: Slowly. People at legal aid, or the Sheriff's Office, or the Army (which, incidentally, is a great source of referrals), aren't going to plug your business unless they truly believe in it. It's up to you to prove that you are worthy of their trust.

RW: *And how do you accomplish that?*

RS: As I've said, offering good service is essential, but you also have to make sure the key people who make the referrals know who you are. One excellent way to do that is to send good solid information to them on a regular basis. Your best bet is to adopt many of the strategies followed by nonprofit consumer organizations. In other words, draft informative newsletters, contact the media when you have something to say, and generally tell the world what a truly good, innovative, and cost-effective job you are doing.

RW: *What about talking to people at public agencies, courts, and law libraries directly?*

RS: Yes, sure, but a hard sell won't work. Remember, these people are motivated to help the people they deal with on a daily basis, not to help your business. You have to convince them that when a person is referred to your typing service, you will really provide a great service. This takes time.

RW: *What about the media? Does People's Paralegal get much free coverage?*

RS: Definitely. The lack of access the average person has to the legal system is a story of continuing media interest, which means our business is newsworthy. I've been providing consumer help and information for over ten years now, which means I know a number of local news, feature, and consumer reporters.

RW: *How often are they interested in hearing from you?*

RS: It's a fine line. If you self-promote too much, too often, you'll turn people off. Reporters are interested when there is something new, as would be the case if your business changes significantly.

RW: *What about the bar association? Does their hostility to the self-help law movement help you?*

RS: Absolutely. Whenever the bar makes a negative statement about non-lawyer legal form preparation, two things happen. First, the press needs to get the other side of the story, which means they are likely to call an IP they know and trust. Once the article is printed, many people who need help with legal paperwork and can't afford a lawyer will find out that alternatives exist and are likely to call the IP who is quoted in the article.

RW: *What else does an IP need to know to deal with the media effectively?*

RS: Tell the truth, and if you make any promises, keep them. For example, if you send out a press release about a protest event that doesn't happen, or promise exciting news you can't deliver, your credibility will be shot. Finally, let me make one more point. No matter how clever your promotional efforts, they will avail you little in the long run unless your business really delivers what it says it will. In this age in which all sorts of mediocre products and services are vastly over-hyped, people are looking for performance, not promises. ∎

Computers, the Internet, and the Independent Paralegal

W hen the first California independent paralegals opened their doors in the early 1970s, a typewriter was the main tool required for the job. Now, 30 years later, its fair to say that the computer has, for all practical purposes, replaced the typewriter. Of course, typewriters still come in handy for preparing documents that are not yet published in electronic format by the courts or private vendors. But in the new century, fewer and fewer documents need be typewritten, in a literal sense. Now the operative term is "print out."

A. Cost Is Not a Significant Barrier

Even when it became evident some years back that a computer could greatly increase an independent paralegal's efficiency, many balked at purchasing one because of the cost. Now, however, price is no longer the barrier it once was. Used computers loaded with all the necessary software can be purchased for several hundred dollars, and new computers, with the minimum necessary software, can be purchased for far less than in past years. Powerful computers complete with a monitor, printer, and basic office software can now be purchased for less than $1,000. For a new version of Microsoft Office (a suite of applications that includes Microsoft Word, Excel, and PowerPoint), tack on an additional $400 or so. And if your business warrants the purchase of one or more special applications, such as bankruptcy software or a child support calculator, figure roughly $200-$400 a program. All together, $1,500-$2,000 should get you up and running.

B. Do I Buy a PC or a Mac?

As you undoubtedly know, there are two main types of computers: the Mac and the PC. As a general rule, you will find a PC more convenient for the IP business, primarily because virtually all new legal software is developed solely for the PC platform. While many new Macs can run PC software if you have the proper conversion program installed, the extra expense and hassle that goes with this "cross-platform" approach probably tilts towards using a PC in the first instance. But if you are a dedicated Mac fan, by all means get a Mac or use the one you have.

C. Choosing Software

Once you have your computer set up, you'll want to explore what types of software are available for your special niche. For instance, if you are a bankruptcy petition preparer, you'll probably want to find a bankruptcy program that meets your requirements. Although attorneys were later than other professionals to adopt the computer as an everyday tool, virtually all attorneys are now computer literate, at least to some degree. And even if they are not, the chances are great that their office staff is totally up to speed.

Because of this, lots of programs are being created and marketed to attorneys for a broad range of legal tasks. Unfortunately, products marketed to attorneys tend to be pricey. It may be, for example, that your budget just won't accommodate the purchase of bankruptcy software for $300 to $400 a pop. But you may find some attorney software that is reasonably priced and does fit within your budget.

There is also an increasing amount of software being marketed directly to the consumer. Nolo publishes a lot of it. Although you often must purchase a separate license from Nolo or other software publishers to use this consumer software for commercial purposes, the license may be a lot cheaper than software intended for attorneys.

We are often asked what software is available for various tasks, such as divorces in North Dakota or incorporations in Maine. The truth is, we usually cannot answer these questions off the top. But we can suggest three basic approaches to finding the answer yourself:

1. **Visit Nolo at www.nolo.com.** Nolo has a lot of software that can be used by IPs. Wills, living trusts, living wills, durable powers of attorney for finances, partnership agreements, corporations, limited liability companies, patents, provisional patents, and residential leases can all be created with Nolo software products. Many Nolo books also come with CDs that contain the book's forms. Nolo's website pro-

vides all the information you'll need about these products, as well as information about how to obtain a commercial license.

2. **Ask a competitor.** In Chapter 8 we suggest that you can learn a lot about the area you choose to operate in by talking to an existing business. Even if there is no existing business in your particular locality, there is likely one somewhere in your state. And, as a general rule, if software works in one part of your state, it will work in all parts of your state. In our experience, independent paralegals are usually willing to share this type of information with others, even if you are likely to be a competitor down the road.

3. **Use the Internet.** If any software exists for your area of practice, you can depend on it being marketed in some way on the Internet. See Section F, below, where we provide some pointers on finding information on the Internet.

D. Create Text Files

As an alternative to purchasing software, you may be able to use your computer to create a set of text files that accomplish the same purpose. A number of legal areas don't really require software in the traditional sense. Rather, it's simply a matter of assembling all the necessary clauses in separate files and then merging the clauses to match the customer's answers in the questionnaire. For example, assume you offer a will preparation service and require your customers to purchase Nolo's *Simple Will Book* as the underlying legal material. Assume further that you obtain a license from Nolo to copy the *Simple Will Book* clauses onto your own computer. The book comes with a CD-ROM containing these clauses. You can then organize the clauses according to how you construct your questionnaire.

Your questionnaire in this example should provide specific references to the sections of the *Simple Will Book* that relate to the specific questions. This turns your questionnaire into a set of directions, from the customer to you, that are clearly based on the information and clauses contained in the Nolo book. This satisfies the basic model advanced throughout this book. That is, your only role as an IP is to prepare legal documents under the direction of your customers. Business entity formation, estate planning documents (wills, living wills, living trusts), landlord/tenant transactions, contracts of various types, and, in many states, divorces, are all tasks that lend themselves to this approach.

E. Committing UPL by Computer

Many IPs who use software (for instance, a bankruptcy program) commonly fall into a trap that may get them charged with UPL. Here's the problem. Most legal programs use an interview format and require that certain decisions be made in the course of producing the final document. For instance, if you have minor children, Nolo's will software (*Quicken WillMaker Plus*) asks you whether you want to choose a personal guardian. If you indicate that you do, then the program prompts you for certain choices. To make these choices intelligently, the user needs access to the program help. However, if you, as the IP, are the only one who is operating the program, your customer won't have that access. This puts you in the role of passing on the information from the help system to the customer. As we emphasize throughout the book, it's far better from a UPL prevention standpoint if your customers have direct access to the information that informs their choices.

What to do? The best solution we can think of is to find a way to give your customers access to the help files. For this you will need permission from the software publisher. Another possible approach is to find a print resource that covers the same choices offered by the program and create a questionnaire that refers to the print resource every time the questionnaire asks for a choice. For instance, if you are using a bankruptcy program, you may want to key your questionnaire to the appropriate sections in one of Nolo's bankruptcy products available in print or electronic form.

F. Living in the Internet Age

If current developments are a prelude to the future, much of the discussion in this chapter about "software" will be obsolete. Every week the Internet sees new sites with new "wizards," form generators, and calculators that provide assistance with completing one legal task or another. Some of these sites also offer step-by-step instructions.

It is also possible to use the Internet to find:

- State and federal statutes, regulations, and cases
- Local ordinances
- Collections of articles on virtually every legal topic
- Forms
- Frequently Asked Questions and Answers about various legal topics (FAQS), and
- Information about current events.

Once you become comfortable with Internet research, it is very much like having your very own law library. And, the more you can help make this information available to your customers, the better informed they will be and the less likely you will be accused of engaging in UPL. Nolo's *Legal Research: How to Find and Understand the Law,* by Elias and Levinkind provides step-by-step assistance for finding legal information on the Internet. Probably the two best websites for starting your research are www.findlaw.com and www.law.cornell.edu. If your business is in California, you can take advantage of the official California website created for the self-represented public, located at www.courtinfo.ca.gov. This site offers lots of FAQs about a large variety of legal tasks and downloadable official forms (created by the California Judicial Council) that can be filled in on your computer. Other states are busy creating similar sites for people representing themselves.

The Internet is also very good for doing market research (see Chapter 10). Most of the Internet search engines offer a Yellow Pages feature that lets you search by profession. So, if you enter "paralegal" in the search engine and specify your state or city, you will get a list of every paralegal who lists in the actual Yellow Pages for that area. This will provide a good indication of the number of independent paralegals already up and running, although some of the listings will be for paralegals who only work for lawyers (freelance paralegals). Incidentally, IPs who also have websites will usually appear at the top of the list.

Finally, as we suggested above, the Internet is a great place to find software and other legal materials that will support your business. All search engines let you search for software by category and online legal catalogs known as portals (findlaw.com is our favorite) will get you to all sorts of legal materials, some free and some not.

G. Will the Internet Make the IP Business Obsolete?

You have only to visit nolo.com to get a hint of what the Internet promises. Anybody with a link to the Internet (which is available to everybody for almost nothing) can get legal information, forms, and instructions directly from the Nolo site, often for free.

As mentioned, courts all over the country are starting to put their forms and instructions up on their own Internet site, and it's expected that in the near future, most forms may be electronically filed, as is now true with federal tax and trademark filings.

The fact is, the Internet allows anyone to be a publisher, which means that every lawyer, law librarian, and paralegal in the U.S. may be busy creating a killer website, in one legal area or another, as these words are being written. If you view legal information as the traditional lawyer's equivalent of gold, the Internet, by removing all publishing barriers, is working a sort of reverse alchemy, transmuting gold into lead.

As a budding independent paralegal, you may get more than a little depressed by all this. After all, if your customers can do everything online, why pay you to do it for them? Fortunately, you can always count on a number of people to be computer/Internet phobic. Also, especially for tasks that come with emotional distress, such as divorce, many people will want to deal with a human being rather than an inanimate entity called a website. And finally, the more information there is on the Internet, the greater the need for a trusted person to point the customer in the right direction. So, even if you are conducting your business the old fashioned way, in a real office, you may still be able to develop a healthy business for years to come. It's probably safe to say, however, that your customer base is likely to shift in the direction of folks with lower incomes and less education than is currently the case.

The other approach, of course, is to join the Internet Age and figure out ways to conduct your business on the Internet. We go into more detail on this in Chapter 6. However, we need to make one point here, loud and clear. The Internet serves up a severe challenge to every sort of business. Those who figure out how to use the Internet to their benefit are likely to do very well while those who don't embrace it are likely to be left in the dust. Unlike business in physical space, there is only a need for one really good Internet site in a particular niche. For instance, if one site gets known as the quality bankruptcy petition preparation site, all other sites may founder, since there is no inherent limitation in the number of cases that the #1 site can handle. ■

CHAPTER

12

Customer Recourse

T his is one of the shortest and most important chapters in this
book. It deals with what to do if a customer is not satisfied with
your work. We refer to this process as providing customer recourse.

A. The Importance of Satisfying Unhappy Customers

The willingness to provide the dissatisfied customer with an efficient
way to gain recourse is important to all businesses. Huge and successful companies, such as the mail order high flyers Land's End and L.L.
Bean, have been built to a substantial degree on their commitment to
promptly taking care of all customer complaints. In the retail area,
Nordstrom bases much of its marketing effort on convincing customers
that it provides excellent recourse should any of its merchandise fail to
live up to a customer's expectations.

Providing a quick, fair way to resolve customer complaints is
even more crucial to small business success, because it's an essential
element of establishing a good "word-of-mouth" marketing plan. (We
discussed how to do this in Chapter 10.) If you doubt the strong link
between taking care of the occasional customer complaint and generating positive recommendations about a business, ask yourself this: If
you hear about a skilled carpenter who does spectacular work, but also
hear that he is temperamental and has a reputation for not taking care
of problems, would you hire him? And if you did, and were upset by
his refusal to take care of several loose ends as part of an otherwise
competent job, would you recommend him to your friends? Despite his
skill, probably not.

And it isn't only carpenters whose business will suffer if they
don't satisfy customer complaints. The same is true of a dentist, plumber,
computer programmer, and, as you have no doubt guessed, an independent paralegal. If word gets out that you aren't reliable and don't
take care of complaints, your business will not grow.

And don't think it's adequate to simply work out solutions to the
occasional customer complaint as they come up. This is a bad business
practice for several reasons. First, you are likely to be emotionally in-

volved with the particular complaint and thus may not be objective enough to look at the situation from your customer's perspective.

Second, and more important, your failure to establish a complaint resolution procedure in advance and announce it early and often means that your customers, and the agencies and other people who refer your customers, won't know what to expect if something goes wrong and therefore may not patronize you in the first place. Think about how many times you have patronized one store or service provider (again, L.L. Bean, Land's End, and Nordstrom are excellent examples) instead of another because you know you'll be in good hands if a problem develops.

Third, if you fail to reassure all customers that you will promptly take care of any problems, you risk a dissatisfied customer complaining to the bar or to the District Attorney or State Department of Consumer Affairs instead of to you. This reason for adopting a good recourse policy deserves emphasis. Never forget that you are working under the always mistrustful—and often hostile—eye of organized lawyerdom. The majority of prosecutions for unauthorized practice that are not initiated by lawyers or judges themselves result from complaints from members of the public·who feel ripped off by an independent paralegal.

Here are the key elements of any good customer recourse policy:
- The customer should know her rights (and responsibilities) and how to take advantage of them from the beginning;
- The customer should be encouraged to tell you about any worries or problems;
- The customer should feel in control of the relationship;
- The customer should be able to ask for and receive her money back at any time, with no need to give a reason;
- Once a customer asks for her money back (or any other promised recourse you offer), it should be provided promptly.

One more important point. When you're deciding whether it's worth the trouble to develop a bulletproof recourse policy, consider and learn from the current plight of lawyers. Because bar associations and other lawyer-controlled professional regulatory groups provide such a poor system to handle and resolve complaints about lawyers who are corrupt, incompetent, and price-gouging, the entire legal profession's reputation isn't much higher than that of the Moscow subway.

The reason we belabor the point that it's essential to establish a good recourse policy in advance is that many independent paralegals haven't done so. A few are even proud to say that they never give a refund. Clearly, no matter how good a legal form typing service some of these independent paralegals offer, they have not learned the basics of running a successful small business. It's as if Macy's advertised "The customer is always wrong."

We have found the intransigence of a number of paralegals on this issue to be particularly surprising in light of the fact that many do excellent work and, as a result, receive only a couple of complaints a year. It's surprising that these IPs are willing to fight with customers over the return of a few hundred dollars at the risk of having these people badmouth them to the public at large, or to the bar in particular.

The California Association of Independent Paralegals provides this excellent advice to its members:

A competent paralegal will encounter customers who are not satisfied. It is a usually good business practice and beneficial for the paralegal occupation if such customers are given a refund if they are dissatisfied with the service. This can pacify the customer, create good will, avoid conflict and cost little.

The temptation to contest a complaint because it is unjust or erroneous is frequently harmful to the paralegal and to their profession. The only paralegal who really suffers from an automatic refund policy is one who fails to satisfy lots of customers. This paralegal should take immediate steps to improve her business practices.

B.   The "No Ifs, Ands, or Buts" Recourse Policy

We recommend that you establish a "no ifs, ands, or buts" money-back recourse policy. Not only is doing this a good deal for your customers, it is also a good deal for you. Why? Because assuming you sensibly screen your customers in the first place to eliminate inappropriate people, and you do a good form preparation job, experience indicates that less than 5% of your customers will be dissatisfied. (This percentage may be a little higher for divorces and lower in many other types of form preparation, such as small business incorporations.) The reason divorce seekers are more likely to complain is explained by the fact that these people are often under considerable emotional stress, and occasionally some of this is bound to spill over to their relationship with you.

Here is a recourse policy that we believe makes sense:

The ABC Typing Service is dedicated to providing quality legal typing services under the direction of its consumers for a fair price. If at any time you believe we have not fully met this goal, please ask for your money back. It will be provided promptly, no questions asked.

C. How to Deal With Predictable Customer Complaints

Enough lecturing! Let's assume you are convinced it's not a good idea to have unsatisfied former customers wandering about maligning your reputation and you have adopted the policies we recommend above.

Let's now look at how to handle several predictable situations in which at least a few customers are likely to be unhappy. The first is when the customer simply changes his mind about pursuing the legal action and asks for his money back after you have competently completed the work. (IPs who type marriage dissolution forms call this "divorce remorse.") Some independent paralegals provide no refund, or only a partial one, reasoning that since their work was done before the customer changed his mind, it's the customer's problem. While this policy is logically defensible, we believe it's misguided. As mentioned above, it's far, far easier in both the short and long run, to state a simple policy that if a customer is dissatisfied for any reason, you'll give a full refund—no "ifs, ands, or buts."

Another fairly common refund situation can occur when a legal action that starts out to be uncontested becomes contested while you are typing paperwork. If, as is likely, a lawyer ends up taking over the case, and you do not complete the paperwork, your customer may feel ripped off by having to pay an attorney in addition to having already paid you. Again, the best way to deal with this problem, which probably won't happen more than a few times a year, is to simply refund all, or at least a substantial part, of the customer's money.

Here is some language you may wish to include in your printed material to deal with this problem:

> *Any uncontested legal action has the potential to become contested, often resulting in both parties hiring a lawyer. If this occurs during the course of any legal procedure for which ABC Typing Service is helping prepare paperwork, all fees and charges will promptly be refunded.*

Customer unhappiness can also occasionally develop if, as part of working with your typing service, the customer needs legal information or advice not available from a self-help law book. As discussed above, it's best to cover this possibility in your original information sheet, indicating that the fee for your service does not cover any necessary lawyers' consultation fees. Assuming your customer simply confers with a lawyer (or calls a legal information phone service) who charges a reasonable fee, and comes back to you to complete the paperwork, there should be no problem, since the customer will almost surely understand that your typing fee has been fairly earned.

As part of working with ABC Typing Service to prepare your own legal paperwork, you may need to obtain legal advice or information from a lawyer or legal information telephone service. It is understood that you are responsible for paying for this legal advice separately and that it is not included in the fee paid the ABC Typing Service to prepare your legal paperwork.

One last note. By far the majority of complaints against lawyers result from the lawyer's failure to communicate with the client, by not returning phone calls or responding to email or letters. It is a good business practice, and will serve you well, if you make sure to be as prompt as possible in responding when your customers contact you.

D. What to Do If You Make a Serious Mistake

Finally, we come to the sticky question of what to do if a customer feels that your negligence or lack of knowledge resulted in loss of a substantial right and is not satisfied with a refund. Many IPs we have talked to state that, over the many years of preparing legal forms, this has never occurred. Others say that they have made mistakes that have caused consumers problems, but it's always been possible to fix them at a reasonable cost, usually by redoing the paperwork.

Fortunately, in most situations, the economic harm that an IP's mistake causes is fairly modest. For example, one IP who has been in business for a decade can remember a situation in which she filed a final decree of divorce before the end of the year, forgetting that the customer had asked her to wait until January 2, for tax reasons. The IP immediately asked a trusted tax preparer to compute the customer's extra tax liability and reimbursed her. The amount was only a few hundred dollars.

Even though IPs who know their field and keep good records don't often have customers who claim that their lack of care resulted in a substantial loss, it can happen. For example, let's say you type divorce papers for Mary C. A year later, she claims you neglected to include several valuable assets that she told you about and blames you for the fact that she wasn't awarded this property in the court divorce decree. Assuming you did all the things we discuss in Chapter 3 to establish that you are only a typing service, do not provide legal advice, and it's up to your customers to understand the laws that affect the particular legal area, you are off to a pretty good start. In addition, however, it's essential that you keep a written record of all information provided by your customer (preferably in her own handwriting), and have her sign a clear statement that the information provided is accurate and complete. (We discuss this in detail in Chapter 8.) In addition, after you type the necessary court or agency forms, your customer should read them carefully (or if necessary, have them read to her) and again sign a statement that they are complete.

If your divorce customer did all this, and the missing property wasn't listed, you are in an excellent legal position. Assuming the property existed in the first place, it's your customer's responsibility, not yours.

E.   Malpractice and Business Liability Insurance

Many IPs believe that they should carry the equivalent of a lawyer's malpractice insurance. Fortunately, when you think it through, there is no reason to buy it, even when it's available—which it isn't in most states. Although a few surety companies in California have underwritten errors and omissions polices for Legal Document Assistants (Hartford, among others), the insurance is expensive—upwards of $800 a year. And we believe you do not need it.

So why isn't an errors and omissions policy necessary? Simply put, under the delivery model we teach in this book—which is also applicable to California Legal Document Assistants—the customer is responsible for his or her own case and must direct your activities. Your only duty, in exchange for the money you are paid, is to prepare and file the customer's documents accurately. It is the customer's role to review the paperwork, so if you have made a mistake the customer should spot it and have you make the necessary corrections. And, since paperwork produced by lawyers frequently contains clerical mistakes, the court system has many ways to correct these mistakes without the party being adversely affected. So, you don't really need an errors and omissions policy to protect against clerical errors.

This isn't to say that you won't make a clerical mistake that it may take a few hundred dollars to correct, only that you aren't facing the kinds of large liabilities that trigger the need for malpractice insurance (see Section D above). Incidentally, lawyers in many states, including California, are not required to carry malpractice insurance. According to one survey taken in the early 1990s, about half of California's attorneys "go bare."

What about errors in judgment, or errors like picking the wrong form or choosing the wrong bankruptcy exemption? Again, those are your customer's responsibility. Under the UPL laws of every state except Arizona and Florida, the exercise of judgment, the selection of forms, and the choosing of exemptions is considered to be the practice of law, and you are not authorized to practice law. And since the unauthorized practice of law is illegal, you would be asking your errors and omissions carrier to defend you for illegal activity—something that every errors and omissions policy excludes from coverage. In short, when your only job is to put the customer's information onto the forms the customer selects, paying for errors and omissions insurance is most likely a waste of money.

TRY MEDIATION

Now suppose you establish that it's too late to take corrective action, but you believe your work didn't cause the problem (for example, your customer supplied you with a signed property list that didn't include the disputed property). Your best bet is to suggest mediation. This involves both of you sitting down with a trained mediator to try and work out your own settlement of the dispute. Since the mediator has no power to impose a decision that you don't agree to, there is no risk that the process will result in financial liability on your part, unless, of course, you voluntarily accept it. One of the best aspects of mediation is that it allows your customers (and you, too, for that matter) to air all grievances, not just the one that directly caused the dispute. Once everything is out in the open, a surprising number of apparently intractable disputes are settled.

This being said, one of the authors recently was retained as an expert witness in a negligence case brought against a California Legal Document Assistant. The LDA prepared a will for a customer who was on his deathbed. Pursuant to the customer's direction, the will left his property to all his children equally. Unfortunately, most of the customer's net worth was tied up in an IRA that named only one of his children as the sole beneficiary. Under California law (and the law of most states), IRAs with beneficiary designations are not covered by the will, and so the other siblings received very little money. When the newly enriched sibling refused to share, the other siblings sued her and the LDA, alleging that the LDA was negligent in not arranging for the other siblings to be added to the IRA designation form.

The LDA was forced to hire a local attorney to represent her in the case, even though she only followed the customer's direction and was not directed by him to do anything about the IRA. Although the plaintiffs dismissed the LDA from the lawsuit on the eve of trial, she ended up paying many thousands of dollars for pretrial representation. Had she been covered by an errors and omissions policy, her legal costs possibly would have been picked up (at least after some serious advocacy on her part against the insurance company). The moral of this story is, there may come a time when errors and omissions is worth the cost after all. And even if the unexpected never happens, the sense of security you gain from the insurance may be worth the premium.

BUY INSURANCE TO COVER NORMAL BUSINESS RISKS

You should definitely consider purchasing normal types of business insurance to protect your business—and, especially if you are not incorporated, your personal assets—should customers be hurt in or outside your premises. This liability insurance is often sold as part of a package with fire and theft coverage, which is also a good idea to cover your business equipment. In addition, if your car, or a car of any employee, is ever used to do errands for the business, be sure your auto insurance policy covers you for any liability incurred. (This usually involves paying extra for business coverage.) If an accident occurs while you are or an employee is on a business errand, even if the employee is driving his or her own car, your business is likely to be sued.

■

CHAPTER

13

Working for Volunteer, Community, or Social Change Organizations

The Pittsburgh, Pennsylvania, bar association charged "Legal Advocacy for Women," a nonprofit center that helps mothers get child support they are legally entitled to, with unauthorized practice of law. (See interview with Rose Palmer in Appendix.) In Lackawanna, N.Y., the Erie County bar association called Judy Lamb on the carpet for similar activities. In other areas of the country, similar types of bar harassment have occasionally been directed against nonprofit groups involved in environmental, consumer, and tenants' rights activities. If you work with a good cause and, as part of doing so, help people understand their legal rights and deal with the legal system by filing papers and appearing in court, are you likely to become the target of organized lawyerdom's official ire?

The answer is a qualified "probably not," although, as the Pennsylvania and New York examples illustrate, IPs who work in a nonprofit context are not immune from being charged with the unauthorized practice of law. Why do I say that volunteer groups normally have less to fear? Because by definition these groups work in areas where people traditionally don't have the money to hire a lawyer. And despite lip service to the contrary, the American legal profession has traditionally had little interest in representing people who can't pay their stiff fees. What about all the free (*pro bono*) work lawyers claim they do? It's mostly public relations hooey designed to frustrate any serious reform of the legal system.

Put more directly, when all the professional hype is stripped away, the legal profession defines the practice of law to involve only legal disputes and procedures where there is money to be made. It follows that since lawyers profit handsomely from business formation, probate, personal injury, domestic disputes (especially between affluent people), and estate planning, to name just a few, they are extremely interested in defending their monopoly power in these areas and are quick to charge nonlawyer interlopers with the unauthorized practice of law.

In many other legal areas, however, lawyers have never found a way to collect what they view as decent fees. These include small consumer disputes, the collection of child support, arguments among neighbors, the right of a poor person to die with dignity, domestic violence, and dozens of everyday hassles. So, even though working in these areas may involve giving advice about legal procedures, completing legal forms, etc., lawyers are often willing to look the other way if nonlawyers do it.

You surely get the point. Because many nonprofit organizations work in areas of little or no lawyerly profit, lawyers normally do not initiate charges of unauthorized practice of law against them. This is true even though paralegals who work for these nonprofits often get far more involved in giving legal advice than do independent paralegals who sell form preparation services directly to the public. And once a particular nonprofit legal self-help group exists for several years (say an AIDS support group, where nonlawyers help dying people complete a living will or durable power of attorney), the very fact that lawyers haven't harassed it in the past often results in a politically convenient and widely accepted fabrication that the organization in question doesn't really engage in the practice of law.

A good example of how this process works is the establishment of tenants' rights groups in the 1960s and 1970s in many areas of the country. At first, there was a great deal of anxiety about how organized lawyerdom would react. The fear was that since in most tenants' rights groups nonlawyers routinely counseled tenants about their legal rights and helped them fill out court forms, such as answers to eviction suits, organized lawyerdom was sure to file unauthorized practice charges. Instead, the bar's response in most places was to do nothing. Apparently, this was for two reasons. First, because lawyers never made much money defending tenants in the first place, no one cared enough to get involved in trying to suppress these activities. Second, lawyers were afraid if they put nonlawyer tenant-advocacy services out of business, they would have to do the work themselves, often on a *pro bono* (free) basis.

By contrast, organized lawyerdom has gone after a number of independent paralegals who offer services to landlords. These for-profit landlord paralegal typing services are often charged with unauthorized practice, even though the work they do is the mirror image of what tenants' groups do. There is, of course, one crucial difference between the two: When it comes to landlords, who have traditionally hired lawyers, an independent paralegal eviction service is seen as taking money out of lawyers' pockets rather than providing a community service.

A. Appearing in Court

There is one legal area, besides representing paying clients, over which lawyers are extremely protective of their monopoly. This involves appearing in court on behalf of a client. As you'll see when you read Rose Palmer's interview in the Appendix, this is one of the things that got Legal Advocacy for Women in trouble in Pittsburgh, Pennsylvania. Indeed, the first formal complaint against the group was filed by a lawyer who objected to volunteers from the group attending court sessions and whispering instructions to women trying to petition for adequate amounts of child support. And later, when Pittsburgh lawyers accepted a settlement allowing nonlawyers to come to court to provide moral and legal support to women, one of the stipulations was that nonlawyer advisors not be allowed to touch, or put their belongings on, the lawyers' (counsel) table. Yes, it's sad that the once proud legal profession should stoop to measure its prerogatives in such petty ways, but petty or not, it's a good illustration of the overt lawyer hostility encountered by nonlawyers who try to help people who appear in court.

No matter what the dispute, or how much or how little money is at stake, lawyers are bent upon defending their right to be the only people who can speak for others in court. The reasons for this probably have as much to do with concerns about loss of status as they do with economics, but it is also true that, traditionally, enforcement of this rule has done much to fatten lawyers' wallets. When faced with the need to file or defend a court action, even perennially cash-starved public interest groups such as environmentalists, advocates for the disabled, friends of animals and supporters of the homeless have often been able to raise money, often significant amounts of it, to pay a lawyer.

Lawyers, of course, argue that greed has nothing to do with their position that only they can speak on behalf of clients in court. They contend that only they are trained in, and tested on, courtroom skills and it would risk doing great consumer harm to allow others to represent people in court. Without boring you with many pages as to why this argument is a largely self-interested sophistry, let us simply point out that in the vast majority of American law schools, courtroom advocacy is not a required course, and that bar examinations do not test this skill. In short, lawyers normally pick up courtroom skills by working with more experienced colleagues and by practicing (literally) on clients. The fact that nonlawyer advocates who work in nonprofit organizations gain their skills in much the same way is, of course, ignored by lawyers.

Judges enforce UPL laws in their courtrooms. In Chapter 2, Section D, we discuss how judges use the "inherent powers" doctrine to protect the legal profession's monopoly over the courtroom and in some instances even the preparation of routine legal paperwork.

B.   Defending Yourself From Lawyer Attacks

But suppose you plan to work with a volunteer group in a situation where you will routinely be dispensing legal information and, despite my advice that you are unlikely to experience trouble with the bar, you are worried. After all, like the people who worked with Pittsburgh's Legal Advocacy for Women, you might be targeted for an unauthorized practice of law enforcement action. Certainly it is appropriate to ask what is likely to happen to you personally if organized lawyerdom tries to suppress your group.

As long as you are working in the broad public interest sector, the answer is "little or nothing." We know of no current criminal prosecutions in this area. Instead, even when a complaint by organized lawyerdom is initiated, what almost always occurs is something like this:

1.   The bar, district attorney, or state supreme court threatens to charge your group (let's assume you work at a center that helps with the legal problems of students) with unauthorized practice. Inciden-

tally, this threat is almost always initiated because a local lawyer handles a dispute against someone who gets legal help from your organization, not because a consumer of your services complains;

2. The media gets involved on the side of your group, asking where else penniless students (or in other situations, mothers without child support, tenants, immigrants, etc.) can get affordable legal help;

3. Organized lawyerdom comes under general attack for not offering free "pro bono" help in the particular area, and for generally overcharging and not providing reasonable access to the legal system for the average student (and by extension, most Americans);

4. Meetings are held between the advocacy group and organized lawyerdom and a compromise is worked out. It typically allows the lawyers to save face by getting the nonprofit group to agree to slightly modify its activities to avoid a charge of UPL (or, if a UPL action has already been filed, to have it dropped). Sometimes this "slap on the wrist" takes the form of limiting some inconsequential aspect of the nonprofit's activities; other times it is accomplished by the nonprofit agreeing to token supervision by a lawyer who is personally interested in the particular activity or cause. Almost always, when you look beyond the surface, the advocacy group is allowed to keep operating much as before.

As Rose Palmer discusses in her interview, the Legal Advocacy for Women situation well illustrates how this usually works. The bar and Legal Advocacy for Women settled their dispute as follows: In exchange for organized lawyerdom backing off, the organization agreed to change its name to "Support, Inc." and clarify a few of its procedures. This consisted of informing all clients that their paralegal helpers are not lawyers (something they knew already), agreeing not to whisper to clients in court, and, as mentioned, agreeing not to touch the counsel table. In short, whispering excepted, Support, Inc., is free to do exactly the same work as Legal Advocacy for Women did. And while the group refused to accept any official supervision by a lawyer or bar association, they were canny enough to partially mollify the local legal establishment by 1) putting a few lawyers on their board of directors, 2) working closely with several local sympathetic lawyers and supportive judges, and 3) beginning a law student intern program under which students from two local law schools help out with Support, Inc., programs.

C. Paying the Bills

Unfortunately, paralegals who work with nonprofits often face a larger problem than the threat of lawyer harassment. Their problem is economic. Most nonprofit groups, whether organized to help people with AIDS, artists, alcoholics, animals, or any of thousands of other worthy endeavors, are severely underfunded. All too often they try to survive from one inadequate grant to the next, existing in large measure because of the personal economic sacrifices made by their own staff. Put more bluntly, a paralegal who works in this setting is typically either unpaid or underpaid. For the rare persons with plenty of money in the bank, this may not be a problem. For everyone else, it is a severe one.

The result is that many nonprofit organizations that try to help their members, or the public generally, with legal problems usually experience rapid staff turnover. Often it seems that as soon as a competent paralegal is trained, she has moved on. Commonly, this isn't because the person wants to leave, but because the hard rock of their altruism has been ground into dust by the even harder economic reality of being poor in America. Obviously, rapid turnover is not only harmful to the paralegals involved, but also takes a toll on the quality of the legal services delivered by the group.

In our view, many of the problems nonprofits have paying paralegals to deliver good legal services could be avoided. The key to doing this is understanding one of the great lessons of the independent paralegal movement—people are willing and able to pay for competent, reasonably priced legal help if charged for it at paralegal, not lawyer, rates. In other words, the seeming conclusion of many nonprofit groups that there are only two alternatives to the delivery of legal services—hire a lawyer and pay the market rate, or provide free services—is just plain wrong.

PARALEGAL SERVICES AND NONPROFIT TAX LAW

Most nonprofit organizations are exempt from income taxation under Section 501(c)(3) of the Internal Revenue Code as educational or charitable organizations. Since education is defined by IRS regulations to include "instruction of the public on subjects useful to individuals and beneficial to the community," and since "charitable" generally means "promotion of the public good," nonprofits that provide paralegal services should fall well within the guidelines of their tax exemption requirements.

Can tax-exempt nonprofits charge hourly fees for paralegal services? Yes they can. (Just think of the substantial service fees collected by other nonprofit organizations, such as nonprofit colleges, trade schools, hospitals, medical clinics, and the like.) As long as the services charged are reasonable, the IRS should not object. In fact, in Ruling 78-428, the IRS decided that a nonprofit group that operated a legal services clinic could charge a fee based upon the income of the client.

This is not the place for a detailed discussion about the mechanics of setting up an economically self-sufficient paralegal office as part of a nonprofit organization. However, it is appropriate to look at one example of how an independent paralegal could provide low-cost legal help at the same time he charges enough to support himself.

Artists of all stripes and spots (dancers, painters, sculptors, jugglers, to mention but a few) often form nonprofit corporations when they want to come together to further their activities, whether it be to establish a performance space, publish educational materials, or sponsor a performance or display. Like the rest of us, most can't afford to hire a lawyer to do this at $200 an hour. As a result, unless they know a lawyer interested in the arts who will volunteer her time, most end up either doing it themselves or knocking on the door of a local nonprofit artists' support group with the hope that someone there can provide free legal help. Because artists' groups are chronically underfunded, they are often unable to do this.

Now, as an alternative, let us propose a different solution. Have the arts support organization work with an independent paralegal, or a paralegal on its own staff, to provide low-cost nonprofit incorporation services to local artists. To establish a fair fee, the first step would be to determine exactly how long it takes to prepare the paperwork to establish a nonprofit corporation and apply for a federal tax exemption. *How to Form a Nonprofit Corporation,* by Anthony Mancuso (Nolo), provides instructions on how to do this in every state and contains the step-by-step instructions necessary to apply for a Section 501(c)(3) federal tax exemption. After reading this book and examining the specific forms and procedures necessary in your state, you are likely to conclude the answer is about four to five hours, assuming someone in the nonprofit group has read Mancuso's book and worked with other members to gather necessary information and make practical choices.

The next step is to figure out a fair hourly return for the person doing this work. Assume after taking overhead into consideration you decide this is $65 per hour. This means you will probably find that a paralegal can prepare a nonprofit corporation for less than $300. Most arts groups, no matter how struggling, can scrape together this amount, especially if they have already checked prices with local lawyers, which are likely to range from $1,000–$2,000. ∎

Political Organizing for Change

L et's start this chapter by reviewing several points that have been discussed throughout this book.

1. The American civil legal system is slow, expensive, and inaccessible. Too often, it's also unjust and corrupt. As a result, the monopoly power of lawyers to deliver legal services in the U.S. is under attack as, increasingly, people see that lawyers are primarily interested in protecting themselves, not the public.

2. The self-help legal movement (and public support for it), has grown immensely in the last 30 years. For example, in several states, including California and Arizona, almost two-thirds of divorces and related family law court actions are now done without a lawyer.

3. The number of people who are running independent paralegal businesses has grown dramatically in the last decade, especially in Florida, Texas, Arizona, California, Minnesota, Oregon, Washington, and Nevada which, taken together, now have thousands of independent paralegals. The past several years have also seen the rapid expansion of a national IP franchise named *We the People*, now doing business in over 80 offices in 22 states.

4. Several studies, as well as a good deal of practical experience with independent paralegal offices, support the proposition that nonlawyers are competent to handle routine legal paperwork.

5. Self-help law software, such as *Nolo's WillMaker Plus*, has sold millions of copies. Ten years ago, these materials didn't exist.

6. The types of legal tasks that the general public is successfully accomplishing on its own using self-help law books and software (often with the help of independent paralegals) are expanding rapidly. In the 1980s, when people thought of self-help law they thought primarily of divorce; today, nonlawyers routinely prepare a wide variety of basic legal forms, including those for stepparent adoption, incorporation, probate and wills, living trusts, and house purchases.

7. The twenty-first century has seen a proliferation of self-help law websites on the Internet. Sponsored and operated by various state court systems, these sites provide legal information and step-by-step procedural instructions tailored to the tasks at hand. Private

websites also are offering a variety of online services, including trademarks, bankruptcies, and incorporation. See, for example, www.legalzoom.com and www.incspot.com/public/index.html. As universal access to the Internet becomes a reality, more and more customers will be turning to the Internet for information about their case. However, as we note earlier, there is still likely to be plenty of business for brick and mortar IPs.

This laundry list of trends adds up to the fact that America is in the midst of a period of fundamental and powerful change in the ways routine legal services are delivered to the middle class. This switch, which is of truly historic proportions, is clearly towards low-cost alternatives to the traditional ways lawyers deliver legal services. As one of these alternatives, the independent paralegal movement is in an excellent position to both help this trend along and to profit from it.

The fact that independent paralegals have made significant strides towards public acceptance in the last few years is not the same thing as saying this new profession is bound to succeed. As noted throughout this book, independent paralegals still face serious political and legal problems because of the hostility of organized lawyerdom. This brings us to the central question of this chapter—how can IPs best protect the advances their occupation has already made and take sensible steps to further expand their role in delivering routine legal services?

MORE ABOUT *WE THE PEOPLE*

We the People use a somewhat different model than the one we teach in this book. Each *We the People* office is an independently owned and operated franchise. The office provides its customers with a workbook and questionnaire prepared by an attorney licensed to practice law in that state. The paperwork is then shipped to the *We the People* headquarters in Santa Barbara, California, where the forms are prepared according to templates provided by the state-licensed attorney. The completed paperwork is then returned to the local office for delivery to the customer, or in some types of cases, for filing with the court. For information on franchise opportunities with *We the People*, contact Fran Distenfield, We the People Forms and Service Centers, U.S.A., Inc., 1501 State St., Santa Barbara, CA 93101, 805-962-4100. Because *We the People* does not provide its customers with comprehensive and reliable written self-help law materials, it has, on occasion, had difficulty explaining to bankruptcy trustees, local prosecutors, and bar association officials how customers get their information without the assistance of a licensed attorney.

A. Independent Paralegals in Arizona, Florida, and California

Because Arizona, Florida, and California are three of a handful of states where the modern independent paralegal movement was born, and currently have the most practicing independent paralegals, let's briefly look at the history and current political situation in each to illustrate the growth of the movement. Sorry, but it's simply beyond the scope of this book to do this for every state.

Arizona

In July 2003, the Arizona Supreme Court passed a law establishing regulations for IPs there (see below). For the preceding 20 years, Arizona was without a UPL law (excepting a court rule barring non-attorneys from providing representation in court). This arrangement allowed

IPs to pretty much do what they wished in the services they provided outside of court. The reason for this laissez-faire approach to IP out-of-court activity stemmed primarily from Arizona's general political leaning against occupational regulation of all types. As a result, Arizona has had a proliferation of IP practice.

While the Arizona legal establishment had long been unhappy about the situation, there was precious little they could do, given the political climate. As the number of Arizona IPs increased exponentially, however, the lawyers decided that something had to be done. And so, with significant input from the IP community and Arizona State Bar, the Arizona Supreme Court fashioned a regulatory scheme that holds great promise (assuming you accept the initial premise that regulation is necessary).

The governing rule is Rule 31, Rules of the Supreme Court of Arizona, which authorizes legal document preparers to provide services in compliance with Arizona Code of Judicial Administration, Section 7-208. The agency administering Section 7-208 is a division of the Arizona Supreme Court known as the Administrative Office of the Courts, Certification and Licensing Division. They can be contacted by mail at 1501 West Washington, Suite 104, Phoenix, Az 85007-3231. The agency website is at www.supreme.state.az.us/cld/ldp.htm. You can email the agency at LegalDocumentPreparer@supreme.state.az.us. The contact phone number is 602-364-2378.

Rule 7-208 defines "legal document preparer" as follows: "'Legal document preparer' means an individual who is certified pursuant to this section to prepare or provide legal documents without the supervision of an attorney, for an entity or a member of the public who is engaging in self representation in any legal matter. An individual whose assistance consists merely of secretarial or receptionist services is not a legal document preparer."

To be certified, the LDP must be a citizen or legal resident of the United States, at least 18 years of age, of good moral character, and must comply with the laws, court rules, and orders adopted by the Arizona Supreme Court to govern legal document preparers there. The applicant must also possess a minimum level of education and experience, meaning:

- a high school diploma or GED and two years of law related experience under the supervision of an attorney or LDP, or actual experience preparing documents prior to July 1, 2003
- a BA from a four year accredited school and one year of law related experience, or
- a certificate of completion from various types of paralegal programs (or law school).

After July 1, 2005, applicants will also have to pass a test regarding the rules of the Supreme Court relating to legal document preparers.

LDPs are allowed to prepare forms for, and deliver legal information to, their customers. They cannot, however, counsel their customers about possible options and strategies. Specifically, under Section F of 7-208, "[A] certified legal document preparer may:

- prepare or provide legal documents, without the supervision of an attorney, for an entity or a member of the public in any legal matter when that entity or person is not represented by an attorney
- provide general legal information, but not any kind of specific advice, opinion, or recommendation to a consumer about possible legal rights, remedies, defenses, options, or strategies
- provide general factual information pertaining to legal rights, procedures, or options available to a person in a legal matter when that person is not represented by an attorney
- make legal forms and documents available to a person who is not represented by an attorney, and
- file and arrange for service of legal forms and documents for a person in a legal matter when that person is not represented by an attorney.

Additional rules require identifying information on all documents prepared by the LDP, annual certification renewal, and ten hours of continuing legal education. The certification may be revoked. Section 7-208 provides considerable due process (procedures for notification and objection) surrounding a decision to deny or revoke certification.

Rule 7-208 also provides a code of conduct for LDPs. Even if you are not doing business in Arizona, these are good rules to operate by. We set them out in full for your convenience in Appendix A.

Florida

In the 1970s and early 1980s, Rosemary Furman, a former court reporter, began to help nonlawyers prepare legal paperwork. Along with the original WAVE Project members, who did the same thing in California, Furman was a true pioneer. (See interview in the Appendix.) When the Florida bar mounted a campaign to close down her office in Jacksonville, Florida, culminating in a 30-day jail sentence from the Florida Supreme Court in 1984 (it was later commuted), Furman fought back. When she appeared on TV shows such as "60 Minutes," she did much to convince American consumers that the lawyer monopoly over legal services was so fraught with self-interest that it had to be broken.

In addition to Rosemary Furman's courage and determination, the battle to allow IPs to operate in Florida was aided by several lawsuits prepared by the Washington-based consumer rights group, Public Citizen. Filed on behalf of Florida citizens who could not afford to hire lawyers, these suits argued that low-income people were being denied reasonable access to justice. Eventually, the activities of Furman and Public Citizen embarrassed the Florida courts into taking some first steps to provide better citizen access to the law. Specifically, the Florida Supreme Court approved a series of simplified legal forms designed to be used without a lawyer, including those necessary to obtain a divorce, collect child support, obtain a restraining order against domestic violence, as well as a number of landlord-tenant forms. Since then, a great number of additional simplified forms have been added.

Of great interest to Florida IPs is that, in adopting this simplified form approach, Florida has also changed its UPL rules as they concern the use of these forms. Specifically, the Supreme Court of Florida amended Chapter 10 of the Rules Regulating the Florida Bar to state (with recent amendments):

...For purposes of this chapter, it shall not constitute the unlicensed practice of law for a nonlawyer to engage in limited oral communications to assist a person in the completion of blanks on a legal form....Oral communications by nonlawyers are restricted to those communications reasonably necessary to elicit factual information to complete blanks on the form and inform the person how to file the form...

The result of allowing IPs to prepare many types of basic legal forms has been the formation of many IP businesses in the state. (See the interview with Ian Gardner in the Appendix.) It has also meant that at least some lawyers have begun to accept the idea that nonlawyer legal form preparers are in Florida to stay.

California

The Golden State tends to be a trend setter. Certainly this is true when it comes to the independent paralegal movement. Thanks, in part, to the self-help law books published by Nolo and the organization of the WAVE Project self-help divorce centers by Charles (Ed) Sherman and Ralph Warner (coauthor of this book) in 1972-73, California has always had more independent paralegals than any other state.

In the mid-1980s, this rapidly growing new service industry was attacked by the Los Angeles County Bar. It urged the California State Bar to vigorously police the unauthorized practice of law, especially in the fields of domestic relations (divorce), bankruptcy, immigration, and landlord/tenant law, all of which the Los Angeles attorney group claimed were rapidly being taken over by independent paralegals.

In response, the State Bar appointed the Public Protection Committee to look into the L.A. bar's claims. The committee was made up of a majority of lawyers and paralegals who worked for lawyers. In what is surely the most surprising event in recent California bar history, instead of proposing a crackdown on IPs, in 1988, the Public Protection Committee unanimously recommended that the California legislature completely abolish the state's UPL laws. It further concluded that independent paralegals should be allowed to provide all types of legal services as long as they are registered with a state agency and disclose their nonlawyer status to all customers.

Even though a subcommittee of Bar Governors largely supported the conclusions of the Public Protection Committee, its recommendations were rejected by the State Bar in August 1989, after many local bar associations reacted in horror to the threatened loss of their traditional monopoly power. The California Bar then appointed a third group (The Commission on Legal Technicians) to restudy the issue. This commission largely agreed with the conclusions of its predecessors and recommended that nonlawyers be authorized by the California Supreme Court to deliver legal services in several major areas (bankruptcy, family, immigration, and landlord-tenant), under the terms of a licensing scheme that would be supervised by an independent state agency. However, the State Bar again refused to adopt its own committee's recommendations.

Between 1992 and 1994, with the leadership of the California Association of Independent Paralegals (CAIP, which is now known as CALDA—California Association of Legal Document Assistants), several bills were introduced in the California legislature calling for registration of existing IPs and a study of whether more regulation was needed. These bills were narrowly defeated, largely as a result of lobbying by organized lawyerdom.

In 1995 and 1996, CAIP continued to expand its activities by:

1. Presenting workshops and seminars designed to teach members to complete a wide variety of legal paperwork;
2. Adopting a consumer-friendly code of conduct and professional responsibility;
3. Studying whether to adopt a system of self-testing and certification that would be available to CAIP members who prepare forms for divorce and other types of family law;
4. Joining the National Federation of Paralegals Association (NFPA) as a full member. Joining NFPA gave CAIP significant added credibility in the legal community.

Between 1989 and 1994, the battle to legalize IPs moved to the state legislature. Led by HALT, the Washington, DC, public interest group, and by CAIP, several different bills were introduced to license, register, and study the IP movement. Although narrowly defeated by the lobbying of organized lawyerdom, these legislative efforts proved extremely important in rallying public and media support behind the idea of non-lawyer legal practice.

Finally, in 1998, CAIP struck paydirt. The California legislature passed SB 1418, a comprehensive piece of legislation designed to promote self-help law services, known as the Legal Document Assistant's Bill. While the bill went into effect January 1, 1999, its regulatory features didn't become effective until January 1, 2000. And the bill contained a sunset provision for January 1, 2003, meaning that it would expire on that date unless the legislature extended it.

In its essentials, the bill combines the model set forth throughout this book with the strictures of *People v. Landlords Eviction Services* (215 Cal.App.3d 1599), the leading court case that has been governing independent paralegals in California since 1989.

Under the legislation, independent paralegals may type any type of documents under the direction and control of their customers, but may not provide legal advice or opinions as to possible courses of action. As part of their service, California IPs can provide their customers with published legal materials or written materials approved by a licensed California attorney. However, they may not themselves orally provide the legal information their customers need to decide which forms to use or how to navigate the appropriate procedures.

In order to provide the service authorized by the new bill, the IP, now termed a Legal Document Assistant, must obtain a $25,000 bond (available for as low as $250 a year with good credit) and meet *any one* of the following education or experience requirements:

- A high school diploma or GED and either two years of law-related experience under an attorney's supervision or a minimum of two years experience providing self-help service prior to January 1, 1999.
- A baccalaureate degree (BA) in any field and either one year of law-related experience under supervision of an attorney or one year of experience providing self-help service prior to January 1, 1999.
- Certificate of completion from a paralegal program that requires 24 semester units.
- Certificate of completion from an ABA-approved paralegal program.

All independent paralegals (LDAs) who meet with customers must register in every county where they offer services. Registration costs $175 per county. Every customer must be given a contract that spells out what legal document assistants may and may not do under the law.

The contract specifies where the customer may seek assistance if he or she is unhappy with the services, and prohibits the LDA from holding on to the customer's original records.

Amendments effective January 1, 2003 require that California LDAs provide certain specific disclosures in their advertising and when first speaking with potential clients to the effect that they are not attorneys and cannot provide legal advice. See Chapter 3 for more about this.

There are more details, but that's the gist of the bill. The bill is not without controversy. Many California independent paralegals feel that they should be allowed to provide a broader range of services than are allowed by the legislation, including the giving of personalized legal information in appropriate situations. But many other California independent paralegals are thrilled that for once they will be able to serve their customers in the traditional manner without the fear of prosecution by overzealous district attorneys. Certainly, SB 1418, codified at Bus. & Prof. Code §§ 6400 and following, will serve to legitimize the California IP profession.

For independent paralegals who would like to get organized in other states, the California legislation and the Arizona rule are a good start. They provide a framework for regulation and activity that allows independent paralegals to serve folks engaged in self-representation without, at the same time, posing a threat to the state's lawyers.

A copy of the bill and an excellent set of FAQs are available on the California Association of Legal Document Assistants website at www.calda.org.

Finally, here is an excerpted article that coauthor Steve Elias distributed to the CALDA members at their annual meeting held in October 2000. It provides a more detailed view of what the Legal Document Assistant role entails.

The New Legal Document Assistant Profession in California

By Steve Elias

As a nonlawyer who directly helped the public in their legal matters, you used to be called an independent paralegal. Then, as the year 2000 kicked in, you were an independent paralegal no more. Cinderella-like, you either qualified as a Legal Document Assistant (LDA), or, you became an "outlaw." To add insult to injury, the legislature has now prohibited you from calling yourself a paralegal unless you work for a lawyer.

You may feel angry and betrayed. To you, the term paralegal has always identified you as a member of an honorable calling, one that implied legal expertise, ethical conduct, fair pricing, and concern for your clients. Now, however, you can only identify as a paralegal if the fruits of your labor end up in the pockets of an attorney. Or put differently, if you continue to operate your own business in pursuit of your own interests, you will no longer be able to wrap yourself in the mantle of the professional identity known as "paralegal." Not to worry. You are a charter member of a brand new profession that challenges you to use all the personal skills and legal knowledge you have acquired over the years.

Since I will be using the "profession" word a lot, I might as well define it. In Merriam-Webster, profession is "a: a calling requiring specialized knowledge and often long and intensive academic preparation; b: a principal calling, vocation, or employment; c: the whole body of persons engaged in a calling." Although I've heard many complain that the LDA Act relegates them to the role of a mere "typist," I believe that for many reasons you fit squarely within the dictionary definition of professional. Let's take a look at some of the skills this new profession requires.

Knowledge of resources

As an LDA, you need an intimate knowledge of the available print and electronic resources best suited to each customer's needs—and of how to find them in the law library or on the Internet. In other words, you must really perform the skills of a highly specialized legal reference librarian. The greater your knowledge of available and suitable information—and your ability to retrieve it—the wider your potential customer base will be.

Knowledge of legal elements

As an LDA, you need an intimate knowledge of the elements associated with various types of legal tasks. Even though the customer takes "responsibility" for directing your work, you must know what specific materials will lead the customer to give you the right directions. In other words, there must be a match between the materials you provide the customer and the specific tasks that the customer wants accomplished. For example, if a customer needed to modify a child custody order, you would need to know that the procedure involves an Order to Show Cause in order to steer the customer to materials that provide step-by-step instructions for preparing this particular document.

Expertise in forms, court rules, and transactional document formatting

Especially for court-related tasks, as an LDA you need expertise in Judicial Council forms, local rules, and the statewide Rules of Court so that you will properly prepare, file, and serve the correct documents. For transactional matters (contracts, wills, living trusts), you must have a good grasp of the English language and a firm understanding of how various documents must be formatted so they will be acceptable to third parties such as title insurance agents and probate judges.

Ability to tutor or coach

As an LDA, you must be able to successfully tutor or coach your customers through the process of acquiring information and building the self-confidence necessary for successful self-representation. This involves a number of subtle sub-skills. You must

- communicate to the customer a confidence that self-help law really works. This of course means that you believe it yourself and organize your office and your personal presentation to reinforce the concept,

- orient the customer as to how particular self-help law materials work, that is, how they are organized, which parts may be safely skipped in the customer's particular case, and where the materials may need to be supplemented with other materials or advice by an attorney,
- pull together supportive materials—e.g., questionnaires, checklists, videos—that will help the customer focus on what information and decisions are necessary for each step,
- understand the personalities of courthouse personnel—judges, clerks, bailiffs—and prepare the customer to make a suitable appearance and to deal with any predictable problems that may occur in the course of the self-representation, and
- exercise great patience and self-restraint when the customer stumbles. (It's tempting to "just do it" when the customer complains about something being too difficult. However, the ethics of the LDA profession demand that the customer be encouraged to just keep plugging away until he or she gets it right.)

Keeping up to date

Law changes constantly. As an LDA you will need to continue your legal education to make sure your information is fresh and legally current.

Assessing fitness of customers and issues for self-help law

As an LDA, you must decide whether any particular customer is capable of successfully engaging in self-representation. Some customers do not have the reading skills, intelligence or emotional stability to successfully complete a particular self-help law task. Under the LDA law, these customers must be referred to lawyers. Similarly, some issues or tasks are so inherently complicated that no amount of self-education will adequately prepare the customer for self-representation. These people also must be referred to a lawyer. Your ability to accurately make these assessments is crucial not only to the customer's legal well-being but also to your business, since "getting in over your head" can bring your LDA business to its knees and make it much more likely that you will be charged with a violation of the LDA law.

These then are the core competencies required for a successful LDA practice. In addition, if you are a LDA who owns your own business, you must acquire the necessary expertise, or associate with those who already have it, to manage the customer service, financial and marketing sides of the business.

LDA practice is both challenging and extremely helpful to customers who wish to minimize their legal fees and control their own legal affairs. It is also a vital part of the growing movement to improve access to our legal system. Because of the complex skill levels and knowledge base required of an LDA, the LDA community is definitely a profession in the fullest sense of the word.

B. Paralegal Political Organizing

The best way to accomplish both of these goals is to organize politically. As long as the independent paralegal movement consists of isolated individuals, and lawyers are organized through bar associations and judges' associations, the trend toward acceptance of paralegals can be slowed, if not contained, by lawyers. Once organized and politically active, however, independent paralegals obviously have a much better opportunity to get the message across to the public that they represent a low-cost, high-quality alternative to lawyers. (If you doubt this, see Virginia Simons's interview in the Appendix.)

There are several important elements to any successful political organizing effort. One is to establish an efficient way for IPs to communicate with each other at both the state and national level. It is particularly essential that IPs in the same state be in close touch, as most unauthorized practice of law is regulated at the state level. It's important to realize that while IPs may all be competing with each other to some degree, the organized bar, with its dedication to putting everyone out of business, is the real adversary. Or, put more directly, it is essential that IPs avoid squabbles with each other at least long enough to present a united front to the bar. If you doubt this, think back to what it cost the Native American tribes to continue their intertribal spats after the Europeans arrived.

Jolene Jacobs, one of the first successful independent paralegals, advises:

Develop, if possible, good relationships with your competitors. Try to have a friendly, positive relationship with them rather than an adversarial one. It can not only make life and your business environment more pleasant, you will build relationships that will help all independent paralegals if the bar gets aggressive.

Once all the IPs in your state are talking to each other, your next job is to establish a solid statewide organization. There are a number of ways to do this, no one of which is the best in all circumstances. With this caution in mind, let us tell you some of the things that were done in the early 1970s as part of establishing California's pioneering WAVE Project:

- Established a central office which, for a small fee, coordinated state-wide efforts of project members, and was available for counseling when the bar threatened any WAVE Project member.
- Produced a quarterly newsletter to serve as a training vehicle and to give WAVE Project members a forum in which to share good ideas and good gossip.
- Held regular meetings and training sessions. After an initial training course for new counselors, which lasted about four days, follow-up two-day training sessions were held periodically in different parts of the state. Incidentally, if you conduct this sort of training, keep things interesting by bringing in outside speakers who are expert in the area of the law you are working in. Also, leave plenty of time for your own political strategy sessions. Keep costs to a minimum, but be ready to chip in whatever it takes.
- Established the idea of centralized legal defense help for the 15-20 independent paralegals in the WAVE Project. To accomplish this, the WAVE Project assessed members a couple of dollars from every fee-charged customer. The idea was to have each member know that he could get quick, effective legal help and counseling by

picking up the phone. We strongly recommend that all paralegal organizations do this. If organized lawyerdom tries to put you in a small room with bars on the windows, your ability to deal with your inevitable feelings of fear and paranoia will be greatly enhanced if you have already set up a legal defense fund.

■

Appendix A

Arizona Code of Conduct for LDPs

LAKE COUNTY SELF-HELP LAW CENTER, INC.
MARKETING STRATEGY

General Overview

Business Strengths

Our extensive knowledge of the legal form preparation industry is our greatest strength. Our positioning in the region in terms of our location and services offered is another strength.

Business Weaknesses

The greatest weakness our business faces is our ability to handle new competition. Currently, we are the only true LDA provider of our services in the area. Any competitor that moves in will pose a minor threat to our stability.

Business Goals

Profit

Our current profit goals are:

Year Two: $204,000 post tax profit

Year Three: $296,000 post tax profit

We have not established any other long-range profit goals at this time.

Sales

Our long-term sales goals are to be profitable from Year One onward and to operate at or close to cash flow break-even by Year Two. We would like our profit margin to be 7 percent by Year Three.

Marketing

Our long-term marketing goals are to develop an extensive website, increase our public relations activities, and create an informative store window to draw in more customers. We intend to move to Main Street and establish an office near the courthouse.

Position in the Marketplace

Description of Our Customers

Our customers are 25- to 85-year-old professionals, married or unmarried, with and without children, who are seeking low cost legal form preparation services with attorney review.

Our Customers' Needs

Our target customers are people who are looking for customized legal document preparation services that will provide them with all the information necessary to successfully complete a legal task.

Why Our Customers Choose Us

Our well-informed, up-to-date staff, combined with our extensive knowledge of self-help law services, allows us to provide better services than those offered by other agencies.

What Sets Us Apart From the Competition

What sets our company apart from our competitors is the fact that we sell top-notch self-help law materials written by attorneys, and all paperwork is reviewed by an attorney. We ask the customer the right questions, find out exactly what they want and need, and direct them to the appropriate legal solution.

Marketing Campaign Specifics

Goals of the Campaign

We would like to increase our visibility, attract new customers, and display and disseminate special offers that are currently available.

Campaign Focus: Specific Products or General Promotion?

Our primary focus is to expand our customer base. We would also like to keep our current customers aware of special promotions we are offering in order to secure their future business with us.

Products to Be Advertised

We will be advertising our complete range of estate planning services, special discounts for couples, and sales of estate planning software.

Measurements of Success

We will measure this ad campaign's success by the number of inquiries received after its launch. This includes phone inquiries as well as inquiries made in person at the office. We will keep records of inquiries received and will ask all callers how they heard about our business.

Evaluation of Effectiveness

We will be reviewing the campaign's effectiveness one month after its launch. We will evaluate its effectiveness based on the number of inquires we receive and any corresponding increase in revenue.

Message

Our Marketing Message:

"No one knows more about helping you legally help yourself."

Time Frame

Campaign Start Date

We will launch this marketing campaign in February, 2004.

Length of Campaign

This campaign will run through June, 2004, for a total of five months.

Budget

Annual Marketing Budget

$12,000

Budget for This Campaign

$5,000. This includes $1,500 for website and database design, implementation, and hardware purchases, which will be useful for more than one year and will be capitalized and depreciated accordingly.

Cost-Saving Measures

We plan to keep advertising costs down by targeting the most appropriate advertising methods for our business, which include estate planning seminars, online advertising, newspaper ads, and classified ads.

Arizona Code of Conduct for Legal Document Preparers

Preamble. This code of conduct is adopted by the Supreme Court to apply to all certified legal document preparers in the state of Arizona. The purpose of this code is to establish minimum standards for performance by certified legal document preparers.

Standard 1. Ethics.

a. A legal document preparer shall avoid impropriety and the appearance of impropriety in all activities, shall respect and comply with the laws, and shall act at all times in a manner that promotes public confidence in the integrity and impartiality of the legal and judicial systems.

b. A legal document preparer shall be alert to situations that are conflicts of interest or that may give the appearance of a conflict of interest.

c. A legal document preparer shall promptly make full disclosure to a consumer of any relationships which may give the appearance of a conflict of interest.

d. A legal document preparer shall refrain from knowingly making misleading, deceptive, untrue, or fraudulent representations while assisting a consumer in the preparation of legal documents. A legal document preparer shall not engage in unethical or unprofessional conduct in any professional dealings that are harmful or detrimental to the public.

Standard 2. Professionalism.

a. A legal document preparer shall treat information received from the consumer as confidential, yet recognize and acknowledge that the privilege of confidential communications is not extended to certified legal document preparers.

b. A legal document preparer shall be truthful and accurate when advertising or representing the legal document preparer's qualifications, skills or abilities, or the services provided, and shall refrain from denigrating or otherwise calling into disrepute the products or services offered by any other legal document preparer or attorney.

c. A legal document preparer shall maintain and observe the highest standards of integrity and truthfulness in all professional dealings.

d. A legal document preparer shall keep abreast of current developments in the law as it relates to legal document preparation and shall fulfill ongoing training requirements to maintain professionalism and the skills necessary to perform their duties competently.

Standard 3. Fees and Services.

a. A legal document preparer shall, upon request of a consumer at any time, disclose in writing an itemization of all rates and charges to that consumer.

b. A legal document preparer shall determine fees independently, except when otherwise established by law, entering into no unlawful agreements with other legal document preparers on the fees to any user.

c. A legal document preparer shall at all times be aware of and avoid impropriety or the appearance of impropriety, which may include, but is not limited to:

  (1) Establishing contingent fees as a basis of compensation;
  (2) Directly or indirectly receiving of any gift, incentive, reward, or anything of value as a condition of the performance of professional services; and
  (3) Directly or indirectly offering to pay any commission or other consideration in order to secure professional assignments;

d. A legal document preparer may consult, associate, collaborate with, and involve other professionals in order to assist the consumer.

Standard 4. Skills and Practice.

a. A legal document preparer shall provide completed documents to a consumer in a timely manner. The legal document preparer shall make a good faith effort to meet promised delivery dates and make timely delivery of documents when no date is specified. A legal document preparer shall meet document preparation deadlines in accordance with rules, statutes, court orders, or agreements with the parties. A legal document preparer shall provide immediate notification of delays.

b. A legal document preparer shall accept only those assignments for which the legal document preparer's level of competence will result in the preparation of an accurate document. The legal document preparer shall decline an assignment when the legal document preparer's abilities are inadequate.

Standard 5. Performance in Accordance with Law.

a. A legal document preparer shall perform all duties and discharge all obligations in accordance with applicable laws, rules or court orders.

b. A legal document preparer shall not represent they are authorized to practice law in this state, nor shall the legal document preparer provide legal advice or services to another by expressing opinions, either verbal or written, or by representing another in a judicial, quasijudicial, or administrative proceeding, or other formal dispute resolution process, except as authorized in Rule 31(a)(4), Rules of the Supreme Court. A legal document preparer shall not attend court with a consumer for the purpose of assisting the consumer in the court proceeding, unless otherwise ordered by the court.

c. A legal document preparer shall not provide any kind of advice, opinion or recommendation to a consumer about possible legal rights, remedies, defenses, options, or strategies. This shall not, however, preclude a certified legal document preparer from providing the type of information permitted in subsection F(1) of this code section. A legal document preparer shall inform the consumer in writing that a legal document preparer is not a lawyer, is not employed by a lawyer, and cannot give legal advice, and that communications with a legal document preparer are not privileged. A legal document preparer shall not use the designations "lawyer," "attorney at law," "counselor at law," "law office," "JD," "Esq.," or other equivalent words, the use of which is reasonably likely to induce others to believe the legal document preparer is authorized to engage in the practice of law in the state of Arizona. ∎

Appendix B

Interviews

This book was first written in the mid-1980s and has been updated and revised a number of times. As part of doing this, new interviews have been added, some old interviews have been updated, and a few interviews have been dropped because the person is no longer in the IP business and his or her remarks are now dated. The interview with Rosemary Furman, one of the true pioneers of the IP movement, appears just as it first did in 1986—some things are just too good to change.

Lois Isenberg Interview

Lois Isenberg has been a very successful paralegal for more than 20 years. She is a past president of the California Association of Independent Paralegals (CAIP).

Ralph Warner (RW): *Take me back a few years and tell me how you got started as an independent paralegal.*

Lois Isenberg (LI): My work background is in advertising, public relations, and film production. In about 1973, I was producing educational films when I got a call for help from a friend who had started a WAVE Project do-it-yourself divorce office.

RW: *What sort of help?*

LI: She had no customers and she obviously needed some in a hurry if she was going to survive. I was on a two-week break between films and agreed to do what I could. I helped her define her market and we designed flyers. After a few days she literally got up from her desk, walked to the door of her office and, as she was exiting the door, said over her shoulder, "I don't want this business, it's yours."

RW: *She gave it to you?*

LI: Yes, but, of course, since there were no customers, she didn't give me much.

RW: *What did you do?*

LI: Got in touch with the WAVE Project people—you and Ed Sherman, among others—and got trained in how to fill out divorce forms. Then I moved the business to my house, where it stayed until 1979. During that time I bought the Hollywood WAVE Project office and moved it into my home also. Eventually, I opened an office on Wilshire Blvd. in Los Angeles.

RW: *Was the business supporting you decently by that time?*

LI: Yes and no. I was still doing other things and wasn't really focused on it. Then around 1980 I met a helpful lawyer, Anne Lober, who was actively involved in promoting mediation for divorcing couples. She encouraged and helped me to learn how to do other types of family law paperwork, including restraining orders and child support and custody modifications. After that I was able to find other helpful attorneys who taught me to do stepparent adoptions, guardianships, and paternity.

RW: *Did this put you over the hump financially?*

LI: It was really ten years after I began that I had a viable business. But again, part of what took me so long was being serious about it. My business grew substantially when I moved it from my home to an office. Visibility is a very important part of a business's success, and even though divorce is not exactly an impulse buy, when people see your sign day after day they will remember you when the need arises.

RW: *After a while, I'm sure you got lots of referrals from satisfied customers.*

LI: Definitely, referrals are about 50% of my business. But, obviously, it takes time to build a referral base. In the meantime, you must develop referral sources. In my case, one of these was working closely with the divorce mediation community—lawyers and others who understood that contested court actions were a terrible way to settle domestic disputes and encouraged people to arrive at their own solutions.

RW: *Do you work alone?*

LI: No. I have a full-time assistant as well as a part-time receptionist-clerk.

RW: *Today, you are the President of the California Association of Independent Paralegals (CAIP). I'll ask you more about CAIP in a minute. Now I want to know when it dawned on you that lawyers didn't approve of what you were doing and that if the independent paralegal movement was going to survive you would have to be politically active and organized.*

LI: Well, it was obvious from day one that low-cost competition was going to annoy lawyers. I can't tell you how many times I was verbally attacked by an attorney in a social situation when I mentioned my work. And, of course, the fact that lawyers were maniacally opposed to what we were doing was a reason why the IP business was semi-underground for many years.

RW: *They couldn't swat you if they couldn't find you.*

LI: Precisely. Most of the early independent paralegals worked from their houses and, at least as far as lawyers were concerned, pretended not to exist. This strategy worked up to a point, but it also prevented us from finding each other and, worse, the public finding us.

RW: *Why did you stick your head above ground?*

LI: To see if I cast a shadow?

RW: *C'mon—seriously.*

LI: I am serious. Sooner or later, IPs have to climb out of their holes and fight for their right to exist. Here in California, in about 1986, ten or fifteen of us, led by Glynda Dixon, who worked in Oakland, began meeting alternately in Northern and Southern California. We adopted the name California Association of Independent Paralegals and decided that CAIP would work towards improving the professionalism of the legal form preparation business.

RW: *How?*

LI: Continuing education for ourselves, establishing ethical standards for the business, and lobbying the state legislature in Sacramento to pass decent laws defining our occupation.

RW: *I know CAIP has close to 200 members these days, some from other states, but I know it hasn't been easy.*

LI: No. At first, getting members was tough. Many people who are attracted to the idea of being an independent paralegal are not joiners. We attract the legal visionary as well as the entrepreneur. The visionary is often focused on the cause of "legal access for all," while oftentimes the entrepreneur is looking for a quick success. What CAIP is trying to do is have all these individuals join together to create a viable force. We need to be able to have legislation passed that will elevate the position of the independent paralegal and provide protection against frivolous lawsuits. CAIP not only wants to encourage a level of excellence among the independent paralegals, but also provide protection for the consumer as well.

RW: *What does CAIP do these days?*

LI: We have come a long way. We have a newsletter called ACCESS, an annual convention, training sessions, and we are extremely active in Sacramento, lobbying to try and open up the lawyer monopoly to recognize that independent paralegals are a viable legal option.

RW: *In addition, you have your own consulting business.*

LI: If running seminars on form preparation skills and business operations is a consulting business, the answer is yes. My major in college was education, but I never actively taught. In doing these seminars, not only do I get a chance to teach, which incidentally I really enjoy, but I also get to teach something I actually know about.

RW: *People fly in from all over, I understand.*

LI: I hope so.

       [Ed. note: Lois does not currently offer these services.]

                          * * * * * *

RW: *Lois, it's now 1996, and two years has passed since we had the conversation set out above. Tell me what has changed in the IP business.*

LI: There has been a big increase in the numbers of people seeking paralegal services. It seems that, as an occupation, we are finally out of the closet, and much of the public is beginning to view us as a truly viable alternative. Here is the good news and the bad news. Obviously the good news is that we can enjoy the business success we are reaping from this awareness and help more people who might otherwise have been denied their day in court. However, this public awareness of IPs has also caused some problems.

RW: *Tell me about them.*

LI: The Los Angeles County Bar Association refers all IP questions and complaints to me. As a result, I hear of problems caused by some inexperienced IPs. Of course, many of the problems are a result of naiveté of the customer. It's a difficult consumer problem that is by no means limited to IPs. How can you protect someone who refuses to protect themselves? For example, one customer called complaining that they had called the number of a typing service they found in the newspaper. The person on the other end of the telephone did not have an office, so they arranged to meet in the parking lot of a casino in Gardena, California. The customer gave the supposed IP $500 cash to do some legal paperwork. When the customer never heard from the person again (his phone number was promptly disconnected), he wanted someone to help him. Obviously, there is little a legitimate IP can do to protect people from this type of fraud. But there are other, less extreme, situations where I believe independent paralegal associations such as CAIP should play a more active role.

RW: *Such as?*

LI: Basically, educating the public. We need to provide good information about when and how to pick a competent independent paralegal. I'm pleased that CAIP has already started to do this. We have a Professional Standards Committee and have written a good Code of Ethics for IPs. We expect our members to adhere to them if they want to stay members in good standing. CAIP is also looking into the idea of creating a skills-based test for members to take. I favor this idea as long as it is a hands-on, technical test involving how to complete and file forms and navigate the court system effectively.

RW: *I guess a test connects back to the idea of educating the customer, because it would be a way to say that IPs who passed the test knew what they are doing.*

LI: Yes, the idea is to get good information to the consumer so that he or she is empowered to make good choices. One step is for all CAIP members to mention that they are members of CAIP in all their promotional materials. Over time, as members of the public realize that CAIP membership really means something, more independent paralegals will want to become members in order to get that seal of approval. Since this will generally mean they will have to raise their standards, the public will benefit. And of course, if CAIP begins a program of skills-based testing for IPs who prepare different types of legal forms, consumers can look for a CAIP certificate of completion.

RW: *What about working with the courts and other agencies that make lots of referrals to IPs so they can educate the public as to what to expect?*

LI: Absolutely. A referral from an experienced person is one of the best ways to get good services. I love my referral business because the customer usually comes in with a positive attitude. Or, put another way, as long as the customer trusts the referral source, she already likes me and feels confident in my services and expertise. No question CAIP can and should work more closely with the agencies and people who refer customers to IPs.

Jon and Melvin Lebewitz Interview

Melvin and Jon Lebewitz—father and son—are the founders and co-owners of L & M Legal Services, Inc., in Minneapolis, Minnesota. L & M primarily handles form preparation for divorces and landlord-tenant problems. It has been in business since 1987. (This interview was done in 1996.)

Ralph Warner (RW): *Tell me how the two of you got started in the legal form preparation business.*

Mel Lebewitz (ML): Two businesses ago, I was in Los Angeles and I saw some storefront legal form preparation shops. This was in the mid-80s. Since I had never seen anything like that before, it stuck in my mind.

Jon Lebewitz (JL): In the meantime, I had gone to college and graduate school to get an MBA and had been working as a securities analyst. But I didn't find it to be a satisfying occupation and moved to California to have a little time out.

ML: Around 1987, Jon called from California and said he was planning to move back to Minneapolis. When he got back, he began to help me in my lawn sprinkler business. On the side, I'd also opened a process-serving business.

RW: *Is that because you don't sell many sprinklers in a Minnesota January?*

ML: Exactly. It's a strictly seasonal business.

JL: By the fall, we knew the businesses wouldn't support both of us, so we were looking around for other ideas. Almost by accident, we got into divorce typing.

ML: It happened after I saw a TV show—I think it was "20-20"—describing the growth of the independent paralegal business in California. Steve Elias and Catherine Jermany from Nolo.com were featured and emphasized that typing legal forms was not only beneficial to consumers who couldn't afford lawyers, but was also a good business.

RW: *And you remembered the store-front shops you had seen in L.A.?*

ML: Yes. I said to my son, let's try this. It could work in Minnesota.

JL: Our first step was to talk to a lawyer friend about how we could begin preparing divorce forms legally, without being charged with unauthorized practice. We made an informal deal—he would teach us how to do basic form preparation and we, in turn, would refer people who really did need legal assistance to him. Up to a point, it worked. He did help us, but we also had to do a lot of learning and all the business development on our own.

RW: *You needed questionnaires, intake forms, office procedures, and so on.*

JL: All of that and, of course, we also needed customers.

RW: *How long did it take to find them?*

JL: We began advertising in September 1989. It was terribly slow at the start. And then we hit the holiday season and things slowed down even more.

RW: *You mean, the business started badly and got worse?*

ML: Yes, so bad that we considered giving the whole idea up. But we kept our advertising going. Still, we were discouraged; two families don't make a living doing a few $99 divorces per week, even along with the other work we were doing.

RW: *When did things begin to change for the better?*

JL: In May of 1990, business began to pick up very slowly. It kept improving from there. We were still struggling, but now we were optimistic.

RW: *Let's jump forward a few years. How were you doing by 1993?*

ML: Better. Advertising was producing steady business, but it was still quite local. Then a funny thing began to happen—we started to get more and more calls from outside of Minneapolis, from people who had seen our ads when they were in town or had heard of us. We began to mail out form packages on an experimental basis.

RW: *Terrific. I bet that was popular.*

JL: Not at first. Our package of forms was too thick and intimidating. We got very few back. But we thought the idea might work, so we talked to a marketing specialist. He helped us create a simple, attractive brochure called "Questions and Answers about L & M Divorce Services." People could fill out a few lines of information and send us a check. In return, we sent them a simplified questionnaire designed to be far more user-friendly. We also emphasized that help was only a phone call away.

RW: *It sounds like you finally got your mail-in service right.*

ML: Yes, as long as people with problems could call us for help with the forms, it worked. In fact, it worked so well that now we do two-thirds of our business by mail, fax, and phone without ever seeing our customers. Outside of Minneapolis and St. Paul, Minnesota is largely rural, and it allows us to run a statewide business. And, of course, the unlawful detainers remain a steady part of the business.

RW: *Have you had any problems with lawyers?*

JL: Very little. The only problems have been with a couple of judges who believe all people need to be represented by an attorney. In one county, they occasionally make it hard for pro pers. But overall, the legal community has accepted us. In fact, now we get lots of referrals from court clerks, judges, and lawyers.

RW: *What do you do when you run into a complicated problem—for example, valuing a tricky pension plan?*

ML: What's often overlooked by lawyers who sometimes argue that independent paralegals are handling complicated legal matters is that most of our customers have low or very moderate incomes. For the most part, they don't have fat pension plans or lots of valuable property. Preparing a divorce for them really is pretty basic. And when we do occasionally run into people with more complicated problems, we send them to a lawyer. When they obtain the necessary information, they come back to us and we complete the form preparation process.

Jolene Jacobs Interview

Jolene Jacobs, a long-time friend, is one of the first successful, modern independent paralegals. She operated a divorce form preparation business from 1973 until early 1994, when she sold her business. (This interview was done in 1992.)

Ralph Warner (RW): *How did you first become involved in paralegal work?*

Jolene Jacobs (JJ): In 1972, when I was just finishing my undergraduate degree, I was interested in doing some kind of consumer advocacy or public service work. I admired Ralph Nader and his Raiders and other individuals who battled large corporations for consumer rights and protection. In December of 1972, I met you and Ed Sherman. I heard about the WAVE Project from a family friend who told me you were looking for people to train to type divorces based on the information in Ed's book, *How to Do Your Own Divorce in California.* I remember coming over to your old, brown-shingle house in Berkeley with several other recruits. You had samples of divorce forms taped to the dining room walls and we all sat around while you showed us how to fill them out, process them through the clerk's office, and talked about how people could best represent themselves in court. What attracted me to the WAVE Project was that although the divorce book worked well for lots of people, many others obviously needed more personal help than any book could provide—both of a secretarial nature and personal support. I signed on, along with a dozen or so others, to train as divorce counselors.

RW: *Come on, you must have been somewhat scared embarking on an illegal business fresh out of college.*

JJ: You warned us that there would be problems, possibly serious problems, with the bar, and that we might even face criminal charges. Oddly, I wasn't scared at that point. I believed the bar's monopoly control over access to legal information and legal assistance was a bad thing. My perspective on the work was that it was a consumer advocacy project rather than a career as a "paralegal." I was so excited that I didn't really worry about it. The prospect of helping people with very little money, and sometimes without much education, put their own decisions on paper, file their papers at court, and represent themselves before a judge was truly exciting. While people may not have been happy about the outcome of their marriage, they could at least feel good about having done their own divorce.

RW: *When the WAVE Project training was over, where did you start working?*

JJ: I opened an office in San Jose in 1973. I stayed there until 1978 and then moved to San Francisco, where I have been since.

RW: *Was it hard to get your business going?*

JJ: It was both simple and hard. I had never been self-employed and had no family history of self-employment as a model. I had just graduated from college with no debts, no responsibilities, and a lot of enthusiasm, but not much else. Of course, I needed very little money to get by at that point. Incidentally, now I might not take that economic risk, so it was good that the chance to do something new crossed my path then.

      I ended up in San Jose because you and Ed suggested that San Jose was a good place to start because there were no other WAVE Project counselors in that area. It was somewhat difficult to move to a new town, look for a place to live, and start a business in an area where I didn't know a soul.

      The mechanics to set up an office weren't hard: get an office, telephone, typewriter, etc. The furniture and office equipment were particularly simple. I started with two wooden apple boxes and a typewriter. One apple box was for the customer to sit on and the other was for the typewriter. If I only had a picture!

      It was harder to learn how to get the word out that this new self-help service was available. In addition to the fact that I knew nothing about marketing, I faced an old California law, passed in the 1890s but still on the books, which made it illegal to "aid or encourage birth control, abortion or divorce." These were all legal activities, yet, at least according to California law, it was illegal to give out information about them. This prevented me from advertising, so I took brochures around to public agencies such as social services and legal aid and to a local newspaper, which wrote a story about my service. Now and then, I was able to get a classified ad into the paper, but then a lawyer or the DA would see it and call the paper and get them to take it out, based on the 1890 law. Of course, I believed this law was unconstitutional, but it was upheld a few years later, I believe, in a case in Southern California. I think it is still on the books, but was forgotten as soon as lawyers wanted to advertise their own divorce services. At any rate, this old law and the determination of lawyers to enforce it was a serious obstacle to the growth of my business.

RW: *What about the local bar association? What was their position on your typing service?*

JJ: The bar association claimed at every opportunity that the WAVE Project was a "fly-by-night" business, a rip-off, "here today and gone tomorrow," etc. It was difficult for me as an individual, and the WAVE Project as a small group, to combat this. While people didn't particularly trust or like the bar association even then, they had no idea who we were and what our credentials or intentions were. In other words, typing divorce forms was a new field and there was no positive history of such a service to make people feel confident. So, if the bar said it was bad, some people, at least, were hesitant to take a risk. In fairness, I should say, however, that there were individual lawyers who supported me.

        To face the bar alone would have been impossible for me. Being a part of a group backed up by you and Ed made me feel more confident, and help was just a phone call away. Later, the WAVE Project counselors began a legal defense fund that we contributed to monthly. This made most of us feel more secure that we could weather a prosecution financially by pooling our money. And we did use money in the fund several times. But the risk of being put out of business, or being arrested, was always there.

RW: *How long were you in business before the bar figured out what you were doing?*

JJ: They noticed me almost immediately. The bar association had already criticized Nolo.com in general, and *How to Do Your Own Divorce in California* specifically, so they were watching everything you and Ed did, especially the WAVE Project. Also, remember, there was an article about my new business in the newspaper and classified ads I placed, so my business wasn't a secret. I can think of five instances when I was investigated that I know about. There may have been others.

RW: *Can you tell me a little about the five?*

JJ: One involved an investigation by the District Attorney. The WAVE Project responded by hiring one of the best constitutional lawyers in the state. The DA was so impressed with the quality of the lawyer's work, and the apparent seriousness of the WAVE Project in fighting prosecution, that the case was dropped "for the time being." The DA did successfully prosecute another paralegal who worked in the area, however. This person worked independently and had no support.

Another time an investigation/prosecution was nipped in the bud because my roommate happened to be a law school classmate of a staff member in the DA's office who was supposed to write a memorandum recommending prosecution. Both my roommate and the classmate had actually done their own divorces using Ed Sherman's divorce book. This meant I had a friend to argue to the DA that while she had no trouble with a total self-help approach because she had the benefit of a legal education, the average consumer needed, and should be able to get, reasonably priced help preparing their papers.

RW: *That was a lucky coincidence, your roommate knowing the person who was to investigate you.*

JJ: Yes, but maybe it wasn't as important as I thought at the time, because a little later there was another investigation by the DA's office. This one I didn't know about until it was over. The investigator who recommended that I not be prosecuted called up to say how impressed he was with the quality of my work. Later, when he left the DA's office, he called and asked for a job at the WAVE Project.

The next incident was scarier. A judge who usually worked in criminal court, but was hearing domestic cases and was unfamiliar with the new trend of petitioners appearing in pro per—that is, representing themselves—told one of my customers that he would have me arrested if I didn't appear in his courtroom the next morning. I wasn't sure that he could legally pull off this King of England routine, but I went over. My customer was also ordered to be there. She was terrified. It didn't help that she had a heart problem.

The clerk read me my rights, the stenographer took down every word, and so on. The judge assured me I would be prosecuted for all sorts of heinous, but not very specific, crimes if I didn't shut down my business. Afterwards, I raced back to my office and called a criminal lawyer, who called the judge. Also, again by coincidence, I knew the judge's former clerk. This person also happened to have worked as a divorce consultant. So, I called the former clerk, who also called the judge on my behalf. After talking to these two people, the judge decided to "put it on the back burner." I think he still would have pursued the matter with the DA to get me prosecuted, but he died suddenly.

RW: *Your experience really underlines the fact that the legal establishment isn't monolithic. At almost every level, from lawyer to law clerk, you found allies when you needed them. But don't let me interrupt a great story. What happened next?*

JJ: Several times a number of divorce typing offices in the Bay Area were investigated on the phone, with no resulting action. We never knew who was doing the investigating, but it was easy to tell something was going on, because the callers kept asking questions that required legal opinions. You can spot this technique because the questions are usually inappropriate—not what most people ask. I think somehow related to these calls was an incident where an undercover investigator posing as a customer walked in and asked some questions, which I answered. Since my responses were not the incriminating answers she expected, or hoped for, she left the office somewhat curtly.

There may have been investigations other than these. I expect there have been. Sometimes the investigator stands out like a sore thumb, or more like a pain in the neck. But there may have been times when I wasn't able to detect them. The point is, of course, to try to be careful all of the time.

RW: *Do you have any other advice for people just starting out about how to avoid unauthorized practice of law charges?*

JJ: I think the more friends and contacts someone has in the local legal world, the easier it is to find out what is going on, and to deal with problems that come up. Also, I would say it is important to have a good lawyer lined up in advance. This is one context in which lawyers have really done a good job for me. I wouldn't have expected it, but it's true. It's ironic, of course, that I need lawyers to save me from lawyers, but that's the American legal system in a nutshell. Also, you need to have friends in the media who will go to bat for you should things get rough. I certainly would have been prosecuted were it not for the realization that if lawyers go after paralegals who do good work and have access to the press, the public will see the lawyers as trying to unfairly suppress a person who is offering a reasonable alternative to their overpriced monopoly. In other words, you need to know how to play David to the bar's Goliath. This isn't hard, because the legal profession can't really deny that they are a monopoly, that their services are expensive and many people can't pay their fees. They claim that the public does not get competent help when they use paralegals, but this is increasingly being recognized as a diversion from the truth that lawyers go after paralegals because they don't want competition. The public has really come to understand as a result of the many recent revelations that lawyers don't regulate their own profession very well, and that hiring a lawyer is no guarantee of competent legal care.

RW: *Do you still fear harassment by the bar?*

JJ: Sure, remember, I have only related my personal experience. I have friends in the business who have been arrested and had their offices closed down and their livelihood lost. Certain areas of California seem to be safer than others to work in. But still, this is one job where a little paranoia is healthy. Even to be the subject of an investigation is no fun. A long prosecution is horrible. I admire the steadfastness and courage of Rosemary Furman of Florida in standing up to the bar. Because she was so vocal in her anger and her belief in the importance of what she was doing, the bar association came down very hard on her. It would have been so much easier to give up. We have all gained something from her fight and from the national publicity her case received. She went through a great deal, and I think that paralegals around the country should have provided more emotional and financial support—myself included.

RW: *Let's leave the unauthorized practice issue for a bit and come back to some of the practical problems of being an independent paralegal. What price did you first charge for a divorce? What do you charge now? Can you make a good living?*

JJ: Our first price was $55 for typing an uncontested divorce. This covered overhead and provided a small income. It wasn't really adequate, so we raised the price to $65, then $75. In California there are now two forms of divorce; my office charges $80 for the very simple variety and $180 for the more complicated standard form (and up to $210 if support is involved). Other paralegal offices charge slightly different fees for divorce. I think the two primary factors that affect price are the cost of office overhead and the price charged by competition. Initially, I think our services were underpriced. I know I was so into consumerism that I felt uncomfortable about charging very much at all. I had never had the experience of setting a fair market value on my own labor. In addition, I had no idea how much it cost just to run an office. Of course, now I am much more sympathetic to people who are self-employed and who have substantial overhead. I know it is certainly not all profit. The idea of charging a fair fee to cover good work and support oneself decently is comfortable to me now.

RW: *Can you make a good living now as an independent paralegal?*

JJ: My income is good, but my work is stressful and it doesn't always seem enough for the number of years of experience I have, or for the volume of work required and the level of stress that accompanies helping people do divorces. It goes beyond typing forms (that's the first layer). I end up being a social worker, family counselor, helping people find jobs, and providing emotional support. Also, with the unresolved status of independent paralegals, the job never feels secure.

RW: *Why did you move to San Francisco from San Jose?*

JJ: I was in San Jose from 1973 until 1978. At that time, my friends who ran the San Francisco office of what by this time had changed in name from the WAVE Project to Divorce Center, were completing law school and wanted to sell their office. I was ready for a change and I missed the central Bay Area (San Jose is 50 miles south), so I decided to sell my San Jose office and buy the San Francisco office.

As it turned out, though, working in suburban San Jose was much easier than working in urban S.F. In San Jose, people were much more easygoing and trusting that I would do my best job for them. In San Francisco, people were fearful of being ripped off, more hostile, more angry, more demanding—all of the things I myself have started to become since I moved back to San Francisco. Also, in San Francisco I work with people from a number of countries, who speak many languages. The language barrier slows things down and makes the work harder. But I have learned so much about other cultures and have enjoyed these relationships to such a degree that I find this to be one of the most rewarding aspects of working in San Francisco.

RW: *Tell me a little about how your current office works.*

JJ: There are two rooms; one is a reception and secretarial area and the second is the area I work in. Sometimes the secretary and I share the same room, depending on the configuration of the office. Over the years, the office has moved several times within the same large building.

We try to get everyone to call before coming in or to make an appointment. I do all of the initial interviews, pre-hearing interviews, preparation of certain sets of papers. The secretary-receptionist types the other sets of forms and mails them out. The office is bilingual in Spanish.

Normally people come in between one and five times, depending on the complexity and how much people want to visit. For the simple form of divorce, some people come in once to give us all necessary information, pay the fee, and ask that all papers be mailed.

We review all files at least three times a year and send out notes to customers we have not heard from in some time to make sure there hasn't been some misunderstanding about the status of the divorce. But we only send out one note. We want to let them know that their divorce is not final, but we don't want to push them into completing a divorce that they would just as well drop or delay.

The office is open five days a week, 9–6, with later, or earlier appointments possible. The customer who qualifies for the basic $80 divorce usually pays the entire fee at the first visit. For the more expensive divorces, we accept the fee paid in two payments. I've had some problem with bad checks. In addition to our fee, the customer will also have to pay a filing fee to the court, unless they are low-income.

Often people need to get a consultation with an attorney about some unresolved legal issue, such as dividing an expensive asset, like a house or pension plan. Sometimes, the spouse is hiding assets, or the person who wants to file is so emotionally drained that they need someone to do all the work for them. I have a list of attorneys available to refer customers to who want or need to see someone.

Sometimes it's hard to get people to go to a lawyer, even when they should. They fear it. As a society, we're trained to go to the dentist and doctor, but we're not told that probably sometime in our lives we will need to see a lawyer. People feel very insecure in relating to lawyers. They don't know what the parameters of the relationship are, and what rights they have, that they are hiring the lawyer to do work for them. They fear, often with good reason, that once they get involved with a lawyer they will lose all control of their case and will end up with a $10,000 bill. In fact, I have had a number of customers who started with lawyers, spent thousands of dollars, and then felt the lawyer would not respect their decisions. As a result, these people fired the lawyer and decided to do it themselves.

RW: *What happens when you interview a customer?*

JJ: Usually only one person comes in, but sometimes they come with the spouse they are getting divorced from, which I prefer. Occasionally, of course, they come with children, friends, or family. Sometimes, the parent wants to leave the child unattended in the waiting room, which I will not allow. (There is a window with a five-story drop.) I have toys for the children. Friends, of course, are no problem. In fact, sometimes they will speak up and offer information that the customer may not have brought up, and they will give a lot of support to the customer.

My least favorite situation is where the parent comes in with the married daughter or son, and it is the parent who does all of the talking. Occasionally, there will be the married couple and representatives of both sides of the family. So, a good rule for any divorce typing office is to have plenty of chairs.

In most instances, it has been determined on the telephone which type of divorce they need, and they have been told what information they will need to bring. I give them a copy of the book *How to Do Your Own Divorce in California* and review the basic information it contains. I then have them sign a disclaimer that states that I am not a lawyer and they are responsible for all of their decisions. If they don't have any further questions, they can begin filling out the worksheets. If they want to think about it, they can take the book and the worksheets home and make another appointment. If the worksheets are completed right then, I immediately prepare the first set of papers. The customer then reviews the papers, signs and dates them, and they are ready to be filed by the customer. The customer is also responsible for serving the divorce papers on the spouse. In the simple form of divorce, called the "Summary Dissolution," there is no formal service of papers, since both the wife and husband sign the first set of forms.

The first interview can take anywhere from one to two hours, although two hours is unusual. The visits after that are shorter, maybe one-half hour.

I feel strongly that in addition to processing enormous amounts of paperwork, the job entails providing a lot of emotional support, information, and often referrals. People who are going through a divorce are usually going through changes in other parts of their lives as well. They may be changing jobs, looking for child care, having trouble finding affordable housing, having credit problems, car hassles, etc. They may not have family in the area, or even in this country, and sometimes don't even have friends they feel comfortable sharing this part of their lives with, so they really need to find an appropriate support group or get emotional help from another source. The point is that often people need more than just getting their papers typed.

RW: *What about marketing your services? How do people know how to find you?*

JJ: Primarily from referrals from previous customers. Positive recommendation by satisfied customers is a very powerful marketing device. I also get a lot of agency referrals. I also get referrals from the court clerk's office, even sometimes from lawyers and other unexpected sources. Advertising in the phone book and other lists where people look for information is also important. I don't do too much new marketing because I'm operating at maximum capacity—that's 60 to 70 new cases per month. I've given some thought to expanding my business, but haven't figured out how to do it in a high quality way.

RW: *What do you do if a customer says you did a poor job?*

JJ: Out of thousands of divorces, I only remember one time when I didn't do something correctly. This occurred in the first few months; the judge pointed out the problem and I was able to fix it. Generally, my high success rate is because I was carefully trained and give every customer a copy of *How to Do Your Own Divorce in California*, which we go through carefully. I encourage people to see an attorney if they have any questions that are not answered in the book, or if they need more information. The customers make all of the decisions about their divorces.

However, I can think of a few instances where I provided good service but the customer thought I did a poor job. For example, I typed the papers as directed in the divorce book, but a particular court clerk or judge would want them done a slightly different way and a nervous customer might wonder if I initially did them correctly or not. Of course, whenever there is any problem, I redo the papers at no extra cost. It is also the case (and anyone who serves the public will know this) that even though you try to provide excellent service to every single person, there are going to be a few who will find some problem, no matter how hard you try. Remember, for most people, going to a nonlawyer for help with a divorce is a new experience, and a number are unsure. But generally I have had very little trouble with this. By the end of almost every divorce I've typed, people feel that they have had excellent help, and usually refer their friends. Lawyers, of course, make a hue and cry about the "terrible" and "incompetent" work done by divorce consultants/independent paralegals like myself, but I know of hundreds of thousands of divorces typed by IPs and I know of very few problems. Compare this to the number of complaints and lawsuits filed against lawyers!

RW: *How do you relate to lawyers in an organized sense?*

JJ: Not well. I see the California Bar Association, indeed, all bar associations, as monoliths with basically conservative memberships antagonistic to change that might erode their traditional paternalistic role and monopoly control. They represent an enormous concentration of power, money, and legislative influence, and almost always use it to block constructive change.

I don't see individual lawyers as necessarily being part of the monolith, but put them in three general groupings. First, lawyers who may feel the adversarial system is not the best way to solve family problems and who support the development of a reasonable alternative for the delivery of legal services. In other words, they are at least somewhat critical of the legal monopoly the bar association is trying to protect. Second, lawyers who are honestly opposed to "divorce consultants," as we are currently called in California, as not being in the public interest because there are no standards for training, licensing, and we are not monitored in any way. Third, I would guess the majority of lawyers, who constantly and cynically cry "consumer protection" as an excuse to suppress alternatives and maintain their control.

Remember, divorce and family law used to be considered the "bread and butter" of law, and the most common reason the average person sought out a lawyer. Now, close to 60% of California divorces are done without lawyers, which is a loss of many millions of dollars of lawyers' income. And remember, this has all happened since 1971. Wouldn't you be threatened if you lost almost half of your business?

RW: *Do you think some lawyers who want to put you out of business are honestly motivated?*

JJ: Sure, I think that some lawyers actually believe that people want and need lawyers to make decisions for them. I once went to a bar association luncheon in Palo Alto, California, an upper-middle to upper-class area. At the luncheon, a lawyer told me that he thought people were "too stupid to make their own decisions" and that they needed lawyers' "firm guidance." Well, fortunately, a lot of people aren't too stupid to see this sort of arrogance for what it is.

        I am also appalled at lawyers' lack of concern about the unavailability of legal services to poor and low-income people who can't pay lawyers' fees. This sort of attitude makes me think of all the people I have worked with who had very little money, and what a severe hardship it would have been for some of them to come up with the money to pay a lawyer. In fact, many of them couldn't come up with the money and weren't able to file for a divorce until they heard about the WAVE Project/Divorce Center. So, I feel angry when I have any contact with lawyers who think like that. They live in a different world than I do.

RW: *Do you think there is any validity to the attorney charge that many independent paralegals are not sufficiently trained, and therefore may not be competent?*

JJ: Since lawyers have fought all legislation supporting training and licensure of independent paralegals, I question their right to make that charge. How can they work to keep us ignorant and then attack us for being ignorant? I support reasonable requirements for licensing and training and some kind of regulation done by an independent state agency— absolutely not by the bar.

RW: *Do you think lawyers will eventually accept the presence of paralegals?*

JJ: They already have when it suits their convenience. They hire paralegals instead of lawyers and assign them the same type of work I do. So the consumer should have that same right. The way it is now, consumers have to pay lawyers' rates for paralegal work, which of course is the idea, from the lawyers' point of view. I think the future for IPs is bright because the public wants alternatives to lawyers. And, hopefully, through some evolutionary process, lawyers will learn to accept the right of the public to use independent paralegals. They may even find a way to work cooperatively with independent paralegals as they realize that IPs take the pressure off them to provide services to millions of low- and moderate-income people.

RW: *What would be your advice to someone starting out?*

JJ: Do you want me to give you a few bits of general advice, or a laundry list of helpful suggestions?

RW: *How about the whole list.*

JJ: You asked for it. I'd say the following:

- Read books, or attend workshops on starting a small business, but don't let them scare you off.

- Have adequate savings to carry you for a while.

- Get good initial training and periodic updates.

- Be willing to take a risk or start part-time and keep the security you have until you see if your paralegal business is going to fly or not. It's hard to tell. Sometimes it seems best to get your feet wet a toe at a time, and sometimes a new business will only work if you make a full-time commitment.

- Have lawyers quickly available to ask questions, and be happy to pay for the help.

- It is not necessary to spend a lot of money furnishing the office at least to start. Save your money for more important things.

- Select a convenient location, with easy access to public transportation. And, hopefully, an area without much competition.

- Cultivate the attitude that what is best for the customer will be best for your business.

- Give financial breaks to the deserving.

- You do not have to accept every customer. Screen out those not appropriate for a fill-in-the boxes clinic approach.

- Develop a fair refund policy.

- Build a network of supportive lawyers to refer your customers to.

- Build good relationships with the landlord, printer, and other business people you deal with.

- Get known in your community. Dozens of groups will refer customers to you if they know about your service.

- Keep good records—every case in its own file, every disclaimer signed, every worksheet saved, etc.

- If you don't know a bookkeeping system, find a bookkeeper or accountant that specializes in small businesses and have them set up a simple system for you.

- Develop, if possible, good relationships with your competitors. Try to have a friendly, positive relationship with them rather than a cutthroat one. It can make life, and your business environment, more pleasant. You can help each other. In our group, we have shared advertising, even in cases where we were sharing the same area.

- Consider sharing office space, possibly with someone whose business or service complements yours, like a tax preparer.

- Be willing to spend money to improve your service. One way to do this is by using a small computer.

- Get insurance—liability and theft—if you have anything of value.

- Look for safety hazards in your office, especially if there will be children. For example, coffee pots with cords hanging down where the child can pull the pot over.

- Watch for changes or trends in your field by reading a local legal newspaper as well as specialized legal materials relevant to your work.

- Diversify beyond divorce and bankruptcy.

RW: *What about the future? What are your plans?*

JJ: I have an interest in organizing paralegals and I do work to help make more types of paralegal assistance available to the public. There is a lot to be done to establish paralegal work as a "safe occupation." I have organized some community workshops and volunteer work around the subject of people doing their own divorce. I think I have a lot to teach others. And of course, I need to learn new things, too. I have taken some courses that I felt would improve my service: Spanish, business applications of computers, a one-year legal secretarial course, and so on. I've also had to update my legal skills.

After 18 years of this work, I have considered a career change, but I think I am faced with the same thoughts that many who are considering trying to be an independent paralegal face: What should I do? Will I make more money? Do I need to be retrained? How much in debt do I want to go to be retrained? Do I want to move? Should I expand this business? Will I like my new career more, as much as, or less than the career I am leaving? Can I successfully work for someone else, or do I want to only consider careers that will allow me to continue to be self-employed?

Basically I feel that I have invested a great deal of energy in the work I am now doing, and find that hard to give up. So, I have turned a lot of my thinking to considering how the independent paralegal field will develop in the next few years and how to best facilitate and participate in that growth and change.

Ian Gardner Interview

Ian Gardner is the president of Paralegal Associates, based in Plantation, Florida. Paralegal Associates franchises paralegal offices in the state of Florida. (This interview was done in 1996.)

Ralph Warner (RW): *Ian, I understand you began your career as an independent paralegal in Canada and then relocated to Florida.*

Ian Gardner (IG): Yes, I was living in Ontario in the early 1980s when the Ontario courts ruled that nonlawyers could help people with traffic and small claims cases as well as landlord-tenant actions. It's known as the *Points* case, and it really had a profound effect on how basic legal services were handled in Toronto and the rest of Ontario. Actually it was my dad who read about it, and a related business of preparing incorporation documents without a lawyer. I was looking for a business to get into, so I opened an office to help people with small claims.

RW: *What about other actions?*

IG: I expanded to handle traffic and landlord-tenant cases. I also began teaching other people how to do the work as part of a franchise business that I ran from 1984 until 1989.

RW: *Somehow you got to Florida. Were you searching for more sun?*

IG: Sure, but also I had made a few dollars and wanted to get away from business and spend more time with my family.

RW: *Had you planned to do independent paralegal work in Florida?*

IG: Not really, but coincidentally I arrived just as big changes in the law business were happening. The Florida Supreme Court changed Rule 106, which allowed nonlawyers to prepare court paperwork for most family law actions—divorce, stepparent adoptions, custody disputes, and paternity, among others.

RW: *Let me guess—you couldn't resist jumping in.*

IG: Yes. I found that not working didn't really agree with me. So I decided to open a storefront office and run it myself.

RW: *Sounds like Canada all over again.*

IG: Yes, but this time I really didn't want to expand. I only did it after people began beating in my door asking to learn the business. At first I said no, but eventually I gave in and filed the papers necessary to get a franchise permit for Paralegal Associates.

RW: *How do you train new people who buy a franchise?*

IG: I provide about three weeks of formal training in how to do the various types of form preparation. Of course, I've developed lots of form preparation and office operating procedures that I pass along as part of the training. Then I have the new person work in an existing office actually doing the work for a couple of weeks.

RW: *Monkey see, monkey do type training.*

IG: Yes, it's really the best way to do it. The experienced IP prepares a certain type of paperwork and the novice does the same job. Then they sit down and compare the results and iron out any problems. But that's not the end of the training. When the new person opens his or her office, we spend a week or two sitting with them to make sure there are no problems.

RW: *How many offices do you have now?*

IG: Eleven. Two were initially unsuccessful largely because the franchisers weren't good business people. But these people have been replaced and now all are successful and profitable. Paralegal Associates is easily the largest paralegal operation in Florida.

RW: *Given that the Florida Supreme Court has approved nonlawyer form preparation in lots of areas, is the unauthorized practice of law still a problem in Florida?*

IG: Yes and no. We have been aggressive in marketing other services beyond the approved forms. We believe if we create forms based on worksheets prepared by the customer, we are not practicing law.

RW: *Does the bar buy that—for example, if you prepare a will or living trust based on an interview form prepared by a customer?*

IG: I can't completely answer that. A few years ago, the state bar saw that I was preparing a judgment form not part of the state package. A complaint was filed and they took my deposition. Soon after, they dropped the complaint. Later the bar sent me a letter challenging my procedures.

RW: *What was your response?*

IG: That we prepared the forms based strictly on what the customer put on the intake form, which made us form preparers or stenographers, not junior lawyers.

RW: *What happened?*

IG: Again, the bar dropped its complaint. They stated that they were reserving the right to take another look at whether our operations violated UPL rules sometime in the future, but in the meantime, they went away.

RW: *So, in the meantime, Paralegal Associates is helping lots of people accomplish basic legal paperwork.*

IG: Yes, about 1,000 per month.

RW: *How much do your franchises cost?*

IG: $39,000 plus, of course, a small percentage of what an office takes in.

Robert Mission Interview

Robert Mission has been an independent paralegal for well over 20 years. One of the true pioneers in this business, Bob currently coordinates the Superior California Legal Clinic in Sacramento, California. (This interview was done in 1992.)

Ralph Warner (RW): *Bob, tell me about your background. How did you get into the independent paralegal business?*

Robert Mission (RM): In the late 1960s, I was a process server. I did gofer work for a lawyer and also worked with a private detective.

RW: *What does the "creep and peep" business have to do with helping non-lawyers prepare legal forms?*

RM: Well, in about 1971, I developed a package of divorce forms complete with simple instructions. I called it "Divorce Economically," and sold the packets for $35. I also helped people type the forms if they needed it. Then, in 1973, I ran into Charlie Bloodgood, a University of California law student who was running a divorce typing service in Sacramento that was affiliated with the WAVE Project. As you know, the WAVE Project system was based on Ed Sherman's book *How to Do Your Own Divorce in California*, published by Nolo. I immediately recognized that the WAVE Project, which had training sessions, continuing education meetings, as well as the divorce book, embodied a more sophisticated approach than mine, so I got in touch with Charlie, met Ed and you, and joined up.

RW: *How did you and Charlie do?*

RM: Great, at least for awhile. We made contact with all sorts of community organizations, listed our service in the classifieds, and the people rolled in. After all, at about $75 to type a divorce, the price was right.

RW: *And then?*

RM: We had heard rumbles that the bar association was very unhappy about the so-called "do-it-yourself" movement, and was investigating our project. However, nothing direct was ever said until one afternoon in 1974, when a Sacramento County Deputy DA swooped into my office, identified himself, read me my rights, and handcuffed me in front of a client.

RW: *Were you scared?*

RM: I didn't have time to figure out how I felt, I was so busy demanding to make a phone call. They finally let me call my attorney, the man I had worked for for years as a gofer. I was confident he would help me, but was told by his secretary that he had just had a heart attack and was in intensive care.

RW: *Oops!*

RM: Oops, nothing! I was so upset I demanded to talk to him—tubes and all.

RW: *What happened?*

RM: By the time I got downtown, my attorney's secretary had made some calls, and I was released on my own recognizance, charged with the crime of unauthorized practice. My next step was to call Phyllis Eliasberg, a Southern California consumer advocate and lawyer who had taken over the WAVE Project from you and Ed when you guys decided to concentrate on Nolo. Phyllis eventually referred me to a Sacramento County attorney, Jim Reed, to defend me.

RW: *Tell me a little about the defense.*

RM: It was based mostly on constitutional grounds, utilizing Ed Sherman's book and the WAVE Project method. I maintained that I was only a typing service offering scrivener services, using as my guideline *How to Do Your Own Divorce in California*. I pointed out that all my clients received a copy of the book, read it carefully, and made their own decisions. I argued that I clearly had a First Amendment right to refer my clients to Ed's book generally and, if they had a specific question, to the particular chapter that dealt with that procedure.

RW: *Did this defense work?*

RM: Beautifully! When the bar counsel took my deposition, he asked me questions related to complicated matters of contested divorce procedure. I replied, "I'm sorry, I can't answer that question." The bar counsel would ask me, "Why can't you answer?" I replied, "Because that information is not covered in *How to Do Your Own Divorce in California* and so to do so would constitute my giving legal advice."

RW: *What did you say when they asked you something that was covered in Ed's book?*

RM: Since I had directed clients to all the key passages so many times, I didn't even have to open the book. I just quoted the relevant passages verbatim.

RW: *What happened in court?*

RM: The criminal procedures simply stopped. Instead, the bar attorneys suggested to my attorney that we enter a broad stipulation as to how I could and couldn't operate. Their proposal was so strict that it would have effectively stopped our operation. I refused to go along, on my attorney, Jim Reed's, advice. Fortunately the judge agreed with Jim that what the bar wanted to force us to do was unconstitutional. I personally feel that in making this decision the judge was heavily influenced by the fact that I received referrals from dozens of public and private agencies, especially those designed to help low-income persons.

RW: *Could you give me several examples?*

RM: Well, agencies such as the State Department of Justice, County Welfare, McGeorge Law School, the Battered Women's Shelter, various community service organizations, and, believe it or not, even the DA's office. In fact, the funniest thing about the whole thing was that the day the deputy DA arrested me, someone in the DA's office had referred me a client.

RW: *Was that the end of your troubles with the bar?*

RM: Not exactly. To the best of my remembrance, the judge suggested that the guidelines proposed by the bar be amended to allow me to still operate as a scrivener. Since these guidelines were basically the same as the WAVE Project rules, I accepted them. I could see that to survive in Sacramento in the long run, I had to go along with some of what the bar wanted.

RW: *How did your new guidelines work out?*

RM: Well, in a sense I never used them as part of my service because by this time my partner, Charlie Bloodgood, had been threatened with reprisals by McGeorge Law School if he didn't quit the independent paralegal business. Incidentally, Charlie is now a prominent lawyer in the area, who recently ran for judge.

RW: *What did you do?*

RM: My attorney and I worked out a new way of operating. I bought out the WAVE Project and reorganized operations completely, utilizing secretaries, independent paralegals, and attorneys working together. We call it Superior California Legal Clinics, Inc. Charlie Bloodgood was president of our organization until 1984, supervising the operation of the clinic.

RW: *Who owns Superior California Legal Clinic?*

RM: It's a nonprofit corporation with a Board of Directors. Our mandate is to help low- and moderate-income people educate themselves to deal with the legal system.

RW: *Then, legally, you work for the nonprofit corporation?*

RM: Right. I'm an officer, on the Board of Directors and an employee.

RW: *Let me change the subject a little and ask what you really do, day by day.*

RM: In 19 years, I've personally (with secretarial assistance, of course) assisted in preparing about 15,000 uncontested divorces. In addition, I've counseled a great many individuals and couples who were going through changes in their lives. I also schedule the attorneys on their appointments for the actions that the Clinic doesn't do on a paralegal basis. In addition, I supervise the many procedures necessary to provide these services as reasonably and effectively as possible, following the prescribed guidelines of the Clinic.

RW: *Have you figured out what your average charge for typing a divorce has been over the years?*

RM: Well, it's gone from $35 in the beginning to close to $150 today for a fairly basic divorce. I guess the average would be about $90, with the exception of a simple Summary Dissolution, which has gone from $40 to $75 today.

RW: *What do you think the same people would have had to pay if they went to an individual attorney or legal clinic and both were represented?*

RM: On the average, with children and little property, probably about $1,000 using a heavily advertised clinic and a minimum of $1,500 for the same thing using a conventional private attorney.

RW: *So, even figuring that some people might have represented themselves or simply gotten along without a divorce, you saved people several million dollars over a period of 14 years.*

RM: Yes, in the divorce area, but Superior does lots of other things now, still at a very economical rate, using a sliding scale, so that all of our low-income clients receive service very economically.

RW: *Give me an example of the work you do.*

RM: We specialize in family law matters, including uncontested divorces, wills, bankruptcies, child support modifications, nonmarried custody actions, name changes, and the like, but we also handle guardianships, paternity actions, adoptions, restraining orders, and, by use of our attorney-referral procedure, some criminal and personal injury cases.

RW: *How does the Clinic work?*

RM: We use a paralegal approach on divorces, separations, annulments, etc. On the others, we refer to one of five attorneys who work with us,

according to our sliding-fee schedule, which we make clear to everyone in advance.

RW: *What are your charges?*

RM: We have set charges for many actions. For example, a bankruptcy is
        currently $125–$150, a name change is $100, and so on. If a particular
        problem doesn't fit into a predictable category, we charge by the hour
        on a sliding scale based on our clients' income. This is basically $40 for
        low-income and $60 for middle-income people.

RW: *How does this compare to local attorney rates?*

RM: The going rate in Sacramento is $125 to $175 per hour. The heavily
        advertised legal clinics charge at least $150 per hour.

RW: *When you changed your method of operating to include attorneys, did
        the bar's attitude change?*

RM: It was a whole new ballgame from the moment we changed the name
        and included lawyers. I guess you could say it allowed me to become
        almost respectable.

RW: *But when it comes down to typing divorces, you are doing pretty much
        the same thing you always did?*

RM: Right, my approach is identical, only under supervision.

RW: *Does that make you smile?*

RM: Chuckle, somewhat, might be a better way to describe it.

RW: *In 19 years, you must have seen a lot of big changes. What's the biggest?*

RM: Attitude. These days the courts, the District Attorney, social services,
        and law schools all refer cases to us. That would have been unheard of
        ten years ago. Now, when a person picks up a divorce form package at
        the court clerk's office, they get an information sheet with our name on
        it. And that's not only happening in Sacramento. We prepare forms for
        people in 26 counties, and in most of them, one or another county
        agency sends us referrals.

RW: *How do you prepare paperwork for people at a distance?*

RM: They call us and we do a little initial screening. If our service is appropriate for the customer, we send out an information package. The customer fills it out and sends in a money order. If we have more questions, we handle them by phone. Otherwise, we type the paper to send them out.

RW: *What do you think about the future of the independent paralegal business?*

RM: The surface hasn't even been scratched. There are certain to be more clinics with paralegals and attorneys working together on a more-or-less equal footing, because the economics of delivering legal services to low- and middle-income people don't allow for anything else. How can a person who makes $8 to $10 an hour afford to pay a lawyer $150 or more per hour? It doesn't make sense. There have been a lot of changes in our legal system over the past 19 years, and you know what?

RW: *I'll bite.*

RM: The changes in how legal services are delivered to people, whether by phone, computer, lawyer, or independent paralegal, in the next 20 years are going to make what we have accomplished so far look small.

Virginia Simons Interview

Virginia Simons worked as an independent paralegal in Bakersfield, California. With over 13 years in the business, she amassed much valuable experience in how to cope with bar association attacks, work with other paralegals, and develop a paralegal business. She passed away in the year 2000, a deeply felt loss to the IP community. (This interview was first done in 1992. It was extensively updated in 1994 and 1996.)

Ralph Warner (RW): Let's start with your personal history as an independent paralegal.

Virginia Simons (VS): I've been in the business since 1981. In the beginning, I only typed divorces and bankruptcies. Now I also do restraining orders in domestic violence situations, family law restraining orders, harassment orders, child support and custody orders, responses, guardianships, terminations of guardianship, stepparent adoptions, paternity orders, name changes, and joinders on pension plans.

RW: *When did you first run into trouble with the local bar?*

VS: Not until 1988, when two other local typing service owners and I were sued by a bankruptcy court trustee.

RW: *I'm interested in why it took the bar eight years to go after you. In a metropolitan area with a population of about 360,000, your business can't have been a secret. Do you know why it took them so long?*

VS: I'm not sure. I tried to keep a very low profile at first. I figured that if I was a good little girl, no one would bother me.

RW: *But in 1988, they did sue you. Had you done something to be perceived as a bad little girl?*

VS: I wasn't doing anything different. It may have been that over the years, as there were more IPs in Bakersfield, lawyers felt they were losing so much business that they decided to crack down. Remember, I wasn't the only target—Marilyn Marvin and Bobbe Powers were also charged with unauthorized practice of law for bankruptcy form preparation.

RW: *What were your feelings when you learned of the suit?*

VS: I panicked. I really thought I would end up in jail. If you had heard the horrible stories about Kern County Jail that I have, you would have some idea of how scared I felt.

RW: *What did you do?*

VS: The hardest part was telling my husband. When I did, his first reaction was to tell me to quit the business and get a job.

RW: *Obviously, you didn't do that. What did you say to your husband to change his mind?*

VS: I said, "You've never backed away from a fight that you couldn't avoid with dignity. You've always told me there are times when you have to stand up and be ready to fight back."

RW: *What was his response?*

VS: He thought about what I said and replied, "Go for it. I'll back you, even if it means losing our house and savings"; and then he said, "You're right."

RW: *Once you had your domestic ducks in a row, what did you, Bobbe, and Marilyn do?*

VS: First, we needed legal help. We had been sued in federal court and we had to respond. The first lawyer we approached turned us down flat. He refused to go against the local legal establishment.

RW: *Whoa. You mean this was so political, a local criminal lawyer who represents all sorts of unpopular people was afraid to take your money?*

VS: Yes. We finally got an attorney who made no bones about the fact that he thought we were guilty of UPL, but said that he was such a good lawyer he could get us off. I'm sorry I can't mention his name, but we had to promise that we wouldn't publicly associate his name with ours.

RW: *Was this because he feared the reaction of his lawyer colleagues?*

VS: Yes. At this point, local lawyers were determined to do away with our competition. Anyone who represented us was in danger of being seen as a traitor by their colleagues.

RW: *What next?*

VS: Even with a lawyer, we felt terribly lonely and isolated. Finally, we called Steve Elias, who is an author and editor with Nolo.com. Steve doesn't normally provide individual advice, but he got interested in the details of our case and came to Bakersfield. He really gave us the strength to go on. Catherine Jermany and Glynda Dixon of the California Association of Independent Paralegals (CAIP) also helped spread the word about our plight and rallied crucial support. But it was really Steve who turned us around when he looked right at us and said "You have a basic personal choice to make. Either stop crying and moaning and enjoy the fight, or quit right now." We decided to put fear behind us and take the offensive.

RW: *What did you do?*

VS: Lots of things. We told each of our customers that we had been sued by a bankruptcy trustee in federal court in an effort to put us out of business, and got them to sign petitions on our behalf. We went to the bankruptcy court once a month when it was in session and took notes as to any unequal treatment given to nonlawyers representing themselves. We testified at public hearings at the state level, where the subject of whether IPs should be certified or licensed was being considered. In short, we started to have fun.

RW: *What happened at the trial?*

VS: The best thing was that 25 people came from all over California to be there to support us. Then, all of a sudden, it was over and we won. Patrick Kavanaugh, the bankruptcy trustee who sued us, thought it was a violation of UPL to simply type bankruptcy forms and didn't present any evidence as to how we were guilty of UPL. The judge, who would have loved to convict us, had to disagree, based on other court decisions that held that simply typing forms wasn't unauthorized practice. In short, he demanded that Kavanaugh produce evidence that we had given customers legal information. Since he wasn't prepared to do that, the judge reluctantly dismissed the case.

RW: *Great, you won. How did you celebrate?*

VS: We organized a public forum at a conference room at the Red Lion Inn on the subject of whether typing services should exist. A couple of lawyers showed up to speak on our side of the issue and several more who opposed us. The press covered it and began to get interested in our story.

RW: *Was this a continuation of your offensive?*

VS: Yes, we had decided to affirmatively contact and engage our opponents. We wanted to convince individual lawyers that many people who couldn't afford lawyer fees really needed our services. In addition, we wanted our adversaries to know that, personally, we weren't monsters. For example, we contacted each of the lawyers who spoke against typing services at the Red Lion Inn.

RW: *Did you apply the same strategy to Patrick Kavanaugh and Gary O'Neil, the two lawyers who had been your principal adversaries?*

VS: Yes, we did, but first we contacted the Kern County DA, because we heard he was thinking of filing criminal UPL charges against us. We asked for an appointment and discussed all the issues. In fact, there was no plan to go after us, but it was good to clear the air. We also contacted a local judge who was rumored to believe that we were keeping filing fees customers paid to us when we filed fee waivers based on the customer's poverty. Interestingly, the judge wasn't worried about that, but did say that, in his opinion, we were practicing law. He then added that given the difficulty in defining UPL, we were okay as long as we stuck to the types of form preparation we were doing.

RW: *In short, the judge presented you with a sort of horseback deal—you can violate the law a little bit, but don't go too far.*

VS: Something like that. But to get back to Kavanaugh and O'Neil, we tried to open up lines of communication. Initially, this happened at public meetings. For example, Kavanaugh and I were both on a bankruptcy subcommittee of the state bar's committee looking into the possibility of licensing typing services. Of the two trustees and one bankruptcy judge on this subcommittee, Kavanaugh was the only one who provided unbiased opinions on how typing services could operate within the bankruptcy field. At a seminar where Gary O'Neil and I both sat on the panel, he claimed Kern County was unique because they had "all those sleaze-bag typing services." When it was my turn to speak, I introduced myself by saying I was one of the "sleaze-bags," and invited Gary to come to one of our local CAIP (California Association of Independent Paralegals) chapter meetings.

RW: *Did he come?*

VS: Yes, he did. First we invited him to lunch with the five of us who ran the main typing services in town. (Incidentally, to show solidarity, we always went together to meetings with the bar, judges, or lawyers.) We worked out a plan for him to speak at our meeting and he invited us, in turn, to speak to a bar association lunch on the issue of whether legal typing services should be licensed.

RW: *Sounds great. Did the communication lead to anything positive?*

VS: Very much so. We had said to Gary that if he thought we were doing a bad job, why didn't he teach us to do better?

RW: *Did you learn anything?*

VS: Yes. It was extremely valuable,.

RW: *Why do you think you were suddenly beginning to be accepted?*

VS: It's complicated, of course, but I think, at bottom, lawyers are beginning to realize that the independent paralegal licensing issue isn't going away. The fact that IPs are organized at the state and local level, that legislation to legalize IPs has been introduced in Sacramento and that even state bar committees have made some positive recommendations all helps us. Why, we have even been invited to attend bar lunches.

RW: *Hey, that's a big change. Are paralegals who work for lawyers also invited?*

VS: Yes, and I guess you could say we are being included in a somewhat similar way.

RW: *Are there other signs that IPs are now considered to be part of the system?*

VS: You remember a few years ago we were afraid to be identified by some judges? Well now the courts ask us to type the names of our businesses on the top of all legal paperwork we prepare so we can be contacted if need be.

RW: *Just like lawyers do.*

VS: Precisely. And I'll tell you a positive recent development. The Kern County Domestic Violence Advisory Committee, which is made up of a number of public and private agencies interested in the subject, puts out several brochures aimed at battered women that are distributed at lots of places, including women's centers, social services agencies, and so on. Anyway, the great thing is that IPs are officially listed as a place to get restraining order applications prepared.

RW: *Terrific! But tell me, is the District Attorney's office a member of the Advisory Committee?*

VS: They sure are.

RW: *What about your competitors? The fact that you and many other typing services in town have worked so closely together tells me that you value cooperation.*

VS: Very much so. Solidarity in this business is essential. The bar is really impressed by the fact that we stick together and can't be picked off one by one.

RW: *Does this strategy extend to new typing services? After all, they are your competitors, much as you compete with lawyers.*

VS: Our strategy is to train the new people to do a good job. Sure I have mixed emotions at times, but by and large I think we all will prosper if the legal form typing business expands. Also, it just feels good to cooperate. It brings me lots of friends. Also, because I can get help from another knowledgeable IP if I need it, I can serve my customers better. And if I don't do a particular type of legal form typing, I can refer the customers to someone who does, either locally or elsewhere in the state.

RW: *Do you see any major changes in the IP business generally?*

VS: There is more competition in our area for basic form preparation for divorces. To prosper, IPs need to learn new skills. For example, a big part of my business these days is helping people prepare guardianships. Many of my customers are grandparents who, due to the disintegration of their children's families, must raise their grandkids and need legal authority to do so. Paternity is another fast-growing area that I've begun to develop.

RW: *In the fall of 1995, you invited me to speak at the California Association of Independent Paralegals' (CAIP) annual meeting in Bakersfield. I had a great time at this very well-attended three-day event, with close to 150 people participating. Did the fact that so many IPs were in Bakersfield have any affect on the local legal community?*

VS: It sure did. As part of the event, we invited a number of local lawyers to teach classes in various aspects of family law—paternity, grandparent visitation, guardianship, and child custody to name a few. We also had a bankruptcy course. Believe it or not, some of the teachers were the same lawyers who used to ask the DA to put some of our IPs in jail. At the end of the weekend, many of the participating attorneys complimented us on how serious and well-informed about key legal issues we were.

RW: *In short, you appeared competent in the eyes of many local lawyers and the word spread.*

VS: Yes, but more than that, the lawyers who participated saw that we take our role as legal form preparers seriously and don't want to practice law.

RW: *Tell me a little more about that. Are you saying that some lawyers are getting over their obsession that IPs are low-cost competitors who will steal their business?*

VS: Definitely. They are getting a much better sense that we really do limit ourselves to preparing paperwork mostly for working-class people who are very inexperienced when it comes to using lawyers. And that when we identify problems we can't handle, we really do refer our customers to an appropriate lawyer.

RW: *Are you saying you actually create new business for lawyers?*

VS: No question. I know for a fact that my referrals have done a lot to keep a few new attorneys in business. Think of it this way—as a society, we all love to hate lawyers, but as individuals, we would be pretty stupid not to recognize that we occasionally need one. Lower-income people tend not to know lawyers personally, but after many years of our working in the community, they do know IPs. So they call us first. It's our role to prepare necessary legal paperwork for routine problems, such as guardianships, restraining orders, or uncontested divorces, but to make referrals to lawyers when they really need more extensive help than we can provide.

RW: *And as you do, lawyers come to see that people who might never have dealt with their legal problem in a formal way are now doing so because they first contact IPs such as you, and you then send them on to an appropriate lawyer.*

VS: Exactly.

Glynda Dixon Interview

Glynda Dixon is an independent paralegal based in Oakland, California. For many years she typed a number of family law forms, including divorce, guardianship, name change, child support modifications, probates, stepparent adoptions, and wills as part of the business she began in 1984. She is a past president of the California Association of Independent Paralegals and a volunteer arbitrator with Oakland Better Business Bureau. In 1994 she sold her family law typing business and began a successful new venture helping people appeal from the denial of Social Security disability benefits. (This interview was extensively updated in 1996.)

Ralph Warner (RW): How did you start in the independent paralegal business?

Glynda Dixon (GD): I prefer the term "public paralegal" or "legal technician," but to answer your question, my training is as a career counselor. In 1984, I became my own client in that I was looking for a career change for myself. A person I knew told me she was getting a divorce with the help of a nonlawyer divorce typing service in Oakland. I was fascinated that this occupation existed. To make a long story short, I investigated and learned that the divorce typing office was run by Sandra Edwards, who also had another, larger office in Walnut Creek, California. I also learned that Sandra followed a system originally taught by you and Ed Sherman as part of the WAVE Project. It allows nonlawyers to prepare routine legal forms with little risk that they will be accused of practicing law without a license. I worked for Sandra for months—typing divorce forms as sort of a paid apprentice, and then I bought the Oakland office.

RW: *What other training did you have?*

GD: I read all the Nolo divorce materials many times, which, by this time, had been used by thousands of people to do their own divorces without help from lawyers. Also, remember, I was typing divorce forms every day under the supervision of a person who had been doing it for years. Under her training, I learned the appropriate work standards and ethical behavior that later helped build my reputation as a reliable service. In addition, I checked out lots of divorce files at the county clerk's office. Court files are public records, so I just checked dozens of random divorces and studied them. I do this with any new procedure I want to learn.

RW: *Where did you operate your first office?*

GD: On a neighborhood shopping street in a middle-class area, about a half-mile from Oakland's downtown area. At that point I was cautious and didn't want to be too close to the downtown legal establishment.

RW: *How did you build up your business?*

GD: It was slow at first. I didn't have much money for promotion, and anyway, I was worried that advertising might bring me trouble with the bar or the District Attorney. As a result, I concentrated on building a personal referral network. I contacted the personnel offices of big businesses, social services agencies, child and family counselors, and even some lawyers, to tell them who I was and what I did.

RW: *Weren't you afraid of lawyers?*

GD: As I said, I was afraid of the bar association and the District Attorney, but not necessarily of individual lawyers. I concentrated on lawyers I knew, or friends knew, and yes, some of them did refer me customers.

RW: *What advertising did you do?*

GD: I tried a few small classified ads in weekly shoppers and penny saver type papers. That didn't produce much, so finally I tried the big city paper, the *Oakland Tribune*, under the "legal services" classifieds heading. It didn't bring in much business at first, but I kept it in, and before long, the phone began ringing. It taught me a valuable lesson. In this business, you need to have an ad in the same place every day. When you do, lots of people eventually figure out it's there and tell others.

RW: *Okay, you started in 1984, how would you describe your business two years later.*

GD: I was having fun, but the business was in poor economic shape. I took in about $45,000 that year and spent almost all of it on overhead and promotion.

RW: *How did you survive?*

GD: Fortunately, my former husband didn't own a business—he has a "regular" job with a "regular" paycheck—otherwise, I would not have been able to stick with it.

RW: *What did you do to improve things?*

GD: I got frustrated enough to see that I needed help on how to run a good small business and found an excellent small business consultant, Roger Pritchard, in Berkeley. He helped me focus on improving my business in a number of ways. The most important was making a marketing plan to produce more customers and sticking to it.

RW: *Can you give me some specifics?*

GD: For the first time, I kept track of where my customers came from. Once I knew that, I concentrated my marketing efforts on the best referral sources. Before I developed a plan, I was often spending as much time on promotional activities that produced 5% of my business as I was on those that produced 25%.

RW: *What else did Pritchard help you with?*

GD: He talked me out of borrowing money to expand the business. He got me to see that the additional money would be wasted until I had a better plan, and better day-to-day control. I was so frustrated, I cried, but he was right. Lack of money wasn't my problem; it was a symptom of running my business.

RW: *Insights are cheap. What did you do to change things?*

GD: As I said, I focused my marketing money and energy where it would do the most good. In addition, I began to offer more services, including typing name changes, child support modifications, and guardianships. I also made an effort to stay in touch with former customers and others

I had worked with to encourage word-of-mouth referrals. Suddenly, after three years or so, people began to see me as established and trustworthy. Individual lawyers, employees at the public law library, people at court offices dealing with child support, even the local bar's legal help service, began sending me people who couldn't afford a lawyer and weren't eligible for legal aid.

RW: *So you found your market niche?*

GD: Exactly. Whether or not they always want to admit it, in the high-cost Bay Area, lawyers can't afford to provide services to working people who have a family income of $50,000 or less. At the same time, they hate to admit that the American legal system is closed to the average person, so they refer these people to me.

RW: *Okay, your business improved; what next?*

GD: I got excited about running an excellent small business and began to see ways to improve it more. My biggest step was to move to an older professional building in downtown Oakland. Now I was near the courts, county offices, such as social services, and the DA's child support collection offices. I was also in the same neighborhood as the majority of Oakland's law firms.

RW: *Were you worried about becoming more visible to the legal establishment?*

GD: Not in the least. I had been threatened by a few lawyers and was investigated by the DA for unauthorized practice when I first started, but I was confident that I knew how to type forms without giving legal information. In short, I felt my business could stand scrutiny and there was no need to hide it. Also, by now, most of the people who might investigate me were sending me customers. I believed that if someone in the legal establishment tried to close me down, a number of conscientious lawyers who respected and trusted my work and knew I didn't practice law would stand up for me.

RW: *How did the move work out?*

GD: Business increased substantially right away. I began to get referrals from lawyers in my building, and when the feedback was good, from others in the downtown area.

RW: *Which leads me to ask whether lawyers, who have been enemies of the Independent Paralegal movement, are turning out to be friends.*

GD: Surprisingly, to some extent, some are. It's like a dual reality. At the state level, bar association types want to put IPs out of business, or to so limit what they can do that it amounts to the same thing. But at the local, day-to-day level, dozens of individual public and private lawyers, and even establishment legal agencies, which I won't name so as to not embarrass them, absolutely depend on the fact that legal typing services such as the one I ran exist. They know something bar associations don't know or won't admit; despite all the hoopla about providing legal access to ordinary Americans, the legal profession is economically completely unable to do it. In the S.F. Bay Area, lawyers claim they need a minimum of $150 an hour or more to get by; how in the world can they get that from people who make $10 an hour?

RW: *Are you pussyfooting around, saying that you have had referrals from court clerks, judges, the local bar associations, and even the District Attorney's office?*

GD: I'd better not comment.

RW: *Okay, let me change gears a little. Rose Palmer, who runs a service in Pittsburgh, Pennsylvania, to help women with divorces and child support, has reported that while the organized bar has been hostile to her organization's efforts to help women deal with issues of divorce, support, custody, and domestic violence, she has gotten support from some judges, who see clearly that many of the people who need help can't afford lawyers. Have you had encouragement from the bench?*

GD: Yes, to a limited but very welcome degree. Some judges never grow up—they keep their narrow lawyer attitudes forever. But it's a mistake to see the judiciary as a monolith. A few judges helped me refine my paperwork technologies and generally supported my efforts. Also, after I became established, several court clerks became very supportive.

RW: *Have you done anything to encourage or institutionalize your relation-
       ship with judges or the courthouse personnel generally?*

GD: I made a habit of filing papers in person so that I could speak to the
       clerks, and I would drop by the law library often. Our local Indepen-
       dent Paralegal Association invited one of our area's most prominent
       family law judges to give us a training session. He did, and has gener-
       ally let it be known that he supports IPs who do top quality form
       preparation and stay away from complicated areas of the law, where
       they don't have expertise. When he told me, "Glynda, I recognize your
       paperwork because it's of such high quality," it made my month—or,
       more so, it made my year!

RW: *You raised the issue of how careful you are to avoid practicing law. Let
       me follow up on that. What did you do when people asked a question
       that requires legal expertise?*

GD: I didn't answer it. All my customers signed a statement saying they
       know I am not a lawyer and I don't give legal advice, so I am very clear
       on this point from the start. In addition, there was a prominent sign in
       my office that said, "We are not attorneys. We do not give legal advice."

RW: *Sure, but that didn't stop them from asking.*

GD: First, you must realize that most questions on the preprinted forms I
       typed aren't legal—it's the same sort of name, address, and age type of
       information that any other government form requests. When questions
       on a form depend on a customer having some legal knowledge, it was
       typically fairly routine and accessible. For example, someone might ask
       if a certain type of property is community property and therefore owned
       by both spouses 50-50. I simply referred them to the relevant discus-
       sion in *California Marriage and Divorce Law*, or *How to Do Your Own
       Divorce in California*, both of which are available on my desk or in any
       bookstore in the state. If the answers weren't there, the person prob-
       ably needs more in-depth information. An example might be a divorce
       where one person has a job that will provide a pension, or there's a lot
       of property involved and the couple is unclear about how to divide it.

RW: *So what did you do then?*

GD: Most legal information or help my customers needed could be efficiently provided by one of three sources. The first were lawyers who knew me and were willing to see a customer for a modest fee, provide the necessary information, and perhaps do a property agreement before sending the customer back so I could finish typing the divorce. In many cases, though, the lawyer didn't really need to do any form preparation. There is a sample property settlement agreement in *How to Do Your Own Divorce,* which I could prepare under the customer's supervision once they have the legal information they need.

The second is mediation. Suppose spouses haven't decided important issues, such as property division; in that case, I recommended mediation. Usually, after two or three mediation sessions, which might cost $200, the couple worked out their own compromise and the mediator wrote it down in a form that I then included with the papers I typed and submitted to the court. You might be surprised, but people are more savvy and knowledgeable than most lawyers want to admit, and given the sort of positive framework mediation offers, they will usually work out a mutually satisfactory and reasonably fair solution, whether it involves property division, custody, visitation, or whatever.

Finally, there is a Divorce Helpline in Santa Cruz, California. This is a phone-in service where lawyers provide legal advice about self-help divorce for a reasonable fee. They even provide a service to compute the value of pensions, which can be complicated, especially if the person covered by the pension hasn't retired yet. Assuming the customer talks to the lawyers at Divorce Helpline for 15 or 20 minutes, they can get the legal help they need for $30 or $40, and I could finish typing their paperwork.

RW: *Sounds good. But you sold your divorce and family law form preparation business and moved on to preparing Social Security Disability Appeals. Why the change?*

GD: After ten years, I was burned out on preparing paperwork for divorces, stepparent adoptions, guardianships, and so on. When I realized I couldn't get my volume up high enough to afford to hire an assistant to do the routine but very fussy and time-consuming form preparation, I decided I simply needed a new professional challenge. Obviously, I am not alone in starting as an IP by typing divorces and then going on to other things. These days, many IPs have become far more imaginative in the types of work they do.

RW: *Give me some details about what you do now.*

GD: I help claimants with the final stages of their application for Social Security Disability—SSDI or SSI. If a person's disability application has been denied twice, they can ask for a hearing before an Administrative Law Judge, who determines if their disability meets the Social Security regulation defining disability, called the Listings. I represent them in preparing for and conducting this hearing.

RW: *What does that involve?*

GD: I help obtain my clients' medical records, prepare written legal arguments (briefs), and represent them at a hearing, all with the idea of explaining why my client is disabled and unable to work.

RW: *Nonlawyers are allowed to do this?*

GD: Yes, a provision of the Federal Administrative Procedure Act authorizes nonlawyer representation. There are many federal and state administrative agencies that allow advocates to represent an applicant. At the hearing, the Administrative Law Judge refers to me as a "nonattorney advocate."

RW: *Do lawyers handle Social Security Disability cases?*

GD: In the S.F. Bay Area, where I'm located, a few do—often the type of lawyer who prefers being in a relatively nonadversarial type law practice. But there is also room for nonlawyer advocates, since there are more potential clients than the lawyers can handle. Except for Legal Aid paralegals, I am one of the few local nonlawyers providing this kind of representation.

RW: *Was it scary when you first represented someone in a court-like setting? After all, you weren't trained as a lawyer.*

GD: Especially with my first few appeals, I would come out of the hearing before the Administrative Law Judge feeling like there was more I should have said. Or I would want to kick myself for not being more pointed in my cross-examination of the expert medical witnesses presented by the government. But since my client almost always won—that is, was judged eligible for disability—and I knew I was preparing very thoroughly, I always felt that I was doing a better than competent job.

RW: *How do you get paid?*

GD: My ad says, "No fee unless we win! No fee for a consultation." In short, I only get paid if the client does. The federal code states I can collect a percentage of any retroactive disability benefits a client obtains with my help—up to a maximum. I can also request fees up front to go into a trust account to pay for medical records or other direct expenses I incur trying to prove a claimant's case. However, with many low-income clients, I must pay these advance fees out of my own pocket. Assuming I help the client achieve a favorable decision, my ability to actually collect my "contingency fee" can be a problem, although by staying in close touch with the client, I'm almost always successful. Of course, I pay great attention to all this, since getting paid is obviously a critical part of running any successful business.

Rosemary Furman Interview

Rosemary Furman began typing legal forms for low-income residents of Jacksonville, Florida, in the early 1970s. Her inspired one-woman fight against the monopolistic practices of the Florida bar took her to the threshold of a Florida jail cell. (This interview was done in 1986.)

Ralph Warner (RW): *Lots of people know at least a little bit about what's happened to you in the last few years, including the fact that the Florida Bar Association tried to jail you for providing high-quality, low-cost legal help to nonlawyers, so I'd like to start a little earlier. I'm curious—how did a respectable middle-aged woman, and mother of three, with no credentials as a radical, get to become Public Enemy Number One to American lawyerdom? What's your background? Were you born feisty, or is it something you just grew into?*

Rosemary Furman (RF): I was born in Alexandria, Virginia, where my grandmother owned a bakery and made a little bootleg beer in the back room. I spoke German as my first language until I was eight. I went to public school, first in Virginia and later in New York state, south of Albany, after being orphaned.

RW: *How did you get involved in the legal system?*

RF: Court reporting. I took classes to become a court reporter. It seemed like a very good income for the hours expended.

RW: *You mean you learned how to key punch one of those little transcribing machines?*

RF: Never! I learned Gregg shorthand, a far more accurate system, and one I keep up with today.

RW: *Where did you work as a court reporter?*

RF: Where didn't I work? I married a military man, and when he was transferred, I packed up the kids and went along. When I'd get to a new city I would put my name on the court reporter list and eventually I'd have a job. At one time or another, I worked in Trenton, New Jersey, Nassau County, Long Island, Boston, Washington, DC, and Jacksonville, Florida.

RW: *So, it was as a court reporter that you first started seeing the legal system as being flawed?*

RF: If that's a polite way to say that I began to see lawyers as barracudas, preying on the public, you're right. You see, a court reporter quickly becomes part of the furniture, and lawyers and judges would often carry on their self-serving schemes in front of me, almost as if I weren't there. I mean, it isn't hard to understand what's going on if you literally see the money changing hands. How many times can you sit in a judge's office and watch the lawyers and judges bargain and sell clients for the highest fee and then go out into the public courtroom and put on a charade for the benefit of the public before you realize that our American justice system is run by a bunch of self-interested charlatans who call themselves officers of the court?

RW: *You just made some pretty strong statements. How about some specifics to back it up.*

RF: Okay, sure, but first, let me just say I'm an old-fashioned constitutionalist. I really believe in fundamental American values like the Bill of Rights, the right of every man and woman to vote, a court system where the average taxpaying citizen can get a fair shake, and so on. You want an example of what turned me off? I could give you dozens, hundreds, but first let me say that any of the bailiffs, marshals, clerks, and other personnel who work at the courthouse could tell you the same sort of thing. What goes on in the so-called halls of justice is closer to a Persian market, with the buying and selling of cases among lawyers, bargaining for probated sentences, cooling down clients whose conviction is a foregone conclusion to avoid violence in the...

RW: *Sorry to interrupt, but how about the example?*

RF: I was a court reporter in Jacksonville, Florida. I was sitting in the judge's office one morning listening to the local lawyers back-door the judge when one lawyer said he represented Alfredo Fernandez (that's not the real name) and wanted to know how the judge was planning to handle

Alfredo's case. The judge checked the file and determined that Alfredo was barely 18 and had been charged with possession of a controlled substance. I can't remember if it was speed or marijuana or what. As it was the kid's first offense, his parents were solid working people in the community and so on, the judge said he would sentence Alfredo to six months in jail, and then, when the parents were done fainting, suspend the sentence and send him home. Then he would withhold adjudication and if after six months Alfredo didn't get into more trouble, he would expunge the record upon Alfredo's petition.

RW: *That doesn't sound so bad.*

RF: Let me finish, please. The lawyer thanked the judge and walked over to the bookcase and selected the book containing the code section that applied to Alfredo. As it happened, the lawbooks were my responsibility as a chambers clerk, so I followed the lawyer into the court room, which was full of people waiting for the law and motion calendar. To make a long story short, the lawyer opened the book to the relevant page, put on a long face, and told the Fernandez parents that it looked like five years—the maximum penalty under the law in question— unless they could come up with $5,000 that morning, in which case he was almost sure he could get Alfredo off. The stunned parents left the courtroom, and the lawyer said "not ready" every time the case was called. An hour later the parents came back with an envelope full of money. The lawyer counted it quickly, answered "ready" when the case was called, and made a brief argument about what a good kid Alfredo was. The judge then gave Alfredo the six-month suspended sentence that he had planned to all along.

RW: *You have convinced me that there was one dishonest lawyer, but not that the judge knew about what was going on.*

RF: Come on. I saw a version of this same story no less than three times a week. Whenever lawyers spot a worried parent in the courtroom or the hall, they move in for the kill. And as to the judge knowing about it, who do you think judges are but lawyers in black dresses? In many states, you have to pay two-years' salary to the local politicos to get to be a judge. Where do you think the money comes from? To be specific,

I can't tell you how many times I've seen lawyers (the DA and the defense lawyer) work out what was going to happen to a defendant with the judge in his office and then have the defense lawyer say that since he had gotten a good fee he had to put on a bit of a performance when they got into the courtroom. The other DA and the judge would laugh and someone would say, "Great, but don't go on so long we miss our starting time."

RW: *You're saying that lawyers and judges are buying and selling justice for their own ends?*

RF: You're damn right, I am. The lawyers that make their phony speeches to try and justify those big fees turn right around and make hefty contributions to the judge's next election campaign. Who do you think finances most judicial election campaigns? The lawyers who appear before those very judges, that's who. And the judges know darn well who contributes. And I might add, the recent scandals in Chicago, New York and Tampa involving judges taking bribes are just the tip of the iceberg. Ninety-nine percent of all judicial offenders go merrily on their way, playing the system for all it's worth.

RW: *Okay, let's get back to you. How did you break free of working at the courthouse and set up your own business?*

RF: Well, in 1972, I was involved in setting up a shelter for battered women in Jacksonville, Florida. On at least four occasions frustrated, battering husbands set fire to the shelter in an attempt to get at their wives. When we sought police protection, we learned that it was a crime to deny a man access to his wife in Florida. What to do? We concluded the only way we could get police protection was for the woman to file for divorce, so they would no longer be treated as some man's property. The problem was that most of the women who came to us had low incomes and couldn't afford a lawyer, and legal aid had a two-year backlog of divorce cases. If you're getting beaten all the time, two years can be a death sentence.

RW: *What happened?*

RF: As you can probably guess, since I had worked at the courthouse, I was elected to type the divorces. From there, one thing led to another and before long, I was doing a thriving legal typing business, which I called the Northside Secretarial Service.

RW: *What sorts of papers did you prepare?*

RF: Divorces, name changes, adoptions, bankruptcies, etc. I did the typing and my customers made their own decisions which, before lawyers captured the legal system and called it a crime, was an American tradition. Of course, everyone who came into my office signed a disclaimer stating that they knew I wasn't a lawyer.

RW: *Tell me about a couple of them.*

RF: Well, the ones I cared most about were situations in which people's lives were being negatively affected by the fact that they couldn't afford to hire a lawyer. For example, I helped grandparents prepare simple adoption papers to adopt their grandchild so that they could qualify for Navy benefits to repair the child's serious spinal problem. Local lawyers wanted $650, which the grandparents (he was retired) didn't have. Another time, I helped a high school graduate from a very poor family change his name officially to the name he had used all his life and which appeared on his school records. The name on his birth certificate was different, which confused things when it came to his getting a scholarship, loans, and grants.

RW: *How did the bar close you down?*

RF: It's a long story, but part of it involved their hiring a former FBI agent to track down my clients. They found over 100. And even though none would testify against me and there was no proof that I did bad work, I was hauled into court on contempt of court charges for giving people legal advice. As far as the bar was concerned, if I told a person how to find the courthouse that constituted giving legal advice, so you can see the charge was a sick joke.

RW: *You mean, you weren't charged with a crime? I thought you ended up with a jail sentence.*

RF: Both are true. When you challenge lawyers, you have to be prepared for anything. They have usurped the power to simply lock you up, even though there is absolutely no legal justification for their action.

RW: *You're exaggerating.*

RF: The bar association complained about me. I was hauled before a contempt of court proceeding—a sort of kangaroo court where I had no right to a jury trial because I was charged with no crime. I was found guilty of competing with lawyers and sentenced to four months in jail by a judge, A.C. Soud, who said, and I am quoting him, "Only her imprisonment will provide the sting necessary to preserve the integrity of the court."

RW: *Are you serious?*

RF: Sure, and another judge, John Santora, chief circuit judge in Jacksonville, said publicly that people like me who ran public services as legal stenographers are "a cancer on society."

RW: *Did you go to jail?*

RF: I'm almost 60 years old, and the idea of doing hard time to appease a bunch of lawyers who were mad because I charged less than they did didn't appeal to me. I appealed and was eventually turned down by everyone, including the U.S. Supreme Court in the fall of 1984. Incidentally, in the whole process, everyone who passed on the question of my freedom was a lawyer. I was never charged with a crime, and never had a jury trial.

RW: *So, how come I'm not visiting you in jail right now?*

RF: A day before my sentence was to start, in November 1984, the Governor of Florida commuted my sentence in exchange for my promise not to run my business any longer.

RW: *What made him commute the sentence?*

RF: Tens of thousands of ordinary people wrote, called, and telegraphed to support me. The interesting thing is that the governor, who as you can probably guess is also a lawyer, had no power to commute my sentence because I had never been charged with or found guilty of a crime. Remember, I was held in contempt of court, so only the original judge could have relieved me of the contempt citation.

RW: *Did the governor know he was acting illegally?*

RF: Sure, he went to Harvard Law School, but that isn't the point. When it comes to protecting their own, lawyers are perfectly willing to act illegally, and the public outcry produced by "60 Minutes" and other TV shows had made me a huge embarrassment to the Florida bar. In a way, it was funny. They became desperate to keep me out of the very jail they had conspired so hard to put me in.

RW: *What are you doing now?*

RF: Rabble rousing in what I consider to be the best tradition of men like Tom Paine, Tom Jefferson, and Patrick Henry. I travel around the country talking to paralegal groups and others in the legal system who do the real work to tell them to challenge the bar by opening their own offices. I am particularly interested in pushing for a basic change in how our courthouses work. Instead of telling people they can't practice law, court clerks should actively help people prepare forms in most routine uncontested actions. After all, the public pays the salaries of these people. Why shouldn't they get help filling in the blanks on forms which are contained in the codes of civil procedure of the various states? We must break the monopoly of the lawyers over the delivery of legal services. The practice of law in the U.S. is a confidence game, nothing more.

When I'm home in Jacksonville, I train others to help the underserved Florida people of low and moderate incomes who have been abandoned by the bar association and who are suffering from economic hardship.

RW: *Do you expect the Florida bar to leave you in peace now?*

RF: Absolutely. They never dreamed that by attacking me they would bring the whole country down on themselves. But if they do come after me again, I'm ready to fight.

Robin Smith Interview

Robin Smith provided independent paralegal services at People's Paralegal, in Beaverton, Oregon, until she was driven out of business by the Oregon State Bar. She has been involved in the consumer movement for nearly 15 years and was an independent paralegal for ten of those years. (This interview was first done in 1994 and updated in 1996 and 1999.)

Ralph Warner (RW): *Robin, why don't you start by telling me who works at People's Paralegal.*

Robin Smith (RS): We have a staff of three, counting me. Our receptionist screens new customers on the phone, makes appointments, and when a customer comes in she helps them fill out our intake form. Our office manager helps customers complete the necessary substantive questionnaire based on the type of legal procedures they want. Incidentally, we used to ask customers to complete these questionnaires themselves, but doing so sometimes intimidated them, or they provided incorrect information which slowed things down.

RW: *Can you give me an example?*

RS: Sure. A divorce that involves minor children requires information about visitation. Seeing a question on a form that asks what type of visitation they want often confuses people. By contrast, in an interview setting, we can tell people that as long as both spouses agree, they can settle on any visitation terms they wish, or simply provide for reasonable and seasonable visitation under Oregon law. If they still have questions, we can then give them written information on the subject. For example, we often provide people with a copy of an Oregon court case in which the judge clearly explained the options and defines what reasonable and seasonable means.

RW: *Great. But let's get back to staffing. What do you handle?*

RS: Our office manager does most of the form preparation, which often involves inserting customers' information into a computerized form preparation system. Incidentally, our basic word processing program is Wordstar 5.0. We also use a document generation program called OverDrive. A few forms still must be prepared using a typewriter. I handle interviews and form preparation in several areas, including living trust, incorporation, and divorce modifications where the former spouses agree. I also handle the business side of our operation, which involves marketing, dealing with the media, supervising bookkeeping, and so on.

RW: *What does your office look like?*

RS: People's Paralegal operates out of an upstairs, two-room office on a commercial street with older office buildings and storefronts. One room, which is very large, is divided by partitions into three spaces. One space functions as a reception-intake area with a play space for small children. It also houses our receptionist's desk and our computer. A second, more private space has two work tables where our office manager or I work with customers to fill out the questionnaires. My office, which serves as a file room as well, is just down the hall.

RW: *What sorts of legal actions do you handle?*

RS: Quite a range—divorce, bankruptcy, wills, living trusts, probate, stepparent adoption, and small business incorporations make up most of it.

RW: *That's a lot. How do you get enough information to customers so they can sensibly tell you what to type?*

RS: In a remarkably high number of areas, people have a good grasp of what they want. For example, a customer might read about a probate-avoiding living trust and then go to a lawyer's "free" seminar at which the lawyer will provide a lot of basic information and then try to get a $1,500 fee. Similarly, a small businessperson who wants to incorporate is usually pretty savvy. In these situations, the customer doesn't need more information. Of course, in other types of form preparation, such as probate or adoption, they are more likely to. We give them procedural information, such as what forms are necessary to accomplish a particular task. Under Oregon law, we don't believe doing this is the unauthorized practice of law. When it comes to substantive questions, we have a whole library of information we've gathered from a number of sources, including Nolo.com publications, and we put the customers' hands on the information they need. Once they have educated themselves, we can go forward. For more complicated questions, we advise people to see a lawyer.

RW: *Have you been hassled by the bar around unauthorized practice issues?*

RS: We have been contacted several times, mostly based on our typing of probates. To do a probate, you need the original will. Sometimes this is in a lawyer's safe and that lawyer is hoping for a nice fat probate fee. When the executor asks the lawyer for the will and says she plans to handle the probate pro per with our help, the lawyer may complain to the bar, which then results in our being called.

RW: *How do you respond?*

RS: That we use the forms provided by the same legal printer that Oregon lawyers use, and that we type and file them in the order required by the court. All information is supplied by the executor, who often has a copy of the will. So far, that seems to satisfy the bar.

RW: *Do you make a good living?*

RS: Charging $175 for a divorce, $225 for a stepparent adoption, and $225–$275 for a living trust (which includes transferring real estate deeds in the name of the trust) and so on, you don't get rich. But we make a decent living and, even though I work very hard, I love what I do. I really feel I provide services people need at a fair price.

RW: *What's your attitude about companies who advertise kits, training packages, and franchises to get people started as IPs and charge huge fees?*

RS: It's often customer fraud, especially when people are conned into spending lots of money based on a promise of big dollar returns. In fact, many of these promoters act like they are selling a franchise but don't comply with state franchise laws. But even more basically, the IP business is not one where huge returns are possible. We are not mass-producing anything—if an office does lots of form preparation, they must hire people and buy equipment to do the intakes and process the forms. In short, the overhead increases with the growth of the business. At the prices we charge, there isn't a big profit margin and that isn't likely to change. If IPs try to raise prices too much, someone new will open an office and undercut them.

RW: *Let's shift gears a little. How do you do your marketing?*

RS: Our biggest source of customers is the positive recommendations from people we have worked with before. Every day we get calls from new customers who have heard about us from someone we worked with previously. To help this along, we keep a mailing list of all our customers and once a year send them a letter reminding them of our services and telling them about anything new we offer. We include a discount coupon that they can use or give a friend.

RW: *What about public agencies and community organizations? Do you market to them?*

RS: Definitely. It's our second largest source of referrals. We contact all sorts of agencies—from the military to battered women's shelters to sheriff's victims' rights office to senior organizations. We have a large list that we regularly update and add to. We make every effort to stay in touch with people who are in a position to refer others. For example, one of our referral sources is the Boys and Girls Aid Society, a prominent legal group that handles adoptions. We prepare the court petition and other documents necessary to adopt.

RW: *What else do you do?*

RS: Lots of community activities. For example, the Chamber of Commerce to which I belong has an event called "Good Neighbor Days," a sort of local fair to raise money for area nonprofits. It's fun—you know, baby races, pie throwing, chili cook-off, crafts booths and so on. Along with a lot of other small business, we take a booth. We also do some advertising—our Yellow Pages ads under "divorce" and "paralegals" produces the most. We also have a classified ad in the big Portland daily and also in the local free classified paper called "The Nickel," and in a paper for seniors. In each, we target our message to our audience. For example, in the senior paper we list wills and trusts.

* * * * *

RW: *It's over two years since we did the first part of this interview, and a lot has happened to you. Give me the highlights.*

RS: On June 28, 1994, without warning, the Oregon State Bar served me with court papers asking for an injunction to shut down my business for the Unauthorized Practice of Law. They had been secretly investigating me for six years, all the while giving lip service to the need to provide better access to law for average Oregonians.

RW: *What did you do?*

RS: After I nearly had a nervous breakdown, I tried to figure out why me. I had testified at both the Oregon State Bar's Task Force hearings in 1992 and the American Bar Association hearings in 1993 on nonlawyer practice, without being attacked. During the intervening months, I hadn't changed how my business worked, so why was I being singled out now? Just to be sure the bar wasn't responding to consumer complaints about the quality of my services, I called the state bar, the Attorney General's consumer complaint department, and the Better Business Bureau to see if anyone had filed complaints about my services. None had.

Still in a quandary, I had to deal with the problem of shopping for a lawyer to represent me and my company. (An Oregon law designed to protect the interests of the legal profession requires that a corporation must be represented by an attorney.)

RW: *Were you beginning to feel any better?*

RS: No. I was just plain shocked. I thought that the elaborate studies bar groups had produced bemoaning the average person's inadequate access to law—all of which emphasized the need for an affordable nonlawyer alternative—meant that the bad old days of lawyers persecuting their competition were over. I truly believed that the bar was moving in the right direction. Obviously, I was wrong. When it came to making a decision to try and put me out of business, the bar's traditional "stamp out the competition" voices won.

RW: *How did you find your lawyer?*

RS: I started with lawyers I knew and had referred people to. For various reasons—fear certainly being one—none wanted to help me. I then tried the ACLU. They weren't interested, but gave me some names of attorneys to call. Then I remembered my Professional Liability Insurance that I purchased through the National Federation of Paralegals Association (NFPA) as soon as it became available to independent paralegals. My policy number in Oregon was 002. I read the policy and was relieved to see that it covered UPL defense. They accepted my case and assigned me an attorney—Gary Abbott.

RW: *What happened?*

RS: Gary Abbott and Karin Phalen worked hard to create a compelling defense. Basically, it included the following points:

1. The practice of law can't be defined, so how can I be prosecuted forcommitting it?
2. I was not treated with basic fairness by the bar (in legal lingo, I was not given due process). For example, they gave me no prior notice of their intent to sue or even sent me a cease and desist letter (which is what the OSB usually does).
3. My First Amendment right to free speech was violated. In hindsight, more should have been done to present this compelling argument, as developed by Steve Elias. [Ed. note: See Chapter 2, Section F.]
4. I was singled out because I had filed a petition for a statewide initiative to repeal the UPL statutes, lobbied in Salem, and otherwise publicized the need for legal reform. This defense was based on the concept of selective or malicious prosecution.

My trial before a judge (I was not entitled to a jury) lasted four days. On April 27, 1995, my son's birthday, it ended. We lost, even though the judge agreed with our contention that the practice of law is undefinable. In essence, the judge said the practice of law is like pornography—it's difficult to define, but I know when I see it, and I see it here. Although taking away my right to do business on the basis of this sort of biased subjective standard (the judge is a lawyer, after all) is indefensible, that's exactly what the injunction the judge issued in my case did.

RW: *Give me the specifics.*

RS: It forbids me from practicing law, which it says includes:
   1. Personal contact in the nature of consultation, explanation, recommendation, or advice regarding legal matters.
   2. Obtaining information orally, in writing or in any other manner relating to individual facts and circumstances.
   3. Advising customers regarding procedural functions of the court system, specifically jurisdiction or venue.
   4. Selecting particular forms, documents, or pleadings.
   5. Assisting in any way with the preparation or filling out of legal forms, or any parts of such forms.

   In short, if I have customers fill out questionnaires dealing with the facts of their situation in order to help them represent themselves, I'm practicing law under this definition. This is a dangerous precedent and should be overturned.

RW: *Wow—they hit you with every weapon in their arsenal. What next? Have you appealed?*

RS: Yes, Bill Fry at HALT, in Washington, DC, provided a huge lift when he contacted Tom Mack, a Washington, DC, lawyer with a strong background in helping the legally left-out. Tom very generously agreed to handle my appeal for no fee, proving that a few lawyers really do take their responsibility to serve the public seriously. We filed our brief, which emphasizes freedom of speech issues, in March, 1996. The paralegal insurance policy I obtained through NFPA didn't pay for the appeal, but they did settle the bar's money judgment against me (issued along with the injunction), so I didn't lose my house. Some of my loyal customers and a few independent paralegals helped fund appeal costs, which, of course, are pretty hefty, even with Tom waiving his fee. [Editor's Note: Unfortunately, Robin lost her appeal. She filed a petition for review with the U.S. Supreme Court, but they declined to hear the case.]

RW: *What are you doing now?*

RS: After taking the entire summer of 1995 off to recover, my husband and I switched roles. After eight years in business, I stay home and he hustles for our bacon. I'm also writing *How to Do Your Own Uncontested Oregon Divorce*, to be published by the infamous and ever helpful Nolo.com. And I keep a bit of sanity by training on my bike preparing for Cycle Oregon, an annual 500-miles-in-a-week group ride. [Editor's Note: Robin went on to complete her divorce book, which is helping many Oregon residents do their own divorce. (Order information is available at the nolo.com online store.) It is ironic that Robin is barred from orally providing to customers the identical information contained in her book.]

RW: *You built a business for eight years and then lost it because lawyers wanted you off their turf. Would you do it again?*

RS: Yes, but in hindsight I should have followed more of the suggestions in your handbook—specifically to give published books to customers to read and regurgitate as part of the form preparation process. Had I done this, the bar would not have been able to scapegoat me using the UPL statute. Just the same, I do not believe I did anything wrong. Low- and moderate-income people need high-quality legal access. They can't afford lawyers, but thousands of them could, and did, afford my help. I feel my efforts made lots of people's lives better.

Rose Palmer Interview

Rose Palmer is executive director of Support, Inc., a Pittsburgh, Pennsylvania-based organization that informs, counsels, and provides advocacy assistance for women on issues of child support, custody, visitation, and domestic violence. This interview was done in 1992.

Ralph Warner (RW): *Rose, take me back a few years and explain how you got involved in helping women with support issues.*

Rose Palmer (RP): It all began in the late 1970s with my own personal struggles as a single parent. I was literally depriving my kids of necessities to pay lawyer fees to try and collect support I desperately needed. And to add insult to injury, I wasn't getting any results.

RW: *You were in the same situation as millions of others. What was the catalyst that led to your decision to make a career out of helping other women learn how to cope with the legal system?*

RP: At one point during my case, when we were in court, I saw that a legal mistake was being made. I interrupted and pointed it out. Even though I was correct and the error had the potential to jeopardize my rights, the Allegheny County hearing officer (in the role of a judge) told me to "shut up." She stated, "You have an attorney; he will speak for you. You do not talk unless I ask you to." Her attitude made me furious. It was as if I had no right to speak, even when the lawyers were messing up. It was a real turning point for me. I went home determined to learn how to do my own legal research and to take charge of my own legal destiny. Soon after, I got in touch with other women who were in the same situation, and Legal Advocacy for Women was born.

RW: *Where did you start your new work?*

RP: At the Pittsburgh YWCA. They gave us space in December of 1979. We stayed there for more than a year, but eventually left and ran our program out of a spare bedroom, because we were simply too controversial for the Y. They had a conservative board, and challenging the legal power structure worried them.

RW: *When did you come out of the bedroom and really get established in Pittsburgh?*

RP: October 1983, and like so many things in life, the story of how we got our first grant has an odd twist. The wife of a city councilman came to us for help with a long story of how she was being victimized by her husband. We were doing consciousness-raising activities at the time—marches, picketing, and other events—to focus attention on how divorced, separated, and single women with children were being discriminated against, and we saw her situation as a chance to further dramatize the issue.

RW: *So you took it public?*

RP: In a big way. And, of course, we got lots of publicity. There was only one problem. The heroine of our little drama was lying.

RW: *Oops. You mean the city councilman hadn't mistreated your client?*

RP: Nope. James O'Malley was a nice guy—such a good man, in fact, that despite our part in unfairly attacking him, he took an interest in what we were doing, applauded our goals, and counseled us to form a formal nonprofit corporation. He then used his influence to get us our first grant.

RW: *What a wonderful story, but don't stop. What happened next?*

RP: With a real office and a few dollars to pay staff, we were much more visible. In fact, in 1985 we saw 700 clients in person and counseled another 2,000 by phone. There was only one problem—all of this activity got us in hot water with the county bar association.

RW: *How exactly did it occur?*

RP: We helped a woman with minor children involved in a divorce, whose husband was represented by a prominent local lawyer. Our client was awarded everything she asked for—child support, day care, and medical care. The same day the judge made the award, the lawyer filed charges with the Unauthorized Practice of Law (UPL) Committee of the Allegheny County bar association, charging us with practicing law without a license.

RW: *So that started a brouhaha about what you could do and not infringe on lawyer turf?*

RP: You bet. They challenged everything, right down to our right to use our name, which at that time was Legal Advocacy for Women. They questioned our right to go into court with women and counsel them as part of court proceedings, as well as helping women prepare budget sheets and other court forms.

RW: *I know you are doing all these things and lots more today, so you must have prevailed.*

RP: We are, and you're right, we eventually did, but it was a real struggle. Fortunately, the media was very sympathetic. Lawyers, after all, do not and cannot provide affordable legal services to the average person, so if we were put out of business, it was obvious that no one was going to help a lot of desperate mothers. Also, we had (and still do, I should add) some brave people on our board of directors. Several local lawyers, judges, and other prominent people who spoke out on our behalf. The result was a compromise in the form of a consent order. We agreed to change our name from "Legal Advocacy for Women" to "Support, Inc.," not to whisper to our clients in court, and not to use or touch the counsel table when we sat next to our clients in court. We could talk to our clients in a normal voice in court and ask for a recess at any time to confer privately in the hall, all of which was fine with us and, of course, made whispering unnecessary.

RW: *No, you can't be serious! The lawyers actually claimed that someone using their tables made you guilty of unauthorized practice of law?*

RP: Funny isn't it? But they were so desperate to draw a bright line between us and them that they drew it along the edge of the table. Since our clients can sit at the table, we had to be able to be there too in order to provide counseling and support. But since it's called the counsel table, and lawyers see this as a synonym for lawyer, we can't touch it or put our papers or research materials on it.

RW: *Lawyers go to law school for three years to make distinctions like that.*

RP: Apparently.

RW: *But otherwise, you carried on the same services as before? You still taught women how to use the legal system and helped them prepare paperwork and accompanied them to court?*

RP: Yes. In a way, it was as if the bar backed down but declared victory.

RW: *Does the Gilbert & Sullivan aspect of this story continue?*

RP: You bet. The next year, Councilman O'Malley helped sponsor an art show/benefit at the main city-county building, with all proceeds going to our organization. The opening was great—fancy dress and so on. Even the mayor presided at the opening ceremonies. There was only one hitch: the invitation went out saying the benefit was for "Support, Inc. (Legal Advocacy for Women)." There was no AKA before Legal Advocacy for Women, or other explanation that this was our former name. Even though we had nothing to do with printing or paying for the invitations (the city did that), attorney James Victor Voss, the same person who had gone after us before, filed another UPL complaint. Fortunately, this one died quickly when we showed that we weren't really using the old name.

RW: *What's new? What are you doing now that you didn't used to do?*

RP: For one thing, we have grown. We now see over 1,000 people in person each year and help 4,000 more by phone. In addition, since there are now more types of pre-printed forms available for the confirmation of child custody, visitation, and so on, it means we help clients with more paperwork. We also have worked with courts to set up a court-approved visitation room so fathers can visit their children during the time when allegations of violence that form the basis for temporary protective (restraining) orders are being investigated. Incidentally, this gives us status as a public service with the courts. Also, I should mention our clinical program. Working with the two local law schools, third-year students are assigned to work with us as part of a family law clinical program, for which the students get credit. Since they are bar-certified to appear in court and supervised by Lesley Grey, a practicing lawyer who works with our program, it's a real plus.

RW: *Has the bar caused further trouble?*

RP: We have been investigated more than once. You can often tell when you get an inappropriate telephone call or visit, but officially we have been left alone.

RW: *Perhaps you have convinced them that you are too determined an opponent.*

RP: I don't know, but we do have allies. The media, particularly, gives us fair treatment. We are well into our second decade of service, so we have built a reputation as being a trustworthy news source. When you are under attack, it's terribly important to have access to the media to get your story out. To achieve this, you must make yourselves available, tell the truth, and be ready to substantiate your statements.

RW: *Support, Inc., has obviously grown in lots of ways. Personally, what have you been doing to stay excited and not get stale?*

RP: I have done general mediation training at the college level and then followed up with specific courses in family mediation. I also host a TV show on our local city cable station that allows me to teach large numbers of women how to deal with the support problem. In a sense, I do self-help law on TV. It's exciting. I've even had family court judges appear in mock courtroom scenes to teach women how to handle the court process.

RW: *Didn't I also hear that you ran for public office?*

RP: Yes, for the state legislature, against a prominent and very entrenched opponent who had heavy financial backing and had been in office 20 years. I had no chance, but I had a great time and got plenty of opportunity to talk about consumer justice issues. The fact that the average person has no access to law is beginning to be important to voters.

People know that our present system—which provides access to our legal system only for those who can afford high lawyer fees—is unfair.

RW: *Let me ask you one final thing. What about fathers? Aren't they victimized by the legal system, too? Who helps them?*

RP: The answer to your first question is yes, absolutely. The legal system treats everyone shabbily. For example, if a father loses his job or suffers a loss of income and can't afford to pay as much child support, he needs to get his support order reduced. But most fathers don't know how to do this, and if they can't afford to pay their normal bills, including child support, how can they afford a lawyer? The result is that the father, who may be doing his best, becomes a statistic for violating his child support order. In fact, the real statistic should indicate that one more person was denied access to the law. In short, the father who couldn't afford to petition the court to reduce his support order because of changed circumstances now is likely to be prosecuted because the system made it impossible for him to take advantage of his legal rights. Although I don't always agree with the positions fathers' groups take, I certainly support their efforts to teach men how to use the legal system and develop better ways for fathers to get affordable legal access. For example, I often invite fathers' groups to participate in my TV show, and Support, Inc., has dealt with both genders on issues of child support since 1989. Men and women will only achieve real structural reform when they realize that law in America is administered primarily for the benefit of lawyers and victimizes both groups. Men and women must work together to achieve a more democratic justice system, as well as to cooperate to raise good kids.

Catherine Elias-Jermany Interview

Catherine Elias-Jermany is the current director of the National Selp-Help Law Project and a co-author of this book.

Ralph Warner (RW): *What do you mean when you say you knew about self-help law before Nolo was started?*

Catherine Elias-Jermany (CJ): If I really go back to the roots of it, it's because of my grandmother Callie Jackson, who started her own legal-help service, The Listening Post, in 1929. She was a grand old lady who died at the age of 105 in 1978. She lived in the big house of a courtway and was the informal lawyer for everyone around. My memories date from my own childhood in the late 1940s and early 1950s. She ran her business from her home and handled leases, burial rights advocacy (black people even had trouble getting equal rights after they were dead in those days), employment claims, you name it. Remember, in those days few people had access to the formal legal system, except perhaps for the very few who had money. People like my grandmother filled in the void—serving as legal advocates to unserved people. Today we would call her a "paralegal," a term which, incidentally, she would have hated.

RW: *Why is that?*

CJ: Because she was a proud, effective person. She wasn't para-anything or sub-anything. It wasn't in her nature to kowtow to anyone.

RW: *Somehow your being around Callie as a child inspired you?*

CJ: It sure did. For example, she built a library full of notebooks about people's legal rights, which she kept on a shelf beside the sugar bowl. I keep similar types of notebooks today, although in the last ten years, lots of my information has been transferred to computer disks.

    The other big influence was my father, who absolutely insisted on perfection. If you didn't get something right the first time, you could just keep doing it over until you did.

RW: *When did you first become interested in legal advocacy?*

CJ: When I was 14, it was obvious to me that some elderly friends who used to live down the street, and had subsequently gone into a nursing home, were being mistreated. This was before all the modern nursing home regulations, so there were no obvious legal handles to use to help them. To make a long story short, I succeeded in going before the L.A. County Board of Supervisors and getting my friends reinstated in another nursing home (they had been kicked out of the first one when we complained), and having the first home closed down. The whole experience taught me that there was a process to deal with everything. This was a powerful lesson—to get things done you simply had to learn the process and then go step by step.

RW: *How did you get involved with paralegals?*

CJ: I was involved with the Southern Christian Leadership Conference before Martin Luther King, Jr., was murdered. I organized in the South and West, and was also deeply involved in the Welfare Rights Movement. In 1968, there was a poor people's campaign in Washington, DC. I handled the parade permits, contracts, and even carried the money. In a sense, I was bag lady for the campaign.

RW: *Where does the paralegal work come in?*

CJ: In 1969, I was back in Los Angeles and I started an organization called the "Dependency Prevention Center," or DPC, to teach poor people how to stand on their own feet. We did welfare, health, housing, and education rights training. I was also still very involved with the local welfare rights organization. Both organizations were doing all sorts of things that were basically legal advocacy. In short, we were doing work that the Legal Aid Society of Los Angeles was unable to do because they didn't always understand the needs of the community. At any rate, a series of confrontations with Legal Services resulted in a number of community people who were trained by DPC being included on the Legal Services board.

        The next step, of course, was to get community people into the Legal Services offices themselves. We did this by doing welfare rights advocacy on a volunteer basis right at the Legal Aid office, throughout California and other states. Then, when openings for interviewers, receptionists, and eventually case advocates happened, our people got the jobs. Of course, these new employees were short on traditional legal skills. They had plenty of fire to change things, but most had never worked in an office before. Through DPC, we provided the training.

RW: *What next?*

CJ: Because of all these activities, I ended up on the Board of Directors of the National Paralegal Institute in 1971, and I worked as a paralegal for the Children's Defense Fund.

RW: *You sure got around.*

CJ: I'm only telling you half of it.

RW: *What is the National Paralegal Institute and when did you start to work there?*

CJ: In 1973, the National Paralegal Institute, which is still in operation today, was founded to determine and define the role of paralegals. It had done numerous studies and was the first to design and implement training for the nonlawyer staff of Legal Services offices. Then, in 1976, when Legal Services brought all its training in-house, I did the same work for the federally funded Legal Services Corporation, as director of training.

RW: *What exactly did you do?*

CJ: Our job was to figure out what the various types of people who had stumbled into paralegal jobs in Legal Services offices needed to know to do their jobs better. For example, since lawyers don't like to interview people, or attend welfare or unemployment hearings, we taught laypeople how to do it. I trained people from Mississippi to Maine to Micronesia. Eventually we even trained lawyers how to run their offices better by the effective use of paralegals.

RW: *Looking back, how do you feel about the work you did in the early- and mid-1970s?*

CJ: On balance, great. We taught people lots of good things, but maybe in retrospect some not so good ones, too. For example, we trained paralegals to make lawyers more efficient. You know, things like tickler systems, efficient filing, doing their client interviews, etc.

RW: *And you see that as a mistake now?*

CJ: Well, in the sense that we taught paralegals to be somewhat dependent, yes. We supported the traditional lawyer-dominated system of delivering services that I now see is often a mistake. Let's get rid of the label "para" and call them legal specialists. Let's get specialists thinking and acting like entrepreneurs. The age of the deregulation of lawyers' monopoly is at hand. People need to be ready.

RW: *So you see paralegals escaping from lawyers?*

CJ: Sure, legal specialists should be able to work with or without lawyer supervisors as they choose. And they will be able to very soon now. The age of legal entrepreneurs providing routine legal services is already upon us because the public demands it. People are sick of our inefficient, overpriced, uncaring legal delivery system. It's got to change. And you know it's funny—in many ways people in low-income communities are open to change because they have had such minimal access to lawyers that their tradition of legal self-reliance is stronger.

RW: *And they have less to lose.*

CJ: That too.

RW: *If you wanted to open your own independent business to help nonlawyers deal with the legal system, would you go to a two- or three-year paralegal school?*

CJ: Personally, no. The reason is simple. Paralegal education is almost always general in nature. It's very weak on usable skills. Or, to say that another way, they don't teach you to do specific tasks independently.

RW: *What does an independent paralegal or legal specialist—someone who is working with nonlawyers around specific form filling-out tasks—need to know?*

CJ: Three things. First, they have to be able to deal with real people in the (often frustrating) course of real-life, legal problem solving. That is, they need to have good interviewing, counseling, data management, and hand-holding skills. And don't underestimate the value of hand-holding. People very often are unable to tell you what they really want or need—it's up to you to be able to help them find out not only what they need, but be able to guide them through the self-help law materials that are appropriate to their situation. Second, the independent paralegal must know how to do the mechanics of the particular task. Third, they must have enough general background or breadth in the particular subject area to be able to help the customer avoid the obvious pitfalls and get legal advice when needed.

RW: *How do people who have never done interviewing in a legal context, kept files, or run an office learn to do this well?*

CJ: For starters, they need at least some structured interviewing, fact gathering, management, and analysis training skills. There are definite techniques in conducting a customer visit and being able to assist the customer to use the information properly.

RW: *You think about the independent paralegal movement every day. Tell me what's going on.*

CJ: The growth is unbelievable. There are now many thousands of IPs.

RW: *Where do all these people come from?*

CJ: All over the U.S. The largest concentration is in California, of course. You would expect that, since the IP movement was born here and it's also the most populous state.

RW: *What sorts of backgrounds do IPs have?*

CJ: A wide variety. Former teachers, business people, social workers, you name it. About one-third are graduates of a formal paralegal school who often work in law firms now or have done so until recently. The goal of many of these people is to combine freelancing for lawyers with working directly for the public.

RW: *What about the other two-thirds? You said they came from a wide variety of backgrounds. Can you be a little more specific?*

CJ: A large group are business people who already deal directly with the public, such as tax preparers, public stenographers, people who run telephone answering services, and so on. They see learning legal form preparation skills as a way to expand the services they already offer to the public.

RW: *Give me an example.*

CJ: Take someone who runs a credit repair and counseling service—not the sleazy variety, but an honest business. It's not hard to learn how to type bankruptcy forms for those who can't realistically avoid bankruptcy. It's a great combination because credit counseling is generally recognized as a nonlawyer function. This means, in the credit context, nonlawyers can actually transfer legal information and expertise without falling victim to UPL charges. Then, if necessary, they can simply transfer over to the typing service model to prepare bankruptcy forms.

RW: *I gather bankruptcy form preparation is a fast-growing Independent Paralegal area. What are some others?*

CJ: Well, bankruptcy is the second, only after the demand for wills. With hard economic times, there is an unfulfilled need in virtually every community. Also living trusts, immigration form preparation, guardianships, and support modifications are all rapidly growing areas.

RW: *What about the traditional bread-and-butter area—divorce?*

CJ: About 75% of all IPs already do divorces. In some states, such as California, Arizona, and Oregon, the business is pretty well saturated. There are really not enough divorces to go around when you figure that there are lots of low-cost alternatives to IPs—for example, self-help lawbooks, battered woman's shelters, and legal services for the poor all take chunks of the divorce business. And then, of course, lawyers have held on to the most affluent 25% of the market. In other states, where the IP movement is really just getting going, there is still plenty of opportunity to type divorces. But remember, as the U.S. population ages, divorce won't be the fast-growing field it was from the mid-1960s to the mid-1980s.

RW: *Let me pick one of the legal areas you mentioned—living trusts. Tell me what's going on.*

CJ: As you know, lots of lawyers have begun to advertise living trust seminars. These are typically designed to sell living trusts for $1,500–$2,500 each, a vastly inflated price given the amount of work involved. It didn't take IPs and financial planners long to see that they could make a good living doing the same thing for $250–$300.

RW: *Are you saying that IPs are engaging in guerrilla marketing by playing off the lawyers' seminar ads?*

CJ: Sure, many list their services in the same senior papers and newsletters that the lawyers advertise in. And some even stand right up and explain that they help people do much the same thing for much less money using a self-help typing approach.

RW: *Don't the lawyers have a cow?*

CJ: Well, a calf anyway, but there isn't much they can do. Remember it's a public meeting in a hotel conference room, so they can't call the cops. Often they try and retaliate in other ways. They might complain to the bar association or write a letter to a local newspaper attempting to put down nonlawyer services.

RW: *How do paralegals avoid UPL charges?*

CJ: They can give or sell customers Denis Clifford's *Make Your Own Living Trust*, which has sold over 150,000 copies direct to the public. As long as the customer has the book and the IP follows the customer's instructions, there is no UPL problem.

RW: *Isn't this approach hard for some consumers, especially those that aren't experienced in the use of a fairly sophisticated book?*

CJ: Not if the IP is trained properly to act as a coach or guide to help the person extract relevant information from the self-help resource. To go back to bankruptcy for a second, it's important for the customer to locate the exempt property information for the state where he or she lives. For the IP to simply tell the customer this information has been held to be unauthorized practice. This is a ridiculous, lawyer-centric, legal rule, of course, but for now we are stuck with it. At any rate, to circumvent it, a well-trained IP can simply direct the consumer to the part of the book where this information is clearly spelled out.

RW: *Do you see this typing service model in which the consumer is educated to make their own decisions primarily as a cover-your-behind device for the IP?*

CJ: No. It's an affirmative way to do business. The concept of self-reliance is buried deep in the American psyche. When functioning properly, the IP acts as a helper to the self-helper. When you see it that way, it's an exciting business niche. And best of all, approached this way, the consumer doesn't see the IP as a second-class lawyer and feel cheated because he or she can't afford a "real" lawyer. Instead, customers see the IP as a positive adjunct to their own learning process.

RW: *If we make an analogy to adding on a deck to a house, would it be fair to say that the IP should play the role of a teacher to a self-help builder rather than that of a cheap unlicensed contractor?*

CJ: Yes, and the best part is that whether it's a deck or a divorce, once a person really learns to do the particular task, they are empowered to attack other, larger problems. In the legal area, it really builds better citizens.

RW: *How can a want-to-be independent paralegal learn the necessary skills?*

CJ: To actually fill out the forms, you would be better off starting with a good self-help book, such as Nolo's *How to File for Bankruptcy*, hanging around the bankruptcy court, and then volunteering in an office where a lot of bankruptcies are typed, such as a consumer legal services office. Remember, rule number one of learning any skill is to carefully observe the correct practice of that skill and then to correctly practice the skill yourself. This can best be done by volunteering and finding a mentor.

RW: *What else?*

CJ: Take a good course. Any legal area can be broken down into a finite number of discrete variables. These variables are interrelated. Understanding the forest is not only knowing what the main variables are but how they relate to each other. To impart this type of information to independent paralegals necessarily requires the use of outlines, charts, lists of steps, and some basic rules. Many paralegal organizations sponsor lectures and workshops on all sorts of legal tasks, including bankruptcy.

RW: *When you teach IPs, what is your approach?*

CJ: Basically, I've always used an extended and detailed hypothetical case that covers an entire range of variables in the field. In working through the hypothetical, I teach the three skills I mentioned earlier and emphasize the relationships between the various factors that will be present in each individual case.

RW: *Okay, can you tell me why it is so important to have a broad base of background information on a particular subject area? After all, don't most self-help typing services just type forms?*

CJ: If they do, they may find themselves in trouble in a hurry. For example, suppose someone gives you a set of facts and asks for a particular result. You need to know whether their fact situation entitles them to the remedy they want under current laws, and you also need to know whether the remedy they want is appropriate under the circumstances. What's more, you must know the self-help law material better than the customer in order to point out any mistakes they may have made and direct them to the part of the book or other resource that contains the correct information.

RW: *Can you be specific?*

CJ: Let's stick with bankruptcy. Suppose someone lists a whole bunch of bank credit card accounts and you see the dates involved indicate that the person was borrowing money from one bank, then opening another account, paying back the first and so on until they got a very high credit limit. They then borrow a lot of money and declare bankruptcy to avoid getting involved. In short, you need to know what an illegal credit and kiting scheme is so you can decline to type the papers in this sort of situation.

RW: *Is this sort of thing a big danger to an independent legal worker?*

CJ: In any field, 15% or 20% of the people who walk in will be asking for help you can't provide, or there will be some other reason why you should not handle their business, like avoiding the occasional crook. You absolutely need to know enough to spot all the issues that may affect the case. As I've said, you have to live the particular areas of the law you are working in before you open your business. Remember, as with any professional, you have to be extremely careful not to get in over your head.

RW: *I know you have worked with IPs all over the country who are trying to survive in an often hostile, lawyer-dominated legal environment. Tell me what you tell them.*

CJ: The key is to know your limitations. Everywhere throughout the U.S., the UPL laws are interpreted the same. Nonlawyers cannot do what lawyers do. This simply means that to minimize your risk of UPL, you must operate as a self-help law specialist, guiding your customers through published materials, without personally providing legal advice and preparing the paperwork under their direction. Secondly, to get a strong statewide organization in place to help IPs with organizing, training, and fighting back against lawyer harassment. In many of the Western states, especially California, Oregon, and Arizona, IP organizations already exist. In states where the movement is newer, a new IP may need to work to pull an organization together. It's really something IPs need to do, since a strong organization offers obvious protection against UPL charges. It's not hard to see that it's a lot easier for the bar to pick off an isolated IP than it is to go up against a well-organized group.

RW: *The main purpose of the state groups is to protect members from unauthorized practice charges?*

CJ: No, that's only one function. Once the group is in place, it can start training members in the right ways to do business—good skills development, good consumer recourse, and other honest business practices. A consumer needs to know he or she will get good services from an IP. If they do, they will use more services, tell their friends, and won't complain to the bar. It's a virtuous circle.

RW: *How many states currently have formal independent paralegal organizations?*

CJ: Sixteen have organizations that meet on a regular basis and do the things I just mentioned. In quite a few more, organizations are at a formative stage. In some areas—where population density is low—it will be necessary to take a regional approach.

RW: *What do you see for the legal movement in the years just ahead?*

CJ: Right now, the movement is consumer driven—consumers want and need better legal access at a reasonable cost. Unfortunately, some IPs don't see that—they believe they are prospering because of something they are doing as individuals. So the answer is that IPs will do well individually and as a group as long as they see that their continued success depends on their doing an excellent job to meet consumer needs. People are fed up with lawyers—not only because of ridiculous fees, but because lawyers deny them control over their own lives. As long as IPs deliver good services that empower people at a reasonable cost, all will be well. If they begin to act like junior lawyers, they will be in trouble. ■

Index

CATALOG

...more from nolo

	PRICE	CODE
BUSINESS		
Buy-Sell Agreement Handbook:Plan Ahead for Changes in the Ownership of Your Business (Book w/CD-ROM)	$49.99	BSAG
The CA Nonprofit Corporation Kit (Binder w/CD-ROM)	$59.95	CNP
Consultant & Independent Contractor Agreements (Book w/CD-ROM)	$29.99	CICA
The Corporate Minutes Book (Book w/CD-ROM)	$69.99	CORMI
Create Your Own Employee Handbook	$49.99	EMHA
Dealing With Problem Employees	$44.99	PROBM
Drive a Modest Car & 16 Other Keys to Small Business Success	$24.99	DRIV
The Employer's Legal Handbook	$39.99	EMPL
Everyday Employment Law	$29.99	ELBA
Federal Employment Laws	$49.99	FELW
Form Your Own Limited Liability Company (Book w/CD-ROM)	$44.99	LIAB
Hiring Independent Contractors: The Employer's Legal Guide (Book w/CD-ROM)	$34.99	HICI
How to Create a Noncompete Agreement	$44.95	NOCMP
How to Form a California Professional Corporation (Book w/CD-ROM)	$59.95	PROF
How to Form a Nonprofit Corporation (Book w/CD-ROM)—National Edition	$44.99	NNP
How to Form a Nonprofit Corporation in California (Book w/CD-ROM)	$44.99	NON
How to Form Your Own California Corporation (Binder w/CD-ROM)	$59.99	CACI
How to Form Your Own California Corporation (Book w/CD-ROM)	$34.99	CCOR
How to Get Your Business on the Web	$29.99	WEBS
How to Write a Business Plan	$34.99	SBS
Incorporate Your Business	$49.95	NIBS
The Independent Paralegal's Handbook	$29.95	PARA

Prices subject to change.

	PRICE	CODE
Leasing Space for Your Small Business	$34.95	LESP
Legal Guide for Starting & Running a Small Business	$34.99	RUNS
Legal Forms for Starting & Running a Small Business (Book w/CD-ROM)	$29.99	RUNS2
Marketing Without Advertising	$24.00	MWAD
Music Law (Book w/CD-ROM)	$34.99	ML
Nolo's Guide to Social Security Disability	$29.99	QSS
Nolo's Quick LLC	$24.99	LLCQ
Nondisclosure Agreements	$39.95	NAG
The Small Business Start-up Kit (Book w/CD-ROM)	$29.99	SMBU
The Small Business Start-up Kit for California (Book w/CD-ROM)	$34.99	OPEN
The Partnership Book: How to Write a Partnership Agreement (Book w/CD-ROM)	$39.99	PART
Sexual Harassment on the Job	$24.95	HARS
Starting & Running a Successful Newsletter or Magazine	$29.99	MAG
Take Charge of Your Workers' Compensation Claim	$34.99	WORK
Tax Savvy for Small Business	$36.99	SAVVY
Working for Yourself: Law & Taxes for the Self-Employed	$39.99	WAGE
Your Crafts Business: A Legal Guide	$26.99	VART
Your Limited Liability Company: An Operating Manual (Book w/CD-ROM)	$49.99	LOP
Your Rights in the Workplace	$29.99	YRW

CONSUMER

	PRICE	CODE
How to Win Your Personal Injury Claim	$29.99	PICL
Nolo's Encyclopedia of Everyday Law	$29.99	EVL
Nolo's Guide to California Law	$24.95	CLAW
Trouble-Free Travel...And What to Do When Things Go Wrong	$14.95	TRAV

ESTATE PLANNING & PROBATE

	PRICE	CODE
8 Ways to Avoid Probate	$19.99	PRO8
9 Ways to Avoid Estate Taxes	$29.95	ESTX

	PRICE	CODE
Estate Planning Basics	$21.99	ESPN
How to Probate an Estate in California	$49.99	PAE
Make Your Own Living Trust (Book w/CD-ROM)	$39.99	LITR
Nolo's Simple Will Book (Book w/CD-ROM)	$36.99	SWIL
Plan Your Estate	$44.99	NEST
Quick & Legal Will Book	$16.99	QUIC

FAMILY MATTERS

	PRICE	CODE
Child Custody: Building Parenting Agreements That Work	$29.99	CUST
The Complete IEP Guide	$24.99	IEP
Divorce & Money: How to Make the Best Financial Decisions During Divorce	$34.99	DIMO
Do Your Own California Adoption: Nolo's Guide for Stepparents and Domestic Partners (Book w/CD-ROM)	$34.99	ADOP
Get a Life: You Don't Need a Million to Retire Well	$24.99	LIFE
The Guardianship Book for California	$34.99	GB
A Legal Guide for Lesbian and Gay Couples	$29.99	LG
Living Together: A Legal Guide (Book w/CD-ROM)	$34.99	LTK
Medical Directives and Powers of Attorney in California	$19.99	CPOA
Using Divorce Mediation: Save Your Money & Your Sanity	$29.95	UDMD

GOING TO COURT

	PRICE	CODE
Beat Your Ticket: Go To Court and Win! (National Edition)	$19.99	BEYT
The Criminal Law Handbook: Know Your Rights, Survive the System	$34.99	KYR
Everybody's Guide to Small Claims Court (National Edition)	$26.99	NSCC
Everybody's Guide to Small Claims Court in California	$26.99	CSCC
Fight Your Ticket ... and Win! (California Edition)	$29.99	FYT
How to Change Your Name in California	$34.95	NAME
How to Collect When You Win a Lawsuit (California Edition)	$29.99	JUDG
How to Seal Your Juvenile & Criminal Records (California Edition)	$34.95	CRIM
The Lawsuit Survival Gide	$29.99	UNCL

	PRICE	CODE
Nolo's Deposition Handbook	$29.99	DEP
Represent Yourself in Court: How to Prepare & Try a Winning Case	$34.99	RYC
Sue in California Without a Lawyer	$34.99	SLWY

HOMEOWNERS, LANDLORDS & TENANTS

	PRICE	CODE
California Tenants' Rights	$27.99	CTEN
Deeds for California Real Estate	$24.99	DEED
Dog Law	$21.95	DOG
Every Landlord's Legal Guide (National Edition, Book w/CD-ROM)	$44.99	ELLI
Every Tenant's Legal Guide	$29.99	EVTEN
For Sale by Owner in California	$29.99	FSBO
How to Buy a House in California	$34.99	BHCA
The California Landlord's Law Book: Rights & Responsibilities (Book w/CD-ROM)	$44.99	LBRT
The California Landlord's Law Book: Evictions (Book w/CD-ROM)	$44.99	LBEV
Leases & Rental Agreements	$29.99	LEAR
Neighbor Law: Fences, Trees, Boundaries & Noise	$26.99	NEI
The New York Landlord's Law Book (Book w/CD-ROM)	$39.99	NYLL
New York Tenants' Rights	$27.99	NYTEN
Renters' Rights (National Edition)	$24.99	RENT
Stop Foreclosure Now in California	$29.95	CLOS

HUMOR

	PRICE	CODE
Poetic Justice	$9.95	PJ

IMMIGRATION

	PRICE	CODE
Becoming a U.S. Citizen: A Guide to the Law, Exam and Interview	$24.99	USCIT
Fiancé & Marriage Visas	$44.95	IMAR
How to Get a Green Card	$29.99	GRN

ORDER 24 HOURS A DAY @ www.nolo.com
Call 800-728-3555 • Mail or fax the order form in this book

	PRICE	CODE
Student & Tourist Visas	$29.95	ISTU
U.S. Immigration Made Easy	$29.99	IMEZ

MONEY MATTERS

	PRICE	CODE
101 Law Forms for Personal Use (Book w/CD-ROM)	$29.99	SPOT
Bankruptcy: Is It the Right Solution to Your Debt Problems?	$19.99	BRS
Chapter 13 Bankruptcy: Repay Your Debts	$34.99	CH13
Creating Your Own Retirement Plan	$29.99	YROP
Credit Repair (Book w/CD-ROM)	$24.99	CREP
Getting Paid: How to Collect from Bankrupt Debtors	$24.99	CRBNK
How to File for Chapter 7 Bankruptcy	$34.99	HFB
IRAs, 401(k)s & Other Retirement Plans: Taking Your Money Out	$34.99	RET
Money Troubles: Legal Strategies to Cope With Your Debts	$29.99	MT
Stand Up to the IRS	$24.99	SIRS
Surviving an IRS Tax Audit	$24.95	SAUD
Take Control of Your Student Loan Debt	$26.95	SLOAN

PATENTS AND COPYRIGHTS

	PRICE	CODE
The Copyright Handbook: How to Protect and Use Written Works (Book w/CD-ROM)	$39.99	COHA
Copyright Your Software	$34.95	CYS
Domain Names	$26.95	DOM
Getting Permission: How to License and Clear Copyrighted Materials Online and Off (Book w/CD-ROM)	$34.99	RIPER
How to Make Patent Drawings Yourself	$29.99	DRAW
Inventor's Guide to Law, Business and Taxes	$34.99	ILAX
The Inventor's Notebook	$24.99	INOT
Nolo's Patents for Beginners	$29.99	QPAT

	PRICE	CODE
License Your Invention (Book w/CD-ROM)	$39.99	LICE
Patent, Copyright & Trademark	$39.99	PCTM
Patent It Yourself	$49.99	PAT
Patent Pending in 24 Hours	$29.99	PEND
Patent Searching Made Easy	$29.95	PATSE
The Public Domain	$34.95	PUBL
Trademark: Legal Care for Your Business and Product Name	$39.95	TRD
Web and Software Development: A Legal Guide (Book w/ CD-ROM)	$44.95	SFT

RESEARCH & REFERENCE

Legal Research: How to Find & Understand the Law	$39.99	LRES

SENIORS

Choose the Right Long-Term Care: Home Care, Assisted Living & Nursing Homes	$21.99	ELD
The Conservatorship Book for California	$44.99	CNSV
Social Security, Medicare & Goverment Pensions	$29.99	SOA

SOFTWARE
Call or check our website at www.nolo.com
for special discounts on Software!

LeaseWriter CD—Windows	$129.95	LWD1
LLC Maker—Windows	$89.95	LLP1
PatentPro Plus—Windows	$399.99	PAPL
Personal RecordKeeper 5.0 CD—Windows	$59.95	RKD5
Quicken Legal Business Pro 2004—Windows	$79.95	SBQB4
Quicken WillMaker Plus 2004—Windows	$79.95	WQP4

SPECIAL UPGRADE OFFER
Get 35% off the latest edition of your Nolo book

It's important to have the most current legal information. Because laws and legal procedures change often, we update our books regularly. To help keep you up-to-date we are extending this special upgrade offer. Cut out and mail the title portion of the cover of your old Nolo book and we'll give you 35% off the retail price of the NEW EDITION of that book when you purchase directly from us. For more information call us at 1-800-728-3555. This offer is to individuals only.

Order Form

Name _____

Address _____

City _____

State, Zip _____

Daytime Phone _____

E-mail _____

Our "No-Hassle" Guarantee

Return anything you buy directly from Nolo for any reason and we'll cheerfully refund your purchase price. No ifs, ands or buts.

☐ Check here if you do not wish to receive mailings from other companies

Item Code	Quantity	Item	Unit Price	Total Price

Method of payment

☐ Check   ☐ VISA   ☐ MasterCard
☐ Discover Card   ☐ American Express

Subtotal	
Add your local sales tax (California only)	
Shipping: RUSH $9, Basic $5 (See below)	
"I bought 3, ship it to me FREE!"(Ground shipping only)	
TOTAL	

Account Number _____

Expiration Date _____

Signature _____

Shipping and Handling

Rush Delivery—Only $9

We'll ship any order to any street address in the U.S. by UPS 2nd Day Air* for only $9!

* Order by noon Pacific Time and get your order in 2 business days. Orders placed after noon Pacific Time will arrive in 3 business days. P.O. boxes and S.F. Bay Area use basic shipping. Alaska and Hawaii use 2nd Day Air or Priority Mail.

Basic Shipping—$5

Use for P.O. Boxes, Northern California and Ground Service.

Allow 1-2 weeks for delivery. U.S. addresses only.

For faster service, use your credit card and our toll-free numbers

**Call our customer service group
Monday thru Friday 7am to 7pm PST**

Phone	1-800-728-3555
Fax	1-800-645-0895
Mail	Nolo
950 Parker St.
Berkeley, CA 94710

**Order 24 hours a day @
www.nolo.com**

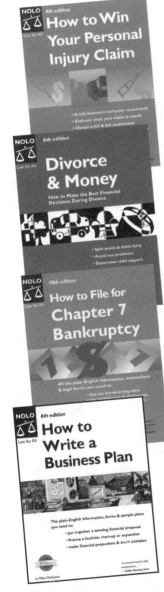

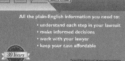

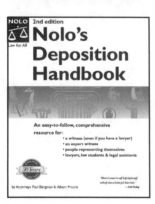

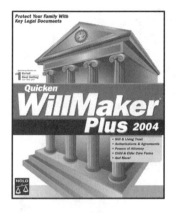

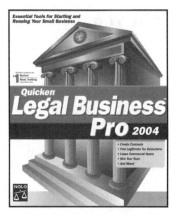